# Defending Interests

## *Public-Private Partnerships in WTO Litigation*

Gregory C. Shaffer

BROOKINGS INSTITUTION PRESS
*Washington, D.C.*

ABOUT BROOKINGS

The Brookings Institution is a private nonprofit organization devoted to research, education, and publication on important issues of domestic and foreign policy. Its principal purpose is to bring knowledge to bear on current and emerging policy problems. The Institution maintains a position of neutrality on issues of public policy. Interpretations or conclusions in Brookings publications should be understood to be solely those of the authors.


1775 Massachusetts Avenue, N.W., Washington, D.C. 20036
*www.brookings.edu*



*Library of Congress Cataloging-in-Publication data*

Shaffer, Gregory C., 1958–
Defending interests: public-private partnerships in WTO litigation / Gregory C. Shaffer.
p. cm.
Includes bibliographical references and index.
ISBN 0-8157-7830-9 (cloth : alk. paper)
ISBN 0-8157-7831-7 (pbk. : alk. paper)
1. World Trade Organization. 2. Actions and defenses. 3. Public-private sector cooperation. 4. Foreign trade regulation. I. Title.
K4610.S52 2003
343'.087—dc22 2003018462

9 8 7 6 5 4 3 2 1

The paper used in this publication meets minimum requirements of the American National Standard for Information Sciences—Permanence of Paper for Printed Library Materials: ANSI Z39.48-1992.

Typeset in Sabon

Composition by Cynthia Stock
Silver Spring, Maryland

Printed by R. R. Donnelley
Harrisonburg, Virginia

# Defending Interests

*To Robert E. Hudec*
(1934–2003)

# *Contents*

*Text tables*



*Appendix tables*

# *Preface*

I dedicate this book to Robert E. Hudec, modest giant of the field in whose footsteps we follow. Bob was my mentor, as he was for so many. He generously read our work and told us what was good, and what did not speak well of us. He kept us honest. He pushed us toward excellence. This is for you Bob, *cordially*.

I likewise owe this book to my colleagues and friends at the University of Wisconsin Law School. Besides Bob Hudec's voluminous work, I am indebted to that of my colleagues, particularly Howard Erlanger, Marc Galanter, Neil Komesar, Stewart Macaulay, and David Trubek.

In the Wisconsin tradition, this book takes a sociolegal, actor-centric approach. It examines the intersection of public law and private interest in litigation before the World Trade Organization and bargaining within its shadow. In a legal realist, "law-and-society" tradition, it evaluates the legalization of the international trading system in terms of its *effects* on private behavior, as opposed to its formal rules and judicial decisions. Thus the book focuses on the operation of public-private networks as seen in the actual handling—the *law-in-action*—of most commercial trade disputes. The book builds on over one hundred interviews with former and current officials at the USTR, other U.S. agencies, the European Commission and EC member states, representatives of U.S. and EC business trade associations, and private lawyers based in Washington and Brussels, complemented by primary documents concerning the use of U.S. and EC procedures for challenging foreign barriers to trade. The book focuses on the deployment of public-private partnerships in international trade relations from 1995, with the creation of the WTO, through January 2003.

This book began as a presentation at the annual conference of the American Society of International Law, to which Amy Porges invited me. It was my second year of teaching, and I told Amy that I would like to investigate what lies behind trade claims brought by the European Community. Hugo Paemen, Jeff Lang, and Jacques Bourgeois were on the panel and kindly listened to this newcomer from Wisconsin and encouraged me to push further. From there, I researched the same question regarding U.S. trade complaints. After presenting a comparison of the two approaches at the biannual conference of the European Community Studies Association, I was pressed to examine more deeply the explanations for these differences, as well as their broader implications. Over the years, with more probings, more trips to Brussels and Washington, the book grew.

I thank those who helped finance this project, in particular, the Smongeski Fund of the University of Wisconsin Foundation, the UW European Union Center (European Union grant), the UW CIBER fund (U.S. Title VI grant), the UW Center on World Affairs and the Global Economy, and the Jarchow Research Award. Chapters were presented at the American Bar Foundation (Chicago 2002); the ASIL International Economic Law Group biannual conference (Houston, 2001); the Law and Society annual conference (Miami, 2000); the European Studies Association biannual conference (Pittsburgh, 1999); the conference "The New Transatlantic Dialogue: Intergovernmental, Transgovernmental and Transnational Perspectives" (Madison, Wisconsin, 1999); and the American Society of International Law annual conference (Washington, 1998). I thank the numerous friends and colleagues who commented on the manuscript in its various stages, including Karen Alter, Claude Barfield, William Clune, David Coen, Richard Cunningham, Candido Garcia-Molyneux, Jon Graubart, Justin Greenwood, Robert Hudec, Neil Komesar, Hugo Paemen, Amy Porges, Reinhard Quick, Kal Raustiala,

Alistair Stewart, and Alasdair Young, as well as four anonymous reviewers. I thank Steven Coon, Greg Creer, Jon Graubart, Drew Jackson, Matthew Kim-Miller, Brian Larson, Yu Li, Meghan McCormick, Jason Myatt, and Benjamin Rickert for their invaluable research assistance. I thank those at the Brookings Institution Press who believed in the book and helped me to improve it. All errors of course remain my own.

Finally, I thank my parents, Herbert Shaffer and Mary Ann Meanwell; my son, Brook Shaffer; my wife, Michele Goodwin; and my stepdaughter, Sage Cammers-Goodwin. Without their love and support, who knows where I would be. My mother has been there always—a home through time. My father passed away in November 2001 when I had thought that this book was nearing its completion. Always proud, always encouraging, he would have been among the first to read it. In my mind, I continue to converse with him about it.

# *List of Acronyms*

| | |
|---|---|
| AD Agreement | Antidumping Agreement (or Agreement on Implementation of Article VI of GATT 1994) |
| CEPS | European Confederation of Producers of Spirits |
| CVD | countervailing duty |
| DG | Directorate-General of the European Commission |
| DOC | Department of Commerce |
| DISCUS | Distilled Spirits Council of the United States |
| DSB | Dispute Settlement Body |
| DSU | Dispute Settlement Understanding |
| EC | European Community |
| EU | European Union |
| FSC | foreign sales corporation |
| GATS | General Agreement on Trade in Services |
| GATT | General Agreement on Tariffs and Trade |
| GSP | General System of Preferences |
| IFPI | International Federation of the Phonographic Industry |

| | |
|---|---|
| IIPA | International Intellectual Property Alliance |
| USITC | United States International Trade Commission |
| NCPI | New Commercial Policy Instrument |
| PhRMA | Pharmaceutical Research and Manufacturers of America |
| QMV | qualified majority voting |
| SCM Agreement | Agreement on Subsidies and Countervailing Measures |
| SPS Agreement | Agreement on Sanitary and Phytosanitary Measures |
| SWA | Scotch Whisky Association |
| TABD | Transatlantic Business Dialogue |
| TBR | Trade Barrier Regulation |
| TBT Agreement | Agreement on Technical Barriers to Trade |
| TRIMS Agreement | Agreement on Trade-Related Investment Measures |
| TRIPS Agreement | Agreement on Trade-Related Aspects of Intellectual Property Rights |
| USTR | United States Trade Representative |
| WTO | World Trade Organization |

# Defending Interests

# 1 The Blurring of the Public and the Private in International Trade Law

International law long has been faulted for being irrelevant and illusory. According to political scientists of the realist tradition, powerful states simply ignore it when advancing national goals.[1] To positivist legal theorists, international law is not law at all because it does not issue from a central authority and is not backed by a sanction.[2]

1. See Morgenthau (1963, p. 278), who called international law "a primitive type of law primarily because it is almost completely decentralized law." For a critique of legalistic approaches to international relations as based on false assumptions, see Kennan (1951). These political realists considered international law dangerous for the United States were it to be taken too seriously. In their view, a state that focuses on international law as opposed to international politics cloaks strategic concerns essential for its security in legalistic and moralistic garb that rivals may use to seek advantage but ignore when impeding their interests. Kennan (p. 95) maintained that the "most serious fault" in past U.S. foreign policy was its "legalistic-moralistic approach to international relations."

2. Austin ([1832] 1971, p. 352) maintained that international law is not law, but simply a form of "positive morality" because there are no commands issued by a sovereign "armed with a sanction." Kelsen (1942), on the other hand, believed that international law is law, but of a "primitive" form, because it depends on self-help, without any centralized power, to apply it. In a similar vein, Hart (1994, pp. 213–37) argued that international law is like primitive law in that it lacks "secondary rules" to

As Max Weber contended, international law should not "be called law, precisely because there is no legal authority above the state capable of enforcing it."[3]

Whatever one's definition of law, international economic law gained standing during the 1990s with the end of the cold war and growing interest in economic globalization. At the same time, international economic norms and rules penetrated more deeply into domestic systems. Although such rules may not be directly applicable in domestic legal systems, nations, from the weakest to the most powerful, take them into account more frequently when enacting, implementing, and interpreting domestic laws and regulations.[4]

At the international level, the impact of law is nowhere more clear than in the realm of trade. At the conclusion of eight years of trade negotiations, 128 countries and customs territories agreed to create the World Trade Organization (WTO), which commenced on January 1, 1995. Even in a strict positivist sense, WTO law consists of rules that a centralized institution (the WTO Dispute Settlement Body) enforces through adopting judicial judgments that, if not complied with, trigger sanctions. Although the WTO lacks police power, its judicial panels are empowered to authorize the withdrawal of trade concessions.[5] All states, even the most powerful ones, have responded to WTO judgments by modifying

---

assess the validity of its "primary" substantive rules. Consequently, while international law may constitute law, it does not constitute a legal system.

3. See Weber (1947, p. 128): "As is well known it has often been denied that international law could be called law, precisely because there is no legal authority above the state capable of enforcing it. In terms of the present terminology this would be correct, for a system of order the sanctions of which consisted wholly in expectations of disapproval and of the reprisals of injured parties, which is thus guaranteed entirely by convention and self-interest without the help of a specialized enforcement agency, is not a case of legal order." On the notion of an acceptance model of law as opposed to the command model of Austin and Weber, see Gottlieb (1985, p. 187). See also McDougal and Lasswell (1996, pp. 113–43).

4. See Stephen (2000, pp. 66–68). For example, most of the 245 pages of the U.S. Uruguay Round Agreements Act of 1994 modify domestic laws of the United States in order to implement its WTO obligations, even though the act also provides that no person other than the federal government may challenge a U.S. law or regulation before a U.S. court for failing to comply with WTO law. See Uruguay Round Agreements Act of 1994, §§102, P.L. 103-465, 108 Statute 4809 (codified as amended at 19 U. S. Code §3512).

5. WTO texts may not use the term "sanctions," but affected parties, commentators, and legal practitioners commonly refer to them. See Charnovitz (2001, p. 792).

domestic regulations and practices, or, in the few cases where domestic politics blocked modification, have accepted the resulting sanctions.[6] In the first eight years after the WTO was established, 279 formal complaints were filed, as a result of which 68 panel and Appellate Body reports were adopted and numerous settlements reached, with 16 panels pending. International trading relations have been governed increasingly through law—or, better stated, through power mediated by law—with all countries, developed and developing alike, initiating more legal complaints against one another.[7]

The blurring of the public and the private spurs the growth of international economic law. WTO law, while formally a domain of *public* international law, profits and prejudices *private* parties. As international economic relations become legalized, lawyers listen and market their wares. Private parties—particularly well-connected, wealthier, and better-organized ones—attempt to use the WTO legal system to advance their commercial ambitions. A more effective WTO public law incites U.S. and European private legal strategies, which in turn yield further WTO public law. WTO law thereby becomes "harder" law through which private actors exercise influence in its shadow. WTO law represents a significantly enhanced legal framework, even though the dispute settlement system of the General Agreement on Tariffs and Trade (GATT), the WTO's predecessor organization existing from 1948 to1995, was legalized over time, and even though political and social forces still constrain WTO law's deployment.[8] The WTO system is broader in scope and membership, more precise in application, more binding in effect, and more

6. See "EC—Regime for the Importation, Sale and Distribution of Bananas" (EC Bananas case), WTO Document Series WT/DS27/R (May 22, 1997); and "EC—Measures Affecting Meat and Meat Products" (EC Meat Hormones case), WTO Document Series WT/DS26/R/USA (August 18, 1997).

7. See Steinberg (2002, p. 339) concerning how the United States and European Communities shape WTO law. Also Busch and Reinhardt (2003); and Shaffer (2003), concerning structural disadvantages developing countries face in WTO dispute settlement. The impact of WTO law does not necessarily contradict realist notions, since arguably the world's most powerful states have played a central role in drafting WTO rules and have benefited most from their enforcement.

8. The GATT trading system refers to the system under the agreement signed in 1947 focusing on trade in goods. Upon the creation of the WTO on January 1, 1995, GATT became one agreement among many under the WTO's umbrella, including those covering intellectual property protection and trade in services. For an overview of the GATT system, see Dam (1970); and Hudec (1993).

actively used.[9] The reaction of private parties throughout the world in opposition to or support of the WTO system and its stream of legal complaints and verdicts is just one indication of WTO law's relevance to states and their constituents.[10]

The growing interaction between private enterprises, their lawyers, and U.S. and European public officials in the bringing of most trade claims reflects a trend from predominantly intergovernmental decision-making toward multilevel private litigation strategies involving direct public-private exchange at the national and international levels.[11] Given the trade-liberalizing rules of the WTO, this trend has an outward-looking, export-promoting orientation, comprised of more systematic challenges, often by larger and well-organized commercial interests, to foreign barriers to trade. International trade disputes are, in consequence, not purely public or intergovernmental. Nor, however, do they reflect a simple co-optation by businesses, particularly large and well-organized ones, of government officials. Rather, they involve the formation of public-private partnerships to pursue varying, but complementary, goals.

Pundits sometimes apply the term "neoliberalism" to this focus on the elimination of trade barriers. Neoliberalism refers to a model of societal relations in which government regulation and social welfare guarantees are reduced in order to foster the play of market forces driven by private enterprises pursuing profit maximization.[12] The extent to which ideology has changed since the mid–twentieth century is captured by comparing today's use of the term with its use in the 1950s. At that time, scholars

9. Abbott and Snidal (2000, p. 421) have presented a typology of international hard and soft law based on three criteria: the stringency of the legal "Obligation," the "Precision" of detail, and whether there is "Delegation" to an enforcing authority. This book goes beyond these formalist measures by examining how WTO law operates in practice.

10. See, for example, Christopher G. Caine (2000, p. 20) for Business without Borders interview with lobbyists for multinational corporations on their lobbying strategies and goals for the WTO. On the efforts of nongovernmental organizations (NGOs) to gain direct access to the WTO, see Bruce Stokes, "New Players in the Trade Game," *National Journal,* December 18, 1999, p. 3630. Greg Hitt, "Fund Raising for Seattle WTO Meeting Raises Concerns," *Wall Street Journal,* May 17, 1999, p. A28, notes that invitations were extended to large corporations, in consideration of a fee, to attend receptions with trade delegates at the WTO Ministerial Meeting in Seattle.

11. For a review of "intergovernmental" theory (focusing solely on "state" actors), as well as "transgovernmental" and "transnational" theories of international relations, see Pollack and Shaffer (2001b, pp. 20–33).

12. See Shaffer (2001, p. 608), who notes, however, that one can favor both liberalized trade and social welfare protection policies.

such as Robert Dahl and Charles Lindblom referred to "neoliberalism" as an ideology "characterized by an almost doctrinaire fixation on certain means, particularly those legitimized during the critical years of the New Deal, such as unquestioned support for trade unions, a strong preference for action by national government as against state and local units, and support for a more powerful executive and bureaucracy."[13] Today, the term "neoliberalism" has been turned on its head to represent "an almost doctrinaire fixation" on free trade, privatization, small government, and unfettered markets to foster economic growth and wealth generation, as opposed to government action and collective bargaining to promote social and economic equality.

This book evaluates how private firms collaborate with governmental authorities in the United States and the European Union (EU) to challenge foreign trade barriers before the WTO legal system and within its shadow.[14] The term "foreign trade barrier" covers any measure that directly or indirectly results in an impediment to trade. While tariffs and quotas constitute the most transparent forms of barriers, less transparent ones include internal taxes, subsidies, technical standards, licensing requirements, and other measures that result in an unequal playing field for foreign producers. Firms that rely on intellectual property assert that the failure to recognize and enforce intellectual property rights likewise constitutes a trade barrier, although many scholars contend otherwise.[15] Public authorities and private firms have reciprocal, though not identical, goals in challenging these trade barriers. This book assesses the challenges that their partnerships pose.

Public-private partnerships in WTO litigation merit close attention for four primary reasons. First, they reflect the dynamic effects of the WTO

13. See Dahl and Lindblom (1976, p. 516).

14. EU and EC (European Community) are used interchangeably in this book. The technical name for the entity representing European Community interests before the WTO is the European Communities, or EC. Article XI of the 1994 Agreement Establishing the WTO refers to "the European Communities" as an original member of the WTO. The Treaty of European Union (TEU) of 1992 changed the name of the EEC (European Economic Communities) to the EC to denote that the European Community had integrated beyond purely economic matters. The TEU created three pillars of activities for the regional block. The first pillar covers all traditional EC matters, including trade. The title that encompasses all three pillars is the European Union (or EU), which is often used by commentators, even though it is the EC that, technically, is a member of the WTO.

15. See, for example, Bhagwati (1994, pp. 111–14).

legal system. The United States and EC have adopted public-private partnerships to exploit the WTO system. Remarkably, either the United States or EC was a plaintiff or defendant in 75 percent of WTO complaints filed, and in 84 percent of complaints that resulted in judicial decisions.[16] In fact, either the United States or EC participated as a plaintiff, defendant, or third party in every WTO case that was litigated before a panel during the WTO's first eight years (see table 6-1). Hence we learn how most WTO legal disputes operate in practice, as opposed to in theory. A summary of all WTO complaints brought by the United States and EC, together with their outcomes, is set forth in appendix tables 1 to 4.

Second, divergent U.S. and European approaches to public-private partnerships in WTO litigation and bargaining exemplify contrasting U.S. and European political and economic structures, administrative cultures, and traditions of government-business relations. The U.S. approach to public-private networks tends to be more "bottom-up," with firms and trade associations playing a proactive role. The EC approach tends to be "top-down," with a public authority (the European Commission) playing the predominant, entrepreneurial role.

Third, the impact of U.S. and European public-private partnerships in WTO litigation has serious implications for the sustainability, equity, and effectiveness of the WTO system. Whichever approach one prefers—top-down or bottom-up—public-private partnerships can render the political management of U.S.-European trade disputes more difficult. Political mismanagement of trade disputes can affect the stability and solidarity of the transatlantic relationship, as well as the overall WTO system. By exposing how WTO law works in practice, the book provides the necessary groundwork for evaluating proposals to modify the WTO legal system, whether in the context of a new round of global trade negotiations, WTO members' formal review of the WTO Dispute Settlement Understanding, or otherwise. Proposals for amending the WTO system are of little value if they are not grounded in a clear understanding of how the system

16. As of January 17, 2003, the United States or EC was a plaintiff or defendant in 210 of the 279 complaints brought before the WTO, constituting 75 percent of the total. The United States or EC was involved in 57 of 68 (or 84 percent) of fully litigated cases. These figures are comparable to those calculated as of May 2, 2001, when the United States or EC was a plaintiff or defendant in 149 of the first 194 complaints brought before the WTO (around 77 percent) and was involved in 34 of 41 (or 85 percent) of fully litigated WTO cases. See WTO Secretariat, "Update of WTO Dispute Settlement Cases," WTO Document WT/DS/OV/10 (updated as of January 17, 2003, issued January 22, 2003).

operates. As the legal realist Karl Llewellyn maintained in the 1930s, "The argument is simply that no judgment of what Ought to be done in the future with respect to any part of law can be intelligently made without knowing objectively, as far as possible, what that part of law is now doing." Llewellyn called for "the temporary divorce of Is and Ought for purposes of study," a wise counsel that much policy analysis, in the rush to advocate normative goals, ignores.[17]

Proposals vary widely concerning reform of the WTO dispute settlement system. Some argue that it should be reigned in. Supporters of this view range from Claude Barfield of the conservative American Enterprise Institute to Ralph Nader of the political left. Both maintain that the WTO system has become too legalized and should be subject to greater political checks, that WTO judicial panels should show greater political deference toward national regulatory measures, and that political bodies should assume greater control of the judicial process.[18] In contrast, some trade commentators of a liberal bent, such as Ernst-Ulrich Petersmann, a professor and legal consultant within the WTO's secretariat, maintain that WTO law should be expanded by granting private parties direct litigation rights so that corporations and other private actors may enforce WTO law through national courts.[19] Others concerned about the equity and effectiveness of the system, such as Petros Mavroidis and Joost Pauwelyn, both of whom have worked at the WTO, support modifications of remedies that could favor weaker parties.[20] These changes could be complemented by the creation of legal support centers to provide litigation resources for financially strapped countries to offset resource imbalances.

17. See Llewellyn (1931, pp. 1236–37).

18. Barfield is the director of trade policy studies at the American Enterprise Institute. Of course, Barfield and Nader come from opposing political perspectives, and the modalities of their recommendations vary greatly. Barfield, for one, believes in the benefits of trade liberalization. Cf. Barfield (2001, pp. 112–29); and Wallach and Sforza (1999), where Ralph Nader, in the preface (p. ix), lambasts the WTO's "autocratic system of international governance that favors corporate interests."

19. See, for example, Petersmann, (1991, pp. 243, 463), who asserts that lawyers should "recognize freedom of trade as a basic individual right." See also Brand (1992, pp. 95–102); and Symposium (1998, p. 147).

20. Mavroidis (2000, p. 763) argues that "the effectiveness of WTO remedies depends on the relative 'persuasive' power of the WTO member threatening with countermeasures." According to Pauwelyn (2000, p. 335), "a more collective and effective mechanism, one aimed at inducing compliance, is required." See also Shaffer (2003).

Fourth, information on the dynamics of public-private partnerships in litigation before the WTO (the most "legalized" of all international institutions) provides empirical grounding for broader assessment of the reciprocal relationship between international law and private behavior. We live in a world marked by increasing interdependence in which political, legal, and economic governance mechanisms clash and mesh at multiple levels. International economic law matters because of its impact on the behavior not only of states but also of their corporations and other constituents. Understanding the *law-in-action* of the WTO is essential for those assessing international economic relations from the perspective of any academic discipline and for the pursuit of any normative goal. Policymakers, lawyers, economists, political scientists, and sociologists increasingly recognize how international law implicates international economic relations, national regulatory behavior, and private conduct.[21]

Chapter 2 offers a theoretical framework for examining the growing role of public-private networks in international governance. It addresses three central questions: Why do public-private networks play an increasing role in international governance in a world of growing numbers and complexity? Who are the primary participants in these networks? What explains their participation? The chapter elucidates the importance of resource interdependencies among public and private actors and relative stakes in outcomes.

The U.S. and European approaches to the public-private relationship are the subject of chapters 3 and 4, respectively. In the United States, on the one hand, private firms adopt various strategies to spur the Office of the United States Trade Representative (USTR) to challenge foreign trade barriers under WTO law and in its shadow. Through a meshing of law and politics, the USTR, in coordination with private actors, identifies, investigates, and takes action against foreign trade barriers, steadily ratcheting up pressure on foreign countries to expand private access to their markets. Channels for deploying public-private trade networks in Europe, on the other hand, include an interstate process and a private petition procedure. The European Commission, which plays a predominant role in these processes, has shifted resources toward challenging

21. See, for example, Goldstein and others, writing in a special issue of *International Organization* (2000). Cf. Finnemore and Toope (2001, p. 743), who criticize Goldstein and others for their positivist conception of law and for their failure to address law's impact from a sociological perspective, including the perspectives of custom, legitimacy, and legal process.

foreign trade barriers and developing public-private networks. As explained in chapter 5, there are historical, political, economic, and cultural reasons for the more proactive and aggressive role that U.S. businesses—and U.S. private lawyers—take in international trade disputes, as well as for some trends in the EC toward U.S.-style practice. Despite their own rivalries, as noted in chapter 6, U.S. and European private firms at times coordinate transatlantic efforts to more effectively challenge third-country trade barriers, including domestic regulations within the United States and Europe themselves.

U.S. and EC public-private networks offer a useful framework for assessing the impact of a more legalized international trading system. WTO law incites private actors and their lawyers, and these actors spur the creation of more public international law. Chapter 7 assesses the implications of these public-private networks for the ability of governments to amicably resolve trade conflicts, the stability and solidarity of U.S.-European relations, and the effectiveness and equity of the international trade dispute settlement system.

# 2 Public-Private Partnerships in Theoretical Perspective

Traditionally, social scientists have treated government as distinct from civil society—hence the public-private dichotomy. For Max Weber, this public-private distinction underlay his conception of a rational, hierarchical state. In Weber's view, "it was left to the complete depersonalization of administrative management by bureaucracy and the rational systematization of law to realize the separation of public and private fully and in principle."[1] Weber famously defined the state as "a compulsory political association with continuous organization . . . [having] administrative staff [that] successfully upholds a claim to the monopoly of the legitimate use of physical force in the enforcement of its order."[2] Under this conception, the state

1. See Weber (1946, p. 239). Also Weber (1947, p. 331): "The organization of offices follows the principle of hierarchy; that is, each lower office is under the control and supervision of a higher one."

2. Weber (1947, p. 154). According to Weber, "The primary formal characteristics of the modern state are as follows: It possesses an administrative and legal order subject to change by legislation, to which the organized corporate activity of the administrative staff, which is also regulated by legislation, is oriented. This system of order claims binding authority, not only over the members of the state, the citizens, most of whom have

governs civil society; the state does not enter into governance networks with it.

Similarly, the American democratic theorist Robert Dahl conceived of a clear separation between public and private. Borrowing from Weber, Dahl also defined government in terms of its "exclusive regulation of the legitimate use of force in enforcing its rules within a given territorial area."[3] Under Dahl's conception of "polyarchy," however, political leaders' control of the state is legitimated through a pluralist democratic political process. Although Dahl's notion of polyarchy (where leaders are controlled indirectly through a pluralist process) is a reverse image of the notion of hierarchy (where control is exercised unilaterally by the state over its citizens), both conceptions are based on a differentiation of the roles of the government (public) and the governed (private).

International relations theory likewise reflected this public-private dichotomy. Here, theorists focused on the interaction among sovereign states and, in some cases, among states and the international organizations that they created.[4] In the debates between realist and institutionalist scholars, both sides ignored any role for private actors. Realist scholars, such as Joseph Grieco, addressed the role of state power in shaping and deploying international regimes to advance state interests.[5] Institutionalist scholars, on the other hand, pointed out how powerful states may agree to constraints imposed on them by international institutions in order to ensure that reciprocally beneficial bargains are sustained.[6] In neither case do private actors enter the picture.

---

obtained membership by birth, but also to a very large extent, over all action taking place in the area of its jurisdiction" (p. 156).

3. Dahl (1976, p. 10); and Dahl and Lindblom (1976, pp. 171, 227–36, 272–86). Dahl notes, however, that these forms of determining economic policy complement and supplement those of the price system and bargaining between governmental actors and key social groups within the nation-state.

4. Although subject to exceptions, international relations theory generally has begun with a systemic view of states coexisting in a condition of anarchy, characterized by an absence of centralized authority. See, for example, Keohane (1986), including the chapters by Kenneth Waltz.

5. See Grieco (1990) on the importance of relative, as opposed to absolute, gains among competing states.

6. See, for example, Keohane (1984); and Abbot (1989, p. 335). Rational institutionalists borrow from game theory and neoinstitutional economics. See Axelrod and Keohane (1985, p. 226); and Snidal (1985, p. 923). As neoinstitutional economist Douglas North (1997, p. 98) writes, "Effective institutions raise the benefits of cooperative solutions or the costs of defection, to use game theoretic terms." Of course, these theories have a number of variants, covered, for example, in Hasenclever, Mayer, and Rittberger (1997).

Institutional economists, in contrast, are primarily concerned with the mechanisms used to coordinate, control, and ultimately allocate resources, and thereby determine economic outcomes. They refer to these mechanisms as systems of "governance," as opposed to government. The prominent institutionalist economist Oliver Williamson, for example, differentiates between two primary mechanisms for allocating resources: governance by hierarchy and governance by markets.[7] Although Williamson focuses on the operations of firms, his ideas apply to political economy in general.[8] Under the concept of hierarchy, governments allocate resources by command, as through acts of legislatures, courts, and bureaucracies. Governments issue regulations, impose fines, and collect taxes. Markets, in contrast, allocate resources through the uncoordinated decisions of individuals, as reflected in the price system. Markets thus reflect a private ordering of goods, services, and wealth, in contrast to a hierarchical public one.

This book concerns a third form of governance, complementing public hierarchies and private markets: governance through *public-private networks*.[9] These networks bring together public and private actors to address discrete policy issues, thereby blurring the public-private distinction. In a world of growing numbers and complexity, governments are

7. On governance by markets and hierarchies, see Williamson (1975; 1985; and 1996, p. 47), noting that governance mechanisms are chosen to economize on transaction costs. In the latter work, Williamson moves to a threefold classification of market, hybrids, and hierarchies, with markets and hierarchies being the "polar modes" (1996, p. 104). The term "hierarchies" refers to "formal administrative and bureaucratic command systems within a single organization to replace market contracting among autonomous exchange partners as the means by which [economic actors] coordinate the flow of personnel, capital, and goods through the production and distribution processes." See Lindberg, Campbell, and Hollingsworth (1991).

8. See Yarbrough and Yarbrough (1990, pp. 236, 249): "Although the origins of NEO [new economics of organization] lie in the study of the firm, the central *problematiques* of NEO are precisely those of political economy. . . . In the NEO world, mutually beneficial long-term cooperation requires an institutional structure to facilitate that cooperation, a structure that involves both firms and states and both trading and governance across borders." Weingast (1993, p. 288) notes: "In important respects, the logic of political institutions parallels that of economic institutions. To borrow Williamson's phrase, the political institutions of society create a 'governance structure.'"

9. For an overview and application of network theories of governance to transatlantic relations, see Pollack and Shaffer (2001c, p. 301); and Powell (1991, p. 295). Ruggie (1995, p. 507) also differentiates among hierarchies, markets, and networks, defining networks as "a collaborative form of organisation, based on complementary strengths, characterised by relational modes of interaction, exhibiting interdependent preferences, stressing mutual benefits, and bonded by considerations of reputation."

delegating traditionally "public" functions to the private sector.[10] Governments then attempt to "steer" outcomes by overseeing these private actors' activities. According to the English political theorist R. A. W. Rhodes, western societies increasingly are governed through "self-organizing, interorganizational networks" composed of public and private actors pursuing shared goals.[11] Rhodes does not see public actors operating with exclusive control. Nongovernmental actors do not merely influence public representatives (as in Dahl's notion of polyarchy) or respond to them (as in Weber's concept of hierarchy). Rather, mixed networks of public and private actors coordinate in formulating and implementing public policy. As Donald Kettl writes regarding network forms of governance, "Government's role has changed. Government is less the producer of goods and services, and more the supervisor of proxies who do the actual work."[12] To some commentators, governance by networks represents a form of oligopoly of the political marketplace, as opposed to a monopoly (under Weber's definition of the state) and free exchange (in an idealized market, or alternatively, a utopian system of anarchy).[13]

The idea that public functions are governed by shifting combinations of public and private actors is, of course, not entirely "new," as suggested by the term "new governance" used by some scholars.[14] The blurring of the public and the private has long been a subject of interest to legal realists and law-and-society scholars.[15] Its saliency has increased, however, in

10. See, for example, Cerny (1997, p. 251).

11. See Rhodes (1997, p. 15). Rhodes (1996, p. 660) lays out four basic characteristics of governance, which distinguish the term from the traditional notion of "government": "(1) interdependence between organizations. Governance is broader than government, covering non-state actors. Changing the boundaries of the state meant the boundaries between public, private and voluntary sectors became shifting and opaque. (2) Continuing interactions between network members, caused by the need to exchange resources and negotiate shared purposes. (3) Game-like interactions, rooted in trust and regulated by rules of the game negotiated and agreed by network participants. (4) A significant degree of autonomy from the state. Networks are not accountable to the state; they are self-organizing. Although the state does not occupy a privileged, sovereign position, it can indirectly and imperfectly steer networks." Rhodes (2000) characterizes governance by networks as "a complex game," one "in which all actors manoeuvre for advantage."

12. See Kettl (1993, p. 21).

13. See, for example, Rhodes (1997, p. 9): "Policy networks are one way of analysing aggregation and intermediation; the oligopoly of the political market-place." For a critical review of public-private interactions involving "regulatory capture," see, for example, Lowi (1979); and Heclo (1978).

14. See, for example, Rhodes (1996, p. 652).

15. See Macaulay (1986, pp. 447–49), citing examples such as "company towns," trade associations, internal corporate mechanisms for arbitration, and protection against industrial

modern, complex, interdependent societies in which public and private actors attempt to adapt to rapid technological, demographic, and other changes. As a result, public institutions have shifted responsibility for the provision of many services to the private and voluntary sectors through privatization and deregulatory policies.

These networks of government officials and private groups are established, in large part, because of *resource interdependencies*. The diffusion of resources among various actors explains the need for networked forms of governance in an increasingly complex world, since neither central governments nor any other single actor possesses the resources necessary to govern without the cooperation of others. Governments need informational resources that private actors provide. As Jan Kooiman states, "No single actor, public or private, has all knowledge and information required to solve complex, dynamic and diversified problems."[16] Where Weber foresaw bureaucratic organizations' use of "knowledge" to exercise control, these scholars find that state agencies increasingly depend on private entities to obtain knowledge and effectively deploy it in implementing policy.[17] As Walter Powell writes, "A basic assumption of

espionage as examples of private actors performing government's three primary functions: the creation and interpretation of rules, adjudication over their compliance, and the application of sanctions for noncompliance. See also Horwitz (1982, pp. 1423–28), who maintains that the public/private distinction arose in order to define an area free from the influence of the state, and that the distinction has eroded as private entities have assumed more power; Turkel (1992), who explores critiques of the distinction by major social theorists; and Cutler (1997, p. 261).

16. Kooiman (1993). See also Kouwenhovern (1993, pp. 119, 123): "The rise of PPP [public-private partnerships] during the middle of the eighties is therefore explained by the perceived recent increase of the recognition by government and the private sector of the necessity to channel, or even exploit, mutual interdependencies by means of cooperation." And Rhodes (1996). An efficiency-based approach to governance by networks focuses on resource interdependencies as a causal explanation. Compare Cutler, Haufler, and Porter (1999), who distinguish between efficiency, power-based, and historical approaches to explain private authority in international affairs.

17. See Weber (1947, p. 339): "Bureaucratic administration means fundamentally the exercise of control on the basis of knowledge." Weber notes that private business has superior knowledge in its field, an exception to bureaucracy's source of power in the modern state through knowledge. See also Weber (1946, p. 235): "Only the expert knowledge of private economic interest groups in the field of 'business' is superior to the expert knowledge of the bureaucracy. This is so because the exact knowledge of facts in their field is vital to the economic existence of businessmen." He goes on, however, to discuss the development of public-private interactions as a means to increase bureaucratic power: "The system is supplemented by the calling in of interest groups as advisory bodies recruited from among the economically and socially most influential strata. . . . This latter development seeks especially to put the concrete experience of interest groups into the service of a rational

network relationships is that one party is dependent on resources controlled by another, and that there are gains to be had by the pooling of resources."[18] Some analysts argue that lobbying can be viewed as a reciprocally beneficial exchange of access and information—a form of public-private partnership.[19]

Of course, not all public and private actors enjoy equal opportunities to participate in these networks. *The relative power and influence of actors within these networks is determined by the diffusion of resources and actors' per capita stakes in outcomes.* First, actors may hold constitutional, legal, organizational, financial, political, informational, or other resources. For example, public actors hold constitutional and legal powers that endow them with authority. In the WTO context, only member states may bring claims before the WTO Dispute Settlement Body.[20] Private actors thus depend on public authorities to represent their interests. Private actors, however, also have organizational, financial, political, and informational resources that can benefit public authorities. For the private sector, "organizational resources, such as money, staff, and members . . . are the raw materials that can be transformed into assets of greater consequence."[21] In the context of WTO dispute settlement, private associations have the financial means to hire legal experts to help develop legal arguments; hold essential information about the marketplace needed to develop a factual basis for legal claims; and deploy political resources through lobbying, campaign financial support, and public informational campaigns.[22] Public authorities rely on these various

---

administration of expertly trained officials. It will certainly be important in the future and it further increases the power of bureaucracy" (1946, p. 235).

18. Powell (1991, p. 272).

19. Degregorio (1998, p. 139): "Both lawmakers and lobbyists gain by entering into these policymaking partnerships. The advocates need accommodating leaders to interject their points into the formal decision-making process. Legislators need information, brokers, and confidants to help them build congressional support for passage. Because both parties to the exchange get something for their trouble, I call this explanation of events an *exchange theory of access.*"

20. Because some WTO members, such as Hong Kong, are customs territories, WTO agreements adopt the term "contracting parties."

21. Degregorio (1998, p. 146). As Alasdair Young (1998, p. 174) points out, "The logic of collective action also manifests itself in the resource/remit imbalance. Firms and trade associations have more money and often can concentrate their greater resources on more discrete—sometimes technical—issues than civic interest organizations."

22. See, for example, Kosterlitz (1998) concerning corporate initiatives in support of educating the public about the virtues of the global economy and free trade policy.

resources. In short, public and private actors depend on each other's resources to accomplish their respective goals.

Resources alone, however, do not fully explain why actors participate in mixed networks. Because resources are limited and their deployment costly, participation also depends on actors' relative stakes in outcomes, particularly on the per capita *benefits* from participating, as compared with the informational and organizational *costs* of doing so. As Neil Komesar writes: "The character of institutional participation is determined by the interaction between the benefits of that participation and the costs of that participation. . . . Interest groups with small numbers but high per capita stakes have significant advantages in political action over interest groups with large numbers and smaller per capita stakes."[23] Groups with high per capita stakes are more likely to obtain and provide information to the policymaking process. In contrast, those with low per capita stakes are less likely to engage in policy strategizing where the per capita benefits of fully understanding the issues and organizing themselves are too low to justify the costs. Even where they each could benefit by collectively contributing to an association representing their interests, they may hope to free-ride on others. Although this account of public-private interactions is less radical than a "public choice" one in which "law is traded for political support, money, power, and other things that politicians and bureaucrats demand," high per capita stakes, resource interdependencies, and the reciprocal interests of public officials and private firms together spur public-private collaborations.[24]

At the international level, in the context of proliferating international organizational and legal structures, governmental representatives retain significant constitutional, legal, and other resources.[25] They thereby typically remain the most important players in public-private networks in

23. Komesar (1994, pp. 3, 8, 868). See also Olson (1965).

24. Colombatto and Macey (1999, p. 929).

25. See Pollack and Shaffer (2001b, p. 302) in the context of transatlantic relations. In international relations theory, some regime theorists such as Oran Young and postmodern theorists such as James Rosenau have included similar themes in their analysis of "global governance." See Rosenau (1992, pp. 4–6): "Governance is not synonymous with government. Both refer to purposive behavior, to goal-oriented activities, to systems of rule; but government suggests activities that are backed by formal authority, by police powers to insure the implementation of duly constituted policies, whereas governance refers to activities backed by shared goals that may or may not derive from legal and formally prescribed responsibilities and that do not necessarily rely on police powers to overcome defiance and attain compliance." Also Young (1997, p. 4).

international relations. Hence some scholars see the operation of "transgovernmental" networks of government officials as "the real new world order."[26] Anne Marie Slaughter contends that "the primary State actors in the international realm are no longer foreign ministries and heads of state, but the same government institutions that dominate domestic politics."[27]

Private actors, however, also play central roles in cross-border networks, just as they do in domestic regulatory contexts. As enterprises engage in cross-border exchange, their per capita stakes in international economic governance mechanisms rise. They press for greater legal certainty in export markets. Through their encounters with foreign regulatory barriers, they obtain valuable information that they have the incentive to package and forcefully present to domestic and transnational policymakers. As firms and trade associations become repeat players in the legal challenge of trade barriers, they develop a knowledge of how to strategically use the WTO process when needed. Numerous works address the relation of private interests and public officials in the negotiation of international trade and investment treaties and the provision of import protection.[28] Similarly, scholars have addressed the interaction between private litigation strategies and European treaties in the context of European integration.[29] By contrast, this book examines how private actors work with national officials in the WTO's two most powerful members—the United States and European Community—to deploy,

26. See Slaughter (1997, p. 183). See also Devuyst (1995, p.127); and Raustiala (2002, p. 1), concerning transgovernmental networks in competition, securities, and environmental policy.

27. Slaughter (2000, p. 178).

28. See Schattschneider (1935); Bauer, de Sola Pool, and Dexter (1963); Destler (1995, p. 7); Gilpin (1975, p. 140), stating "corporations and the U.S. government have tended to share an overlapping and complementary set of interests"; Goldstein (1993, pp. 137–63); Sell (1999, p. 175), showing public-private networks in WTO negotiations over intellectual property rights; Strange (1985, p. 234), noting "a complex network or web of transnational, bilateral bargains—bargains between corporations and other corporations, between corporations and governments, and between governments"; and Stopford and Strange (1991), addressing what the authors term "triangular diplomacy" involving state-state, state-firm, and firm-firm negotiations.

29. See Alter (2001, pp. 52–53), who "shows how the interaction between private litigants raising cases, national courts referring cases and invoking ECJ jurisprudence, and the ECJ interpreting European law all contributed to the construction of an international rule of law in Europe." Stone Sweet (2000, p. 5) notes the "reciprocal influence of legal rules and private behaviour in the European political-judicial context." And Conant (2002) offers insight into the role of organized interests in EC litigation.

enforce, and shape public international economic law. They do so through WTO litigation and settlement negotiations conducted in the shadow of the threat of a WTO claim. Private exporting firms and industry associations form partnerships with national trade representatives in WTO dispute settlement even more easily than in trade negotiations because other domestic actors are less likely to have clear countervailing interests. Rather, only foreign constituencies typically are protected by the regulatory barrier at stake, and they are not represented in the political process of the country initiating the WTO complaint.

# 3 *The United States's Initial Partnership Edge in Opening Foreign Markets*

The United States was the first country under the GATT trading system to create a legalistic procedure through which private firms could petition their government to challenge foreign trade barriers. Much has been written on this procedure, known as Section 301, from a policy perspective, particularly on its coercive use. The scholarly debate has centered largely on whether the procedure's deployment has promoted or distorted trade liberalization goals. Some contend that Section 301 is primarily a mechanism for private interests to harness U.S. unilateral power and replace "economic efficiency with political clout as the determinate of exports in the world trading system."[1] Others counter that Section 301 "can be a useful tool" for ensuring countries' compliance with trade commitments and for "encouraging additional liberalization in areas not covered by the WTO rules."[2] By contrast, this book

1. See Bhagwati and Patrick (1990, p. 35).

2. Bayard and Elliott (1994, p. 351). See also Sykes (1992, p. 313), who concludes that the statute "is fairly successful at inducing foreign governments to modify their practices when they are accused of violating U.S. legal rights"; and Swan (1999, pp. 48–49).

examines *Section 301 as a mechanism within a broader informal process of public-private coordination behind U.S. challenges to foreign trade barriers*. The procedure's basic function is to facilitate the formation of ad hoc public-private networks to develop and exploit public international economic law in order to advance U.S. national and commercial interests.

## Historical and Contextual Background

Throughout U.S. history, Congress has delegated to the president the power to impose retaliatory duties and other import restrictions on countries that discriminate against U.S. products.[3] During the two decades following World War II, the U.S. domestic economy was by and large insulated from foreign trade, so there was little constituent demand and congressional pressure for an aggressive U.S. trade policy. In the 1950s, foreign imports totaled only about 3 percent of U.S. production, and the country had a trade surplus, which extended through the 1960s.[4] By 1970, however, U.S. imports and exports together accounted for about 11 percent of U.S. gross domestic product, rising to 14 percent by 1980 and increasing to 29 percent by 1999.[5] Most important, starting in the 1970s, imports into the U.S. market steadily outpaced U.S. exports.[6] With the European and Japanese economies revitalized and U.S. trade deficits beginning to bloat, industry pressed Congress to act.[7]

The impetus for Section 301 and its successive amendments, particularly those in 1984 and 1988, was Congress's view that U.S. markets were disproportionately open in comparison with foreign markets in an increasingly competitive globalizing economy. GATT rules, Congress argued, were too narrow and the U.S. executive branch too accommodating. Congress demanded reciprocity and viewed Section 301 as a lever to obtain it. One way to force reciprocity, it hoped, was to expand Section 301 to target areas not yet covered by international trade rules but of

3. See Bhala (2000, p. 1268), referring, respectively, to powers granted to President Washington, an 1890 statute upheld in the Supreme Court case *Field* v. *Clark* (1892), and the U.S. trade acts of 1930 and 1934.

4. See Destler (1995, p. 7). Also Gilpin (1987) concerning the United States as a post–World War II economic hegemon.

5. See ITA (1999, table 1). Also Pollack and Shaffer (2001b, pp. 7–10).

6. On the switch from U.S. trade surplus to trade deficit in 1971, see "U.S. International Trade in Goods and Services" at www.census.gov/foreign-trade/statistics/historical/index.html (March 2003).

7. See Destler (1995, pp. 47–53).

mounting importance to U.S. industry—particularly trade in services and intellectual property protection.[8] Firms in high-technology sectors lobbied for a more aggressive U.S. trade policy under a reinforced Section 301 process.[9] The intellectual property lobby, in particular, "astutely packaged its demands as a solution to America's trade woes."[10]

Section 301 can, in this sense, be viewed as a tool to counter U.S. constituent demands for greater protectionism. By acting more aggressively to challenge foreign measures affecting U.S. high-tech, intellectual property, and services sectors, free trade advocates hoped to fend off pressures on Congress to raise U.S. protectionist barriers.[11] This strategy is analogous to what has been dubbed the "bicycle theory" of trade policy, which claims that "unless there is forward movement, the bicycle will fall over."[12] For some commentators, Section 301 was not so much a co-optation of U.S. government policy by business as a co-optation of business by the U.S. government. As one government official proclaimed in reference to Section 301: "When you let a dog piss all over a fire hydrant, he thinks he owns it."[13]

Sections 301–310 of the Trade Act of 1974 set forth a procedure for the USTR to investigate and take action against foreign trade barriers in response to petitions filed by *private* firms and trade associations. In theory, the USTR also may "self-initiate" an investigation, although such government initiation is typically done at the bidding of an industry or firm.[14] In 1974 Section 301 expanded an earlier provision applying to agricultural trade to cover all goods and services "associated with" trade in goods.[15] In 1979, 1984, 1988, and 1994, Congress passed amendments

8. See Destler (1995, pp. 47–53); and Bayard and Elliot (1994).

9. Milner (1990, p. 171), citing with approval Sylvia Ostry (1990, chaps. 2 and 6).

10. Sell (1999, p. 175).

11. See Feketekuky (1990, pp. 94–96); and Destler (1995).

12. Jackson (1998, p. 24).

13. Quoted in Winham (1986, p. 316).

14. The USTR either self-initiates a Section 301 investigation (under Section 302(b)) or begins an investigation in response to a petition filed by an "interested person" (under Section 302(a)). An interested person includes any domestic association, firm, or worker.

15. Section 301's immediate predecessor was Section 252 of the Trade Expansions Act of 1962. Enacted in response to new agricultural trade barriers under the EC's Common Agricultural Policy, Section 252 authorized retaliation against unjustifiable foreign restrictions on U.S. agricultural exports. Section 252, however, was used only twice, once against the EC in response to EC variable tariffs on chicken exports, leading to the U.S.-EC "chicken war," and once against Canada in response to Canadian restrictions on U.S. meat imports. See Hudec (1990a).

further broadening the scope of Section 301 to cover foreign barriers to services and investment, intellectual property protection, competition law enforcement, and labor practices. These amendments also tightened the requirements on the U.S. executive by establishing narrower deadlines and limiting the president's discretion.

A procedure is of no value, however, if it is not effectively used. Pressure from executive branch departments giving higher priority to cold war foreign policy goals over the expansion of foreign market access constrained Section 301's use. As two former members of the USTR note, congressional representatives complained that "trade is the handmaiden of all other considerations of the U.S. government," so that U.S. administrations "use trade to barter for other non-trade issues."[16] As the era of the Marshall Plan and U.S. postwar competitive dominance receded, private firms viewed the Department of State, which coordinated U.S. trade policy through the 1950s, as particularly unresponsive to their needs. They successfully lobbied Congress to create the Office of the United States Trade Representative in 1962 (originally named the Office of the Special Representative for Trade Negotiations), then to raise the USTR post to a cabinet-level position in 1974, and finally in 1988, to transfer authority for making Section 301 decisions from the president to the USTR.[17] Through these changes, firms and their congressional allies wished to shift power in executive branch deliberations from those agencies that focused on nonexport goals (such as the Departments of State, Treasury, and Defense and the National Security Council) to those more likely to defend private export interests (such as the USTR and, on agricultural matters, the Department of Agriculture). The end of the cold war facilitated this administrative reorganization. The transfer of authority to the USTR permitted congressional committees to call before them the individual who formally made the decision under Section 301 and to press that person to take action or explain the reason for failing to do so. Although congressional committees could not call the president to testify before them, they could grill the USTR.

16. See Bello and Holmer (1990a). Milner (1990, p. 166) also confirms that "congressional frustration with the president's unwillingness to use Section 301 as it was intended impelled Congress to revise the statute."

17. See Destler (1995, pp. 105–06). The USTR's decisions, however, remained "subject to the specific direction, if any, of the President." See Trade Act of 1974, §301(a), 19 U.S.Code §241 (1998).

In creating a more automatic Section 301 process presided over by the USTR, Congress attempted to make the executive more "accountable" not only to Congress but also to industry.[18] By enhancing USTR authority and constraining executive discretion, Congress has, over time, helped foster coordination between government and the private sector to pry open foreign markets. The USTR was to report not just to the president, but also to Congress. And organized industries ensured that Congress knew how the USTR was doing.

Because the United States aggressively challenges foreign market barriers, some criticize U.S. trade policy as a tool for powerful business interests. Sylvia Ostry, former Canadian ambassador during the Uruguay Round trade negotiations, for one, has argued that "America does not have a trade policy. It has clients."[19] Ostry's remarks imply that U.S. interests are up for sale, particularly to those funding presidential and congressional campaigns. She contends, "High policy is seen as a responsibility as much of the senior levels of the business community as of the government."[20]

U.S. support for Chiquita Brands' opposition to the EC's banana licensing regime provides a clear example. Carl Lindner, Chiquita's president and controlling shareholder, was among the top three contributors to the Democratic and Republican parties in 1998.[21] He reportedly had coffee with the president and spent a night in the White House's Lincoln bedroom.[22] The Center for Responsive Politics, a nonpartisan and nonprofit organization, discloses that Lindner contributed more than $2.4 million over the 1996 and 1998 election cycles.[23]

According to one former USTR official, it certainly appeared that Lindner hoped "to buy" the WTO case from the USTR. Apparently, Lindner was present when former USTR Mickey Kantor met in a key breakfast meeting with U.S. Republican Senate leader Robert Dole about

18. See Bello and Holmer (1990a, p. 34).

19. See "At Daggers Drawn: First Bananas, Now Beef, Soon Genetically Modified Foods," *Economist*, May 8, 1999, p. 17 (citing Ostry). Ostry is now with the University of Toronto's Center for International Studies.

20. Ostry (1990, p. 19), also stating, "Paradoxically, the role of the private sector in U.S. trade policy making may be connected to the 'absence' of government."

21. See Brian Morrissey, "Protectionist Clouds Build," *Journal of Commerce,* April 1999, p. 6A.

22. See Michael Weisskopf, "The Busy Back-Door Men," *Time*, March 31, 1997, p. 40.

23. Contribution information available at www.opensecrets.org/index.asp (March 2003).

Congress's approval of the Uruguay Round Agreements Act, whereby the United States would join the WTO.[24] Lindner reportedly was joined by his outside counsel, Carolyn Gleason of the law firm McDermott Will & Emery. Senator Dole allegedly indicated to Kantor not only that he liked the new draft of the Uruguay Round Agreements Act but that he would like the USTR to take up Chiquita's case, which Gleason could confirm was strong. Arguably, Senator Dole and Kantor reached an implicit understanding that the Clinton administration would further the chances of the act's approval were the USTR to take up Chiquita's case. Not only was Congress's ratification of U.S. membership in the WTO at stake. Senator Dole ran against President Bill Clinton in the next presidential election.

With congressional and executive support, the USTR dedicated thousands of personnel hours to challenging EC barriers to Chiquita banana imports. The litigation involved four WTO panels, a total of over one thousand pages of written briefs, buttressed by thousands of pages of annexes, and an eventual settlement in Chiquita's interest.[25] Just as the USTR fended for Chiquita's bananas, so it battled for Kodak's film, cattlemen's beef, and Pfizer's patents, bringing WTO claims on their behalf. Under this conception of privatized trade policy, if business is the USTR's client, then campaign funds and related forms of consideration must constitute the USTR's legal fees.

In bringing a case under WTO rules, however, the USTR does not assume the traditional role of private counsel toward its business client because the office cannot focus solely on winning a case through the strongest arguments. Rather, the USTR almost always has a conflict of interest with its "client" industry or firm. The USTR always must consider potential cases in which WTO members would challenge U.S. government policies, and other U.S. interests would need to be defended.

24. This was related to me in an interview with a former USTR official in Washington, D.C. (October 18, 2001).

25. See DS27 in appendix table 1. The case was litigated before a WTO dispute settlement panel, the WTO Appellate Body, and two subsequent WTO arbitration panels, respectively determining the implementation period, reviewing the EC's failure to comply with the decisions, and determining the extent of U.S. retaliatory sanctions. See Petersmann (2000). As regards the settlement, see Anthony DePalma, "Dole Says Trade Accord on Bananas Favors Rival," *New York Times*, April 14, 2001: "Dole [the company] contends that the agreement favors Chiquita Brands International because it establishes a system under which European import licenses will be distributed based on import levels from 1994 to 1996. . . . Chiquita officials generally expressed satisfaction with the agreement."

Cases involving food and drug standards, subsidies, and antidumping claims, to give just three examples, inherently raise these conflicts. In any individual WTO claim brought by the United States, the USTR also must be concerned about setting precedents for later cases in which the United States is on the defensive.

Under the current WTO system, the relation of U.S. private interests and public authorities is neither, as Ostry suggests, that of lawyer-client, nor, as some trade liberals desire, that of firms acting independently of government. Rather, as a result of the system's intergovernmental structure, firms must work with the USTR as a partner if they wish to successfully challenge trade barriers under WTO rules. The separate, reciprocal, overlapping interests of the USTR and the private sector give rise to ad hoc, hybrid public-private networks. The USTR depends on private sector lobbying in order to obtain support within both Congress and the administration for the USTR's policy goals and for the USTR's practical needs, from the granting of "fast-track" negotiating authority, or the ratification of new trade agreements, to approving the WTO accession of China or Russia, or the allocation of budgetary funds.[26]

The history of government requests for U.S. private sector support in the ratification of trade agreements did not begin in the 1990s. For instance, the overwhelming congressional support for U.S. ratification of the 1979 Tokyo Round agreements has been attributed in large part "to the laborious process of private sector consultation, in which . . . trade officials and industry representatives worked closely together to promote U.S. commercial interests."[27] However, the need for public support

26. See, for example, "House Appropriations Subcommittee Funds Trade Agencies," *Inside U.S. Trade*, June 9, 2000, noting cut in funds to the International Trade Commission on account of lobbying "from lawyers representing integrated steel producers," and an increase in USTR funds, though not as much as requested. "Fast-track" (or "trade-promotion") negotiating authority refers to a procedure whereby Congress grants the executive authority to negotiate trade liberalization agreements under prescribed mandates and subject to congressional oversight, pursuant to which, once an agreement is signed, Congress cannot amend it but must approve or reject it by an up or down vote. For an overview and assessment of "fast track," see Koh (1992, p. 143). Congress's grant of "trade-promotion" negotiating authority was not renewed between 1994 and 2002. In August 2002, Congress granted the Bush administration such authority by one vote, subject to numerous conditions, including an expiration date of June 1, 2005, which automatically will be extended until June 1, 2007, if neither House of the Congress adopts a resolution in opposition to the extension. See Trade Act of 2002, P.L. 107-210, §2103, 116 Stat. 933 (August 6, 2002).

27. Wolff (1985, pp. 320–21). Wolff is a former USTR general counsel who is a leading member of the Washington trade bar.

intensified in the 1990s with the growing politicization of trade policies. When the Clinton administration attempted to obtain congressional approval of China's accession to the WTO, for example, L. Craig Johnstone, of the U.S. Chamber of Commerce, stated, "We were asked by the administration if we could deliver the votes. . . . We said we could and we will."[28] In particular, the USTR depends on export-oriented industries to rally their employees and management to write, call, or otherwise lobby congressional representatives to support the USTR's positions.[29] Following the USTR's successful WTO litigation against Japan and Korea on behalf of the U.S. spirits industry in the late 1990s, the vice president of the Distilled Spirits Council of the United States (DISCUS) declared before the Senate Committee on Finance, "The WTO has played an integral role in our members' efforts to reduce or eliminate trade barriers and expand their imports to foreign markets." DISCUS correspondingly urged Congress "to provide the political and statutory authority [i.e. fast-track] required to strengthen and expand the WTO and reaffirm the leading role of the United States in the international trading system."[30]

In return, the Office of the United States Trade Representative aggressively defends industry interests, be it in multilateral or bilateral trade negotiations, WTO accession negotiations, or WTO litigation or settlement discussions. The USTR also provides exporting industries with a voice in interagency debates so that the president considers their desires when balancing multiple U.S. interests. Responding to U.S. efforts to protect U.S. intellectual property rights, Eric Smith, president of the International Intellectual Property Alliance, noted, "The U.S. government put enormous resources into the effort to convince Ukraine to take action. We thank them for their support."[31] When the process is successful, the

28. See Richard W. Stevenson, "White House and Business Groups to Push Congress on China Pact," *New York Times*, November 16, 1999, pp. A1, 10, quoting Johnson, senior vice president for international economic and national security affairs. See also "Administration Reaches Out to Business on Upcoming China MFN Vote," *Inside U.S. Trade*, December 24, 1999, p. 1.

29. See, for example, Gilligan (1997, pp. 135–37) concerning the importance of exporter lobbying for changing legislators' preferences.

30. Mark Z. Orr, vice president, International Issues and Trade, Distilled Spirits Council of the United States, Inc., *Trade Agreement Compliance,* Hearings before the Senate Committee on Finance, 116 Cong. 1 sess. (Government Printing Office, February 23, 1999).

31. See, for example, "Ukraine Named 'Priority Foreign Country' under USTR's 'Special 301' IPR Provision," *International Trade Reporter (BNA)*, March 15, 2001, p. 429, quoting Smith.

president and other officials at the highest level promote issues on industry's behalf, as President Clinton did when he defended industry interests concerning pharmaceutical patent protection during his 1999 visit with Nelson Mandela in South Africa.

Countervailing forces, however, may intervene. Other commercial interests, such as the generic drug industry, may counterlobby.[32] Or, activists promoting noncommercial causes, such as the provision of low-cost drugs to African AIDS victims, may undermine business-government strategies. For example, the Clinton administration at first advanced the pharmaceutical industry's interests in Africa, designating Vice President Al Gore as cochairman of a U.S.–South African bi-national commission on pharmaceutical issues. When Gore ran for president, however, hundreds of protestors gathered at his campaign events to chant "Gore's greed kills!" The activists pressed the administration to change its policies. The administration stalled and then capitulated.[33] Despite what some commentators suggest, firms are not "clients" that can dictate USTR actions, and the USTR is not a gun for hire. Rather, firms must negotiate ad hoc partnerships with the USTR, collaborating with the office where their interests coincide and domestic politics permits.

Over time, this interaction of public and private actors has intensified on account of structural changes from above (the relative legalization of the international trading system) and pressure from below (firms more aggressively demanding the removal of foreign trade barriers as they become more dependent on cross-border trade and investment in a globalizing economy). Section 301 constitutes a specific legal provision for private solicitation of public assistance on trade matters. However, it also represents much more. It forms part of a larger informal process of public and private actors, holding interdependent resources, working through networks to advance their reciprocal interests in a globalizing economy. They do so by deploying and operating in the shadow of public international trade law.

32. On the negative impact of U.S. implementation of the TRIPS Agreement on the U.S. generic drug industry, see Grygiel (1997, p. 47).

33. See Steven Meyers, "South Africa and U.S. End Dispute over Drugs," *New York Times*, September 18, 1999, p. A8; Doug Ireland, "AIDS Drugs for Africa," *Nation*, October 4, 1999, p. 5; and Gary Yerkey, "President Orders Easing of IPR Policy for Sub-Saharan Africa to Help Fight AIDS," *International Trade Reporter (BNA)*, May 18, 2000, p. 792.

## The Legal and Institutional Frameworks

To understand how U.S. public-private partnerships operate in international dispute settlement, one first needs to examine Section 301's framework and the governmental structure for its implementation. Section 301 sets forth four grounds on which the USTR may bring a WTO complaint or otherwise respond (and possibly retaliate) against a foreign country practice that restricts U.S. exports. Two of the grounds formally trigger "mandatory action": where there is a violation of "any trade agreement" or the violation of any "international legal rights of the United States."[34] In practice, at least in regard to the WTO's members, these "mandatory" grounds should be based on alleged violations of one of the WTO's nineteen agreements. Under the remaining two grounds, the USTR holds the discretionary power to take action where a foreign practice "restricts United States commerce" and is either "discriminatory" or "unreasonable."[35] The term "unreasonable" was used in the original 1974 version of Section 301 but was left undefined until 1984. In 1988 the definition was expanded to refer to any act that is "unfair or inequitable," including the following potpourri of examples:

> *(i) [denial of] fair and equitable—*
> *(I) opportunities for the establishment of an enterprise,*
> *(II) provision of adequate and effective protection of intellectual property rights notwithstanding that the foreign country may be in compliance with specific obligations of the [TRIPS Agreement] . . . ,*
> *(IV) market opportunities, including the toleration by a foreign government of systematic anti-competitive activities . . . ,*
> *(ii) constitutes export targeting, or*
> *(iii) constitutes a persistent pattern of conduct that—*
> *(I) denies workers the right of association, [and a list of other labor rights].*

34. See Trade Act of 1974, §301(a), 19 U.S. Code §2411(a). Prior to the creation of the WTO, private parties also brought Section 301 cases in response to alleged violations of bilateral agreements, such as "Friendship, Navigation and Commerce Agreements." See Bhala and Kennedy (1998, pp. 1024–25). The Bush administration's negotiation of bilateral trade agreements could signal a renewed U.S. focus on bilateral trade instruments. See Gordon (2003, p. 105).

35. See Trade Act of 1974, §301(b), 19 U.S. Code §2411(b).

Foreigners criticize these discretionary grounds, particularly because they open-endedly grant authority to the USTR to impose unilateral trade restrictions on account of a practice that irks some U.S. producer interest, but does not violate any WTO or other legal obligation. As the human rights scholar Philip Alston writes regarding the labor provisions in Section 301, "the form in which the standards [of Section 301's labor provisions] are stated is so bald and inadequate as to have the effect of providing a carte blanche to the relevant U.S. government agencies, thereby enabling them to opt for whatever standards they choose to set in a given situation."[36] As an EC representative states, "Section 301 was designed to be unilateral."[37]

In 1988, under congressional pressure to respond to the growing U.S. trade deficit, particularly with Japan, the Reagan administration agreed to further toughen Section 301 by adopting three new mechanisms, known as Super 301 (which targets "priority" foreign practices),[38] Special 301 (which targets intellectual property protection in "priority foreign countries"),[39] and telecom 301 (which targets "priority" foreign telecommunications markets).[40] Firms relying on intellectual property and advanced technology were a driving force behind these provisions, as their political clout in the United States rose. After the USTR obtained

36. Alston (1993, pp. 7–8).

37. Alistair Stewart, head of DG Trade's Market Access Unit, telephone interview, January 16, 2002.

38. Under the initial version of Super 301, the USTR was to identify "priority practices" and "priority foreign countries." Although Congress provided for no termination date for Special 301 and telecom 301, it initially created Super 301 for a two-year period. When the Clinton administration renewed Super 301 in 1994 by executive order, the criterion of "priority foreign countries" was dropped, so that Super 301 began to look more like the basic Section 301 statute. Under this version of Super 301, the USTR was to identify "priority foreign practices" whose elimination "is likely to have the most significant potential to increase United States exports," thereby triggering the normal Section 301 process. See Trade Act of 1974, 19 U.S. Code §2420(a)(1)(B). The Clinton administration continued Super 301 by executive order during most of its tenure, reinstating Super 301 through 2001–02 by executive order in March 1999. The Bush administration was undecided as to whether to continue it. See "USTR to Weigh Changing Annual Reviews of Foreign Trade Practices," *Inside U.S. Trade*, May 4, 2001; James Dorn, "The Need to Engage China," *Asian Wall Street Journal*, October 9, 2002.

39. Under Special 301, the USTR is to identify, on an annual basis, "priority foreign countries" that "(A) deny adequate and effective protection of intellectual property rights, or (B) deny fair and equitable market access to United States persons that rely upon intellectual property protection." Such a finding triggers an expedited Section 301 process. See Trade Act of 1974, 19 U.S. Code §2242.

40. 19 U.S. Code §3106.

private sector support, the administration developed a sliding scale under Super and Special 301 whereby the government would prioritize relevant countries and practices by placing them in one of three categories: (1) "priority" countries and practices, (2) those on a "priority watch list," and (3) those on a "watch list."[41] Private firms have attempted to use these categories and the deadlines built into the process to steadily jack up pressure on foreign countries to change their legislation and regulatory behavior. If the USTR lists a country or a country's practice in the "priority" category, the United States likely will file a WTO complaint or take unilateral retaliatory action.

In deciding whether to initiate an investigation into a trade matter, the Office of the United States Trade Representative must not act alone but must work through an interagency process. The relevant interagency committees are the "Section 301 committee" and the "Special 301 committee," which bring together lower-level officials from most federal agencies, including the Departments of State, Treasury, Commerce, Defense, Agriculture, and Transport, the National Security Council, the Food and Drug Administration, and the Environmental Protection Agency. A USTR representative chairs the meetings and is typically viewed by firms as their primary supporter in the process. If these agency officials do not agree on a matter, they refer it to committees assembling more senior officials (in order of referral, the Trade Policy Staff Committee, the Trade Policy Review Group, and, ultimately, members of the president's cabinet). In practice, the lower-level Section 301 and Special 301 committees avoid referral by obtaining guidance from their superiors.[42]

Overall, Section 301 does not so much provide a legal right, as it represents a process of public-private collaboration in fact-gathering, strategizing, negotiating, and (potentially) litigating over foreign trade restrictions. As a leading member of the Washington trade bar states, "The petitioning company or industry must develop the facts necessary to demonstrate the existence and effect of the foreign unfair practice. Although Section 301 contains references to an 'investigation,' neither USTR nor any other government agency in fact conducts—or has the resources to conduct—any meaningful investigation."[43] Despite some of

41. See Bello and Holmer (1990b, p. 267).

42. Former chair of Section 301 committee, telephone interview, May 14, 1999. Confirmed by Irving Williamson, another former chair of the Section 301 Committee, May 17, 1999.

43. See Cunningham (1998, p. 282).

its "mandatory" language, Section 301's legal criteria remain sufficiently subjective to grant the interagency committees considerable discretion as to whether to take action. As former USTR Robert Strauss allegedly gibed, Section 301 is "mandatory but not compulsory."[44] Even in "mandatory" cases, there is a gaping hole in the procedure, since the USTR retains discretion regarding whether to start an investigation in the first place. Section 302 of the act provides that "the Trade Representative shall review the allegations in any petition . . . and . . . shall determine whether to initiate an investigation" but does not expressly create any obligation for the USTR to investigate.[45] In the statute's thirty-year existence, no administrative decision involving a Section 301 private petition has been subjected to judicial review because, in practice, private firms and the USTR informally coordinate a strategy before any formal petition is filed or "investigation" begun.[46]

If firms are to successfully challenge a foreign market barrier, they must rely on U.S. public authorities to represent their interests. They thus work the Section 301 process with the USTR as a network partner, and not as a bureaucracy whose actions they can force through a domestic legal proceeding. In short, what is referred to as "Section 301" should be viewed as a process of public-private collaboration more focused on problem solving than on litigation, a process in which formal Section 301 "investigations" are just one means of leverage among a larger arsenal. As outlined in the next section, this process of public-private collaboration is linked to, and conducted in the shadow of, WTO law.

## Private Firms' Strategic Use of the Dispute Settlement Process

A successful public-private collaboration to challenge foreign trade barriers requires interfirm coordination, an intensive exchange of information between public authorities and private firms, strategic use of leverage points against foreign governments, and the harnessing of political clout. This section explains how U.S. private firms work the process.

44. Bello and Holmer (1990a, p. 12).

45. Trade Act of 1974, §301, 19 U.S. Code §2412 (1998).

46. See Bhala and Kennedy (1998, pp. 1045–47), discussing criteria under which a Section 301 determination could potentially be subject to judicial review. In support of judicial review of Section 301 determinations, see Eichman and Horlick (1989); and Kennedy (1987). In opposition, Hudec (1990b).

## *Coordinating through Trade Associations*

Unless one or two firms dominate an industry, as Boeing does in the case of aircraft or Chiquita and Dole in the case of bananas, firms improve their chances of successfully challenging foreign trade restrictions when they coordinate their activities through a trade association. Even where a single firm dominates an industry, it may act under the gloss of an industry association: Archer Daniels Midland, for example, is the dominant member of the Corn Refiners Association, and Seagrams the dominant member of the distilled spirits association.[47] Through a trade association, a large firm declares that it is working for a broader industrial and national interest. Through a trade association, it hopes to more effectively rally political support in Congress when needed.

The trade association's representative is a middleman playing a diplomat's role, explaining positions, receiving pressure, and exercising pressure. As a former USTR official confirms, the association representative often acts like "guys in our foreign embassies," having to explain how Washington works back in Peoria and explain to Washington what Peoria wants.[48] Moreover, dominant firms "can make it tough" for trade association representatives, just as U.S. political officials can make a U.S. diplomat's life tough in an international organization, or the United States can make life tough for a representative of an international organization when the representative tries to balance the views of the United States against those of other members.

There are trade associations for just about everything in Washington. By the mid-1990s, there were more than 23,000 national associations and 64,000 regional, state, and local associations, in contrast to a mere 5,000 national associations in 1955 and 13,000 in 1975.[49] Just to cover the capital's daily special of pork, milk, and corn, there are the National Pork Producers Counsel, the National Milk Producers Federation, and the Corn Refiners Association. For firms relying on intellectual property protection, the Pharmaceutical Research and Manufacturers of America (PhRMA) represents the pharmaceutical industry, and the International Intellectual Property Alliance (IIPA) represents the publishing, film,

47. Interview in Washington, D.C., October 18, 2001.

48. Interview in Washington, D.C., October 18, 2001.

49. Shaiko (1998, p. 7), citing American Society of Association Executives. More than 600 corporations have full-time Washington, D.C., offices with a government relations department (p. 6). "Lobbying expenditures for 1996 totaled roughly $1 billion" (p. 15).

recording, and software industries.[50] These industries are represented by sector-specific associations as well, which, in turn, are members of IIPA, including the Association of American Publishers, the American Film Marketing Association, the Business Software Alliance, the Interactive Digital Software Association, the Motion Picture Association of America, the National Music Publishers' Association, and the Recording Industry Association of America.

Firms also form ad hoc associations targeting specific foreign practices: witness the Coalition against Australian Leather Subsidies. The coalition was formed to bring a Section 301 petition in August 1996, challenging Australia's grant of subsidies to its leather industry. Since the coalition remained unsatisfied with an Australian undertaking to terminate its leather subsidies, it pressed the USTR to bring a WTO case in May 1998 against Australia's subsidies for "automotive leather," which Australia agreed to remove in 1999 and eventually did so in 2000. Under the U.S.-Australian settlement, the Australian firm Howe & Co. agreed to pay back $7.2 million in government grants; Australia agreed to remove the eligibility of automotive leather from government support programs targeted for the textiles, clothing, and footwear sectors; and Australia agreed to prohibit any new direct or indirect subsidies for automotive leather manufacturers and sellers for a period of twelve years.[51]

Under a more legalized WTO system, WTO cases are demanding significantly more time, expense, and effort. The USTR is unlikely to expend scarce resources and limited political capital within the U.S. interagency process when a claim against a foreign government is not backed by broad sectoral support. Where the USTR agrees to form an ad hoc public-private network on a specific trade matter, it wants a strong partner. Smaller claimants may pursue successful public-private collaborations if they are well-organized and present a strong case.[52] Large firms are not

50. PhRMA does not include generic drug companies.

51. The United States was unsatisfied with Australia's implementation of the WTO panel decision, stating that the entire grant package had not been repaid by the Australian beneficiary of the subsidy. See Daniel Pruzin, "U.S., Australia to Renew WTO Battle over Automotive Leather Export Subsidies," *International Trade Reporter (BNA),* October 13, 1999, pp. 1632–33. Further bilateral negotiations resulted in the settlement agreement. See Daniel Pruzin, "U.S. and Australia Tell WTO Details of Auto Leather Dispute Settlement," *International Trade Reporter (BNA)*, August 3, 2000, p. 1213.

52. By well-organized, I mean small companies that effectively work through trade associations, such as members of the computer software industry. As Richard Cunningham, a trade lawyer at Steptoe & Johnson, points out, the USTR may bring a claim on behalf of a

always successful, especially when there is a large countervailing interest that may constrain the United States, as has occurred in the EC's defense of Airbus. In general, however, large and well-organized commercial interests are more successful in working the process.

## *Public-Private Exchange of Information*

Firms do not simply "buy" USTR assistance by collectively garnering congressional backing. To persuade the Office of the United States Trade Representative to take a case to the World Trade Organization, a firm normally must present the USTR with a strong legal case supported by a detailed factual record. The USTR wants a strong partner not only in terms of ensuring broad industry support; it wants a winning case. The USTR does not want to waste its resources, impair its international credibility, and tarnish its reputation before Congress by bringing and then losing a weak legal case before the WTO. As a former general counsel at the USTR, Judith Bello, writes, administrative officials "tend to be institutionally risk-averse" and thus "are likely to feel substantial pressure to win any challenge they elect to make of another government's practice."[53] Some in the Washington trade bar maintain that the Japan–Photographic Film case—also known as the Kodak-Fuji case, after the firms behind the "intergovernmental" suit—exemplifies what can go wrong when the USTR pursues a WTO case for political reasons. The United States (and Kodak) lost the case at vast expense, leaving the USTR on the defensive when it then asked Congress for fast-track authority to negotiate new trade agreements. As one trade lawyer commented, "The Kodak case was a very chilling experience for USTR."[54]

Building a strong legal case requires an intensive exchange of information between the relevant public authority (USTR) and private firms. The process begins with the identification of foreign trade barriers and

smaller, albeit organized interest, because the claim is "too small to make waves." Cunningham cites, as an example, the Section 201 case brought by Harley Davidson resulting in "41 percent duties" against Japanese imports. Interview in Washington, D.C., October 18, 2001. Similarly, the "Border Waters Coalition against Discrimination in Services Trade" successfully used the Section 301 process against Canada. See "Canada and Practices Affecting Tourism and Sport Fishing (301-119)," at www.ustr.gov/enforcement/tradelaw.shtml (December 2001).

53. See Bello (1997, pp. 359–60).

54. Richard Cunningham, interview in Washington, D.C., October 18, 2001. Kodak's attorneys nonetheless claimed partial victory when Japan stated in its submissions to the WTO dispute settlement panel how it would enforce its antitrust laws. See Wolff (1998). However, the attorneys may have simply been making the best of their defeat.

culminates in a negotiated settlement or the bringing of a WTO complaint, and, if successful, the monitoring of compliance. The USTR has limited resources, particularly to compile and organize the factual basis for a successful WTO claim. It thus relies on industry assistance. Since U.S. industries, in turn, rely on the USTR to defend their interests under WTO law, they are pleased to oblige. If the USTR is unsatisfied with the factual dossier provided, it asks for more information. Firms are, in many ways, the USTR's eyes. Although U.S. embassies may help compile information, firms know best the impact of a trade restriction on the market in which they operate or wish to enter. Thus, as another member of the Washington trade bar and former USTR lawyer remarks, private counsel plays an "increasingly significant" role in WTO cases, since government agencies handling WTO matters are "extremely short-staffed" and in particular lack "access to the facts."[55]

Large and well-organized firms are often repeat players who, over time, learn to work the system.[56] As firms become experienced with the process, they learn to anticipate what the USTR needs. The process becomes routinized. In the area of intellectual property protection in particular, industry associations gather and compile information well in advance of the USTR's annual notice in the Federal Register requesting assistance in identifying and prioritizing foreign trade barriers.[57] The International Intellectual Property Association, for example, works with its members to gather information from around the world throughout the year. On the basis of the information gathered, the association prepares a detailed submission to the USTR in early February of each year focusing on copyright "piracy" and inadequate copyright enforcement around the world. In its report, the IIPA stresses the loss of high-wage U.S. jobs and billions of dollars of revenue to the U.S. economy (and implicitly, to the association's members).[58] The association's reports often comprise over 600

55. See, for example, Rossella Brevetti, "Lawyer Sees Growing Role for Private Counsel in WTO Cases," *International Trade Reporter (BNA)*, May 3, 2001, p. 720, noting remarks of Geralyn Ritter of the Washington firm Covington & Burling.

56. The term "repeat players" is from a classic piece by Galanter (1974).

57. See "Request for Public Comment with Respect to the Annual National Trade Estimate Report on Foreign Trade Barriers," 63 Fed. Reg. 619 (1998).

58. See, for example, Corbett Daly, "International Intellectual Property Alliance Urges USTR to Step Up Pressure on Ukraine," *International Trade Reporter (BNA)*, February 22, 2001, p. 301. See also "USTR Seeks WTO Dispute Panel over Korean Airport Procurement," *International Trade Reporter (BNA)*, May 5, 1999, p. 764, citing April 29, 1999, testimony of leaders of the U.S. software industry to the Senate Foreign Relations Subcommittee.

pages specifying how the USTR should prioritize countries in its final Special 301 report—categorizing them for the "priority" list, the "priority watch" list, and the "watch" list. According to an IIPA representative, the association's success in influencing U.S. governmental priorities is demonstrated by the similarity between the IIPA's initial submissions and the government's ultimate findings in the Special 301 Reports.[59]

Since not every country can be a priority foreign country, the IIPA targets those countries of greatest economic value (in terms of lost revenue) and precedential value (in terms of the global impact of winning a case). A sophisticated association thinks like a successful public interest lawyer. As one trade lawyer noted, "You do not bring *Brown* v. *Board of Education* until you successfully establish a supportive case law."[60] To maximize pressure on developing countries to enact and implement more protective copyright laws, the IIPA wants the USTR to choose cases that it clearly can win under the Agreement on Trade-Related Aspects of Intellectual Property Rights.

The USTR uses the submissions of private firms to pressure foreign governments to change their practices before the USTR issues its annual reports. The process is designed to stimulate negotiations. As a result, a fight often erupts over the facts before the USTR initiates a Section 301 investigation or files a complaint at the World Trade Organization.[61] The battle over the facts involves not only U.S. and foreign governmental representatives but also U.S. (and sometimes foreign) firms and their legal representatives. If the foreign government does not undertake to change its practices or otherwise convince the USTR that the U.S. industry has misrepresented the facts, it is listed in the relevant report, and this can trigger the filing of a WTO complaint.

### *Working the Interagency Process*

Once the trade association compiles the relevant information, it attempts to "educate" the members of the interagency 301 committee about the

59. IIPA representative, telephone interview, May 17, 1999.

60. Member of Washington trade bar, telephone interview, May 20, 1999. Similarly, in terms of U.S. domestic constitutional law cases, "cases do not arrive at the door steps of the Supreme Court like orphans in the night." There are usually organized interests behind them, often bringing them as test cases. See Cortner (1975, p. iv). In fact, as Lee Epstein (1991, p. 355) points out in regard to U.S. constitutional law litigation, "[Although] conventional wisdom certainly holds that public interest groups and civil rights/liberties groups dominate litigation, . . . they are far from the leading participants. That distinction belongs to commercial groups and governmental interests."

61. IIPA interview.

facts. Except for agricultural matters, associations typically start with the Office of the United States Trade Representative, since it leads the interagency process and is viewed as their ally and primary partner in the process. The U.S. Department of Agriculture takes the lead in defending U.S. agricultural interests. Associations, sometimes in coordination with their member firms, pay periodic visits to every agency representative on the Section 301 committee, as well as to their superiors within these agencies. Since there are divisions within as well as between government agencies, an industry needs to create strong working relationships with key contacts in each agency in order to teach the agency to appreciate—and support—the industry's concerns. Firms deploy their informational resources to persuade public authorities to work on their behalf. Firms find the Department of Commerce to be a particularly friendly agency, sometimes referred to as a "clientele" agency.[62]

Firms most frequently cite the Departments of State, Treasury, and Defense as "problem agencies." Treasury may oppose challenging a foreign trade barrier because an aggressive trade action could interfere with Treasury's efforts to shore up a country's financial system. The Defense Department will not want to compromise its use of air bases in Turkey over complaints about "pirated" Disney videos or Puff Daddy compact discs, no matter how valuable they may be to a U.S. industry or firm.

Trade associations generally are most concerned with the Department of State. There is an old saying among Washington lobbyists that "in the Department of State, you can find a desk for every country in the world except for the America desk."[63] Ambassadors are promoted because they are "diplomatic" and maintain friendly relations with officials of the countries where they are based. Associations report that they often must work to counter (what they term) "misinformation" provided by a foreign country desk in the Department of State, forwarded from a U.S. foreign embassy, and originally obtained from foreign government sources.[64]

The dialogue over trade barriers, in other words, becomes more than an intergovernmental one. It involves private firms debating factual and legal issues with representatives of multiple U.S. agencies and foreign

62. Interviews with trade association representatives and Washington trade lawyers, May 17–20, 1999. On industry capture of agencies, see, generally Lowi (1979, pp. 77–78).

63. Gary Horlick, telephone interview when a partner at O'Melveny & Myers, May 1999. See also Paula Stern (1990, pp. 193–94), citing congressional concerns with the State Department.

64. A representative from an intellectual property trade association, interview, May 17, 1999.

government officials. To further complicate the process, foreign firms often hire Washington lawyers to present their version of events. In the Kodak-Fuji case, Fuji hired a U.S. law firm to respond to Kodak's Section 301 petition at the U.S. national level, and, ultimately, to assist it (and Japan) in the WTO intergovernmental procedure. The combined legal fees of Dewey Ballantine (for Kodak) and Willkie Farr & Gallagher (for Fuji) were estimated to exceed U.S.$12,000,000 in that case.[65] The fight over the facts, occurring throughout the Section 301 and WTO process, can be an expensive one, favoring large or well-organized commercial interests.

### *Inciting Congressional Pressure*

Industry does not rely solely on persuasion of agency representatives concerning the facts. Firms work the political process as well, contacting congressional representatives directly and in coordination with industry associations, whether through their "government affairs" divisions or through outside lobbyists. Many of the leading lobbyists in Washington are law firms with major international trade practices. In terms of lobbying receipts in the first part of 1999, Patton Boggs ranked number two; Akin, Gump, Strauss, Hauer & Feld, number five; and Hogan & Hartson number seven.[66]

Firms press their case to local congressional representatives and those on the international trade subcommittees of the Senate Finance Committee and the House Ways and Means Committee. Local congressional representatives, in turn, contact their colleagues on these committees. Whenever a USTR official visits Congress, congressional representatives raise specific trade matters—whether about meat, steel rods, or leather—however unrelated to the meeting's agenda. In the WTO bananas case, the Republican congressional representative from Cincinnati, Ohio (the headquarters of Chiquita bananas), helped rally key members of the trade subcommittee of the Ways and Means Committee to demand that the USTR bring the WTO case.[67] When the EC did not comply with the WTO Appellate Body's ruling, congressional representatives

65. See John Maggs, "U.S. Goes to War over Film in Japan," *Journal of Commerce*, June 14, 1996, p. 1A. Confirmed in interview with member of the Washington trade bar, May 20, 1999.

66. See Mel Lewis, "Spheres of Influence Grow in Washington," *New York Times*, November 16, 1999, pp. C1, C27.

67. House staff member to House subcommittees, telephone interview, May 20, 1999.

drafted legislation that would have compelled the USTR to retaliate had the president not responded by committing to retaliate on his own. To assure a doubting Congress, President Clinton, politically vulnerable from the Monica Lewinsky scandal and House impeachment hearings, was compelled to confirm the undertaking by letter to the Senate majority leader and the speaker of the House.[68] At one point, Senate Majority Leader Trent Lott even attached a legislative rider that would "require industry approval of any trade deal the U.S. negotiates to reduce sanctions against the European Union for the Commission's beef and banana policies."[69]

In the EC–Meat Hormones case, the beef industry likewise pressed the USTR to take its case to the WTO and to retaliate against the EC for failing to comply with the WTO Appellate Body's ruling. The beef industry's trade organizations—the American Meat Institute, the National Cattlemen's Beef Association, and the U.S. Meat Export Federation—orchestrated countrywide pressure on the USTR.[70] Thus the beef industry could call on large numbers of congressional representatives to demand action. As one USTR representative stated, "We know the intensity of the issue by how we are approached. A phone call from a Congressman means a lot more than a letter."[71] Phone calls from members of Congress throughout the country mean even more. The threat of draft legislation forcing the USTR to act is most persuasive. Industries with significant operations in politically important states—such as California, New York, Texas, and Florida—can, in particular, effectively work the political process.[72]

In addition to threatening to pass legislation compelling action, Congress retains a number of devices to pressure the USTR on industry's behalf. Even were the president to veto such legislation, Congress can make the administration's life difficult through the "threat of electoral or budgetary reprisals."[73] The USTR may rely on a congressional representative's support for a renewal of "fast-track" trade negotiating authority

68. See Marc Selinger, "Clinton Averts Vote on EU Trade," *Washington Times*, October 13, 1998, p. B9.

69. See "Lott Rider Faces Fierce Opposition from Lawmakers, Others," *Inside U.S. Trade*, October 27, 2000, p. 1.

70. Representative from the National Cattlemen's Beef Association, telephone interview, May 20, 1999.

71. USTR official, telephone interview, May 14, 1999.

72. See Bello (1997, pp. 3590–60).

73. Gormley (1998, 214–15).

or for a vote on Chinese or Russian accession to the WTO. Similarly, a key congressional representative could withhold support for funding a new USTR hire, or for promoting a USTR official to a senior post. Firms attempt to use congressional clout where helpful to facilitate and enhance their leverage in public-private trade networks.

## *The Use of Leverage Points*

Ultimately, the exercise of power is about "who can influence whom to do what."[74] The USTR, as a public authority acting on behalf of U.S. commercial interests, deploys multiple strategies and successive deadlines and leverage points to steadily ratchet up pressure on foreign governments. These leverage points include the following: (1) the deadline for private submissions of information to the USTR concerning foreign trade barriers; (2) the deadline for the publication of USTR annual reports to Congress, which prioritize countries and their practices; (3) the deadline for initiating and concluding Section 301 investigations; and (4) the many deadlines in the WTO dispute settlement system. This is by no means an exhaustive list. Imaginative firms and their legal counsel devise multiple pressure-inducing tools. To name just one, firms can also lobby the U.S. International Trade Commission to conduct sectoral studies of foreign barriers in order to establish facts and political momentum for a U.S. case.[75]

The USTR gathers information from public and private sources and attempts to rank trade matters by their relative importance. Where USTR officials are overburdened, which is often the case, the U.S. governmental reports restate the formulations submitted by private industry. The Super 301/National Trade Estimate reports identify trade barriers on a country-by-country basis, estimating "the impact of these foreign practices on the value of U.S. imports," thereby prioritizing foreign practices.[76] The Special 301 reports categorize countries by their protection of intellectual property rights, setting forth the basis for a U.S. complaint in each case. The reports have become more detailed over time, with the National Trade Estimate Report consisting of over 400 pages since

74. See Gilpin (1975, p. 37), noting the psychological dimensions of power.

75. Trade lawyer Richard Cunningham, interview in Washington, D.C., October 18, 2001.

76. USTR (1999, p. 1).

1998.[77] The USTR likewise issues annual reports on foreign government procurement practices and barriers in the telecommunications sector. These reports have foreshadowed U.S. cases before the WTO regarding Mexico's telecommunications regulations and Korea's government procurement practices.[78]

A report's publication represents a "plateau in an ongoing dialogue" with foreign authorities. As a USTR official confirms, "What is valuable is the deadline. It does not matter what the date is."[79] The USTR even provides "draft" reports to foreign officials in a last-ditch effort to persuade them to change a regulatory policy or practice. If prepublication negotiations are unsuccessful, the practice is listed, forming the basis for initiating a WTO complaint. For example, following earlier warnings to the EC, Canada, and Argentina, the USTR announced, upon issuance of its 1999 Special 301 report, that it was filing WTO complaints against them for violating obligations under the TRIPS Agreement.[80] The USTR

77. The annual Trade Policy Agenda and Annual Report expanded every year from a 112-page report in 1995 to a 289-page report in 1999, to a 309-page report in 2000. With the transition to the Bush administration, however, the report did shorten to 231 pages in 2001, and 229 pages (plus annexes) in 2002. The National Trade Estimate Report grew from 387 pages in 1997, to 411 pages in 1998, to 436 pages in 1999, cutting back slightly to 432 pages in 2000, and expanding again to 472 pages in 2001 and 455 pages in 2002. See USTR, "USTR Resources," at www.ustr.gov./reports/index.shtml (January 2002). Compare "Industry Input to 2001 National Foreign Trade Barriers Report Sags," *Inside U.S. Trade*, January 11, 2002, p. 4: "One factor in some associations' decision not to submit comments was a new request from USTR that parties include the numerical estimates of the impact of trade measures." Another factor could be that the Bush administration appeared less ready to use WTO litigation at the beginning of its tenure.

78. The telecommunications report is required pursuant to Section 1377 of the 1988 act. See, for example, Gary Yerkey, "Telecommunications: U.S. Threatens Trade Action against Mexico, Colombia, South Africa and Taiwan," *International Trade Reporter (BNA)*, April 5, 2001, p. 528, in response to U.S. carrier complaints; and "USTR Seeks WTO Dispute Panel over Korean Airport Procurement," *International Trade Reporter*, noting claim against South Korean discriminatory practices in the bidding for the construction of the U.S.$6 billion Inchon International Airport project. The report on foreign government procurement practices initially was required under Title VII of the Omnibus Trade and Competitiveness Act of 1988 and was reinstated, simultaneously with Super 301, by Executive Order in 1999.

79. Former USTR member, telephone interview, May 14, 1999. The publication date for the Special 301 and NTE reports has been April 30 of each year, setting a deadline that focuses negotiations.

80. See "USTR Initiates WTO Consultations on IPR with Argentina, Canada, EU," *International Trade Reporter (BNA)*, May 5, 1999, p. 763. The TRIPS violations were all identified to the USTR by the pharmaceutical manufacturers' trade association, PhRMA, in its annual Special 301 submission. On September 18, 2000, the Appellate Body upheld a

negotiated in a similar fashion with concerned foreign countries before it published its 1999 Super 301 report, which triggered WTO complaints against the EC, India, and South Korea.[81]

U.S. trade associations, in coordination with the USTR, attempt to strategically use the process. According to a representative of the intellectual property industry, foreign countries now respond to trade association submissions with their own submissions, defending the legality of their practices and explaining why they should not be branded "priority" countries.[82] These reactions demonstrate that foreign governments, particularly developing country governments, take the process seriously. Firms attempt to use this fight over the facts as leverage to induce the USTR to press foreign governments to change their policies. The U.S. intellectual property industry claims that Special 301 has been a huge success, with countries around the world having adopted and strengthened intellectual property regimes. In testimony before Congress, Harvey Bale, senior vice president of PhRMA, argued that "Section and Special 301 have earned a special degree of importance because they have served to drive progress," citing "the most noteworthy successes . . . [of] the Andean Pact, China, Hungary, Indonesia, the Philippines, Taiwan and Thailand."[83]

---

panel decision that declared Canada's Patent Act inconsistent with TRIPS because it provided only seventeen years of patent protection. See DS170 in appendix table 1.

81. Upon publication of the report, the USTR announced new WTO cases against the EC (regarding French subsidies), India (for local content automobile requirements), and South Korea (for discriminatory restrictions on foreign beef). See DS 161, 172, 173, and 175 of appendix tables 1 and 2. See also "USTR to Launch Three WTO Cases in Connection with Super 301 Report," *International Trade Reporter (BNA)*, May 5, 1999, p. 762. On July 31, 2000, a panel ruled against South Korea's restrictive policies on beef. The Appellate Body largely upheld the panel's conclusions on the central Article III.4 national treatment claim. See Bhala and Gantz (2002, p. 488). On April 24, 2001, the United States and South Korea set a deadline of September 10, 2001, to implement the panel decision. See Daniel Pruzin, "U.S., Australia Agree with South Korea on Deadline to Implement WTO Beef Ruling," *International Trade Reporter (BNA)*, April 26, 2001, p. 661. India revised its policies for the automobile sector while the panel proceeding was pending. See Ravi Kanth, "U.S., EU Auto Dispute with India May Be Moot under India's New Policy," *International Trade Reporter (BNA)*, April 12, 2001, p. 580. Nonetheless, the WTO panel ruled against India's policies on December 12, 2001. India appealed, and then withdrew its appeal, of the panel's decision.

82. IIPA interview.

83. Harvey E. Bale, "Pharmaceutical Research and Manufacturers of America, Senate Finance/International Trade Law '301' Designations," Testimony before Senate Committee on Finance, 103 Cong. 2 sess. (GPO, June 24, 1994), concerning implementation of the Special 301 trade remedy law.

An intellectual property lobbyist for the copyright industry agreed: "Special 301 is a wonderful mechanism."[84]

The USTR avoids beginning a formal "investigation" on behalf of a private industry unless, at the end of the process, the United States is ready to retaliate or has another exit strategy.[85] According to a former Section 301 committee chair, "considerable air time" is given to the issue of "exit."[86] The USTR wants to be sure that if the foreign government refuses to make adequate concessions, the USTR has a preconceived plan. An exit strategy was particularly important before the WTO was established because unilateral U.S. retaliation could trigger counterretaliation and thereby infuriate other U.S. commercial constituents. With the advent of the WTO's legalized dispute settlement system, the most common exit strategy in an unsuccessful bilateral negotiation is to file a WTO complaint, which then triggers a new series of deadlines. When the USTR lists a foreign practice or initiates a Section 301 investigation, it signals to a foreign country that the United States will file a WTO claim or take some other action (within the constraints of WTO rules) if a settlement is not reached by a fixed date.

These trade reports serve as shadow WTO complaints and as maneuvers to induce concessionary settlements. Even when the United States initiates complaints before the WTO, it successfully settles most of them during the consultation period before a judicial panel is formed.[87] Moreover, as political scientists Marc Busch and Eric Reinhardt document, about two-thirds of WTO formal complaints that settle "prior to a

84. IIPA interview. Compare the assessment of Patrick Low (1993, p. 93), a leading trade economist and advocate of multilateralism, now at the WTO: "Special 301 has not been a success." Economist Anne Krueger (1995, p. 68) concurs. However, those who have demanded and worked the Section 301 process, particularly U.S. intellectual property firms and associations, would disagree with their conclusions.

85. The deadline by which the USTR must make its determination under Section 301 is eighteen months in the case of the violation of a trade agreement, and twelve months for all other Section 301 cases other than intellectual property cases that do not involve a trade agreement, for which the period is six months (Section 304(a)). Once the USTR makes its determination, it must implement action within thirty days, with a delay of up to six months being authorized in certain limited circumstances (Section 305(a)).

86. Telephone interview, May 14, 1999.

87. See, for example, Busch and Reinhardt (2000, p. 158): "One little-known fact about GATT/WTO is that fully three-fifths of all disputes end prior to a panel ruling, and most of these without a request for panel even being made." Also Busch and Reinhardt (2002, p. 474), noting that "upwards of 55 percent of disputes end in consultation (Table 3)," and the positive impact of the "shadow of the law . . . [on] concessions."

ruling (whether before or after the establishment of a panel), exhibited full or partial concessions by the defendant."[88] Busch and Reinhardt statistically show that "the net effect of invoking adjudication, in the form of panel establishment, is to significantly increase the level of liberalization of disputed measures."[89] This is what happened following a complaint initiated against Mexico in 2000 under the WTO telecommunications agreement, known as the Basic Telecom Agreement: Mexico's formerly government-owned firm, Telmex, agreed to significantly reduce its interconnection rates, opening the Mexican long-distance telephone market to greater competition from U.S. firms, and in 2001 the United States suspended the case.[90] When U.S. telecommunications firms still were dissatisfied with Telmex's concessions, however, the United States renewed its complaint, again increasing the pressure.[91]

At other times, the United States raises industry concerns before the relevant WTO committees responsible for overseeing WTO agreements while it negotiates a bilateral settlement. In 2000 the Slovak Republic, Rumania, Pakistan, and Bangladesh each announced before the WTO Committee on Balance of Payment Restrictions their respective reductions and phaseouts of import controls on balance of payments grounds, to the benefit of U.S. exporters.[92] They did so in the shadow of an earlier U.S. case against India's import restrictions on balance of payment grounds.[93] The USTR similarly announced that "U.S. pressure on Hungary regarding restrictive import policies for beef products resulted in Hungary's decision to open a special quota for high-quality North American beef," and that U.S. pressure on Korea resulted in a favorable

88. Busch and Reinhardt (2000, p. 162).

89. Busch and Reinhardt (2002, p. 474).

90. USTR official, interview in Washington, October 18, 2001. See also John Nagel, "Telmex, Rivals Finalize Connections Accord, Ending Years of Dispute, Easing WTO Battle," *International Trade Reporter (BNA)*, January 4, 2001, p. 6; and Rossella Brevetti, "U.S. Sees Possible Resolution to Telecom Issues with Mexico," *International Trade Reporter (BNA)*, June 7, 2001, p. 901.

91. See Daniel Pruzin, "Mexico Hits Out at U.S. for Pursuing WTO Claim on Mexican Telecom Market," *International Trade Reporter (BNA)*, March 14, 2002, p. 460. See also DS204 in appendix table 2.

92. USTR (2001, p. 84), referring to U.S. interventions in meetings of the WTO committees on agriculture and balance of payments.

93. Report of the Appellate Body, "India—Quantitative Restrictions on Imports of Agricultural, Textile and Industrial Products," WTO Document WT/DS90/AB/R (issued August 23, 1999, adopted September 22, 1999). See DS90 in appendix table 1.

modification of its administration of rice quotas.[94] In each case, the United States did not need to pursue a formal WTO complaint.

It is the threat of U.S. sanctions, and not the sanctions themselves, that induce countries to open their markets to U.S. products: "In fact, in only fifteen of the 119 Section 301 investigations made and disposed before August 9, 1999, were trade sanctions actually imposed."[95] Historically, there are many "significant success stories in U.S. companies' use of Section 301," or threatened use, to open up foreign markets and to protect their home market.[96] To give a more recent example of Section 301's strategic use, when the U.S. steel producer Nucor threatened to initiate a Section 301 case in November 2002 against Polish steel subsidies, it did so "to bring Poland to the negotiating table so that U.S. officials might persuade it to abandon its proposed subsidy package."[97]

Although Section 301 grants private firms legal rights to cause the USTR to act on their behalf, the process in fact induces the USTR and private firms to act as partners in an informal public-private network. In the end, a firm depends on the USTR to defend its interests in intergovernmental negotiations or litigation, and the USTR hopes to successfully remove the foreign barrier in the most effective manner in order to prop its own standing within the government. Firms thus rarely file a Section 301 petition against the USTR's advice.[98] A well-counseled firm approaches the USTR before submitting its petition. The USTR reviews and comments on draft petitions before recommending that one be filed. If the USTR believes that the Section 301 process is not the most effective way to have the barrier removed, it will so indicate. For this reason, the USTR has rarely had to formally reject a petition in Section 301's twenty-eight-year history. The last time it did so was in 1988, when it rejected petitions filed by the governor of Michigan concerning automobile components and by U.S. rice millers' associations concerning Japan.[99] In

94. USTR (2001, p. 40).

95. See Chang (2000, p. 1157): "Experience has shown that the power of Section 301 lies in the threat of a trade sanction, rather than sanction itself." Citing USTR, "Section 301 Table of Cases" (www.ustr.gov/reports/301report/act301.htm [August 1999]).

96. See Cunningham (1998, pp. 281–82); and Bayard and Elliott (1994).

97. "Nucor Threatens Section 301 Case over Polish Steel Subsidies," *Inside U.S. Trade*, November 1, 2002.

98. Williamson, interview, May 17, 1999.

99. The USTR rejected the Michigan governor's petition on the grounds that government officials are not authorized to file petitions under Section 302 and that the U.S.-Canada Free Trade Agreement was in the process of being implemented. The USTR rejected

November 2002, for example, when the USTR declined to initiate a Section 301 proceeding concerning the EC's fishing practices in the Atlantic Ocean, the Recreational Fishing Alliance voluntarily "withdrew" its petition, noting that it would work with the U.S. Department of Commerce to devise a solution with the EC. The trade association emphasized that it had been successful because its petition "received tremendous support from Congress" and the issue was now being addressed within "the highest levels of our government," which would press its cause in negotiations with the EC.[100]

## *Litigating before the World Trade Organization*

If the USTR, in consultation with industry, decides to file a complaint before the WTO Dispute Settlement Body, the exchange of information and general coordination between public trade officials and the affected industry intensifies. Demand for public-private collaboration has heightened since the WTO's formation in 1995 because the WTO dispute settlement system offers greater legal certainty and has become more resource-intensive. No longer may a defendant government block the formation of a judicial panel, the adoption of a panel ruling, or the authorization of sanctions, as under the former GATT regime.[101] Moreover, WTO panels increasingly apply a highly contextualized, case-specific approach, as opposed to generic rules.[102] This trend represents a switch

---

the petition filed by the Rice Council for Market Development and the Rice Millers' Association on the grounds that the Uruguay Round multilateral negotiations were a more effective means to proceed. See "USTR Rejects Michigan Governor's Complaint against Canada's Auto Duty-Remission Plan," *International Trade Reporter (BNA)*, November 23, 1988, p. 1535. Also "Petition by Rice Council for Market Development and Rice Millers' Association for Action Under Section 301; Decision Not to Initiate and Investigation; Reasons Therefore," 53 Fed. Reg. 970 (1988); and "Yeutter Rejects Rice Industry 301 Petition, Says GATT Is a Better Forum for Complaint," *International Trade Reporter (BNA)*, November 2, 1988, p. 1442.

100. See press release on the association's web site at www.savefish.com/pr10282.htm; and Gary Yerkey, "USTR Rejects Industry Call to Threaten EU with Trade Sanctions in Fishing Dispute," *International Trade Reporter (BNA)*, November 7, 2002, p. 1905, quoting an RFA representative as stating that they view "this outcome as a solid win for the U.S. fishing industry."

101. See Bhala and Kennedy (1998, p. 38).

102. See, for example, Report of the Appellate Body, "United States—Import Prohibition of Certain Shrimp and Shrimp Products," WTO Document WT/DS58/AB/R (issued October 12, 1998, adopted November 6, 1998), rejecting a generic analysis based on categories of trade measures in favor of a fact-specific analysis based on the "specific case"; and Report of the Appellate Body, "EC—Measures Concerning Meat and Meat Products

from a civil law to a more common law approach. Given the number of complicated cases that the USTR counsel now must litigate, the need for legally sophisticated factual development and argument, the tight deadlines imposed by the WTO's Dispute Settlement Understanding, and the political stakes of winning or losing WTO cases, the USTR typically requires industry to submit convincing factual and legal memoranda as a prerequisite to its filing of a WTO complaint. In the Korea–Alcoholic Beverages case, the USTR asked industry representatives to take pictures of bars, check websites and advertisements, and prepare a detailed market analysis for the USTR before it filed the suit.[103] As one USTR official states, the USTR wants a commitment from firms to respond to "time-sensitive demands for materials from [WTO] panels." Another confirms, "We at USTR rely on industry."[104]

With WTO cases becoming more factually and legally complex, the demands on WTO complainants and defendants multiply. The EC bananas case, for example, involved over a dozen claims under four WTO agreements.[105] The initial panel decision alone took up more than 470 pages, much of it setting forth the case's factual background, with a detailed description of the EC's byzantine banana quota and licensing regime. In the Japan–Photographic Film case, "twenty thousand pages of original Japanese-source documents were placed in evidence."[106] These WTO judicial decisions are not that far from the norm. The average length of the seventeen WTO panel decisions in 2001 and 2002 was 251 pages. Whereas GATT produced an average of 86 pages of panel findings a year from 1986 to1995, the WTO produced 693 pages of

---

(Hormones)," WTO Documents WTDS26/AB/R, WT/DS48/AB/R (issued January 16, 1998, adopted February 13, 1998), para. 133.

103. USTR representative and representative of distilled spirits association, telephone interviews, May 19, 1999.

104. USTR official, telephone interview in Washington, D.C., May 19, 1999. Confirmed in interview with USTR official, October 18, 2001. See also Bello (1997, pp. 360–61): the "administration's lawyers . . . rely upon and work closely with the directly affected private parties. The input provided by the latter serves as additional resources and thereby reduces the burden on an administration in WTO litigation."

105. The relevant WTO agreements were GATT (1994), General Agreement on Trade in Services (GATS), the Agreement on Trade-Related Investment Measures (TRIMS), and the Agreement on Import Licensing Procedures. Request for Consultations by Ecuador, Guatemala, Honduras, Mexico, and the United States, "European Communities—Regime for the Importation, Sale and Distribution of Bananas," WTO Document WT/DS27/1 (February 12, 1996).

106. See Wolff (1998, p. 956).

panel findings in 1999 alone, and this calculation includes only the findings sections of the decisions and excludes all Appellate Body decisions and follow-up panel and arbitration decisions concerning the implementation period, compliance measures, and sanctions.[107] If one counts the entire judicial reports, then there were 6,008 pages of panel decisions in 2000, and 7,251 pages if one includes Appellate Body and arbitration decisions.[108]

Although the USTR still seeks assistance from U.S. embassies, which may prepare helpful studies, private industry representatives are fundamental for the establishment of the factual record. U.S. attorneys involved in the bananas case maintain that a mark of U.S. success is that the factual description in the WTO panel report was taken largely from the U.S. brief.[109] Much of that factual description had been prepared by Chiquita and its lawyers.[110] In a case challenging Argentina's customs treatment of U.S. footwear and textiles, the USTR provided data on the customs treatment of 118 separate tariff categories.[111] Nike "worked the hill" to incite scores in Congress to press the USTR to litigate the case. Nike then provided the USTR with the required backup material.[112]

Because of the demands of the WTO process, industries typically hire Washington trade lawyers to assist them. The Distilled Spirits Council hired Michael Hathaway of Nalls, Frazier & Hathaway in Korea–Alcoholic Beverages. Chiquita hired Carolyn Gleason of McDermott Will & Emery, as did the American Meat Institute in EC–Meat Hormones. Kodak hired Alan Wolff of Dewey Ballantine in Japan–Photographic Film. Major Washington law firms worked on such U.S. defensive cases as the "foreign sales corporation" (FSC) tax subsidy case and the numerous

107. See Davey (2003).

108. According to the WTO's website, in 2000 there were eighteen panel decisions, eight Appellate Body decisions, fifteen implementation decisions (pursuant to DSU Article 21.3.c), seven compliance decisions (pursuant to DSU Article 21.5), and two decisions on sanctions (pursuant to DSU Article 22.6). Panel decisions took up 6,008 pages; Appellate Body decisions, 401pages; compliance panels, 606 pages; arbitral decisions concerning the implementation period, 61 pages; and arbitral decisions concerning the amount of authorized sanctions, 75 pages.

109. USTR official, telephone interview, May 19, 1999. Confirmed by a member of the Legal Service of the European Commission, interview in Brussels, June 22, 1999.

110. USTR official, telephone interview, May 19, 1999.

111. See Report of the Appellate Body, "Argentina—Measures Affecting Imports of Footwear, Textiles, Apparel and Other Items," WTO Document WT/DS56/AB/R (issued March 27, 1998, adopted April 22, 1998), para. 61. See also DS56 in appendix table 1.

112. A former member of USTR, telephone interview, April 24, 2003.

cases challenging U.S. antidumping laws.[113] In the early U.S.–Reformulated Gasoline case, both U.S. oil companies and environmentalists helped the USTR with its defense. One of the refiners' associations hired law professor and environmental advocate Dan Esty to assist in the formulation of the GATT article XX defense presented by the United States.[114] In many cases, private counsel has entirely written the first draft of the brief's factual section. For the legal analysis, counsel attempts to meet with USTR lawyers throughout the process to develop legal arguments and apply the facts. Counsel provides sample briefs or memoranda from which representatives at the USTR can cut and paste, as well as mark-ups of the USTR's drafts. The USTR does not necessarily take all or even part of what outside private counsel supplies. Yet the USTR often makes use of outside counsel's offerings, whether because it finds the briefs helpful, because it is overwhelmed, or because it is under political pressure. Sometimes lower-level USTR legal counsel receive mixed messages, as political winds shift, being told to "take responsibility for drafting everything," and then to "stop doing it yourself and start farming out to private firms."[115]

Defendant countries also hire private lawyers, including former USTR officials, to defend them against U.S. claims.[116] Defendants' growing legal sophistication heightens the need for cooperation between the USTR and the relevant U.S. industry. Private lawyers now may plead cases for WTO members before WTO dispute settlement panels and the WTO Appellate Body.[117] In the Korea–Alcoholic Beverages case, for example, Korea hired

113. E-mail message from USTR representative, March 12, 2002. For example, Wilmer Cutler & Pickering, among many other firms, worked on the FSC case.

114. Confirmed in e-mail from Daniel Esty, April 27, 2003.

115. USTR officials, interviews in Washington, D.C., August 19 and October 18, 2001. See also Brevetti, "Lawyer Sees Growing Role," p. 720, reporting remarks of Geralyn Ritter, attorney at the Washington, D.C., firm of Covington & Burling.

116. The trade lawyers at the Washington, D.C., firm Sidley Austin Brown & Wood, who worked for Powell Goldstein Frazer & Murphy until spring 2002, often represent developing country interests. There are almost thirty attorneys working for the firm on WTO matters. In 2000 the firm hired one of the USTR's most seasoned veterans, Amelia Porges, author of a 1,220-page, two-volume guide to GATT jurisprudence (see Porges 1995). In June 2000, the Powell Goldstein firm opened a branch in Geneva, which was led by Scott Anderson, who had worked for five years for the USTR on WTO cases, much of the time based in Geneva. See "Une firme d'avocats Americaine ouverts ses bureaux à Geneve près de l'Organisation Mondiale du Commerce," *Le Temps*, June 7, 2000, p. 33.

117. See, for example, Report of the Panel, "Indonesia—Certain Measures Affecting the Automobile Industry," WTO Document WT/DS54,55,59,64/R (July 2, 1998). Report of

a Brussels-based attorney, Marco Bronckers, to defend its interests. According to U.S. industry representatives, Bronckers "threw all sorts of garbage at us" in an attempt to demonstrate that Korea's tax system, which taxed whisky "at ten times the rate" of the rice-based *soju*, was nondiscriminatory because (in GATT terms) *soju* was not a competitive or "like product."[118] That is, Korea's attorney presented factual evidence designed to show that *soju* and U.S. distilled spirits were not competitive products because they were made for different markets.

In responding to Korea's proposed definition of the relevant product market, the USTR required extensive assistance from the U.S. distilled spirits trade association (DISCUS) and its consultants and Washington-based attorneys to compare the products' physical characteristics, distillation techniques, advertising and distribution methods, consumer uses and perceptions, and price elasticities, were the USTR to prevail in the case. The industry commissioned a study to show that the U.S. alcoholic beverages were competitive products, including on account of the positive "cross-price elasticity of demand" for these beverages. The United States presented this evidence to the panel. The panel found that the industry study "provided useful information" and was "helpful" in its determination of the key issue as to whether the U.S. spirits were "competitive" or "substitutable" products.[119] The panel held that they were, and that Korea had violated its WTO obligations by applying a dissimilar internal tax "so as to afford protection." As in the Japan–Alcoholic Beverages case, the WTO Appellate Body affirmed the panel's use of industry-commissioned studies as evidence, and the United States prevailed.[120] Following these decisions, the United States, EC, and their respective spirits industries successfully pressed countries around the world to reduce their taxes on U.S. and EC hard alcohol to the same level applied to local alcohol—the industry's primary goal.

---

the Appellate Body, "European Communities—Regime for the Importation, Sale and Distribution of Bananas," WTO Document WT/DS27/AB/R (September 9, 1997).

118. DISCUS representative, telephone interview, May 19, 1999.

119. Report of the Panel, "Korea—Taxes on Alcoholic Beverages," WTO Document WT/DS/75/R (September 17, 1998), paras. 10.91–.92. See also para. 10.44: a product's "cross-price elasticity of demand," "elasticity of substitution," or price elasticity of demand refers to the impact of one product's price differential (including an account of discriminatory internal taxes) on another product's consumption.

120. See Report of the Appellate Body, "Japan—Taxes on Alcoholic Beverages," WTO Document WT/DS/8/AB/R (issued October 4, 1996, adopted November 1, 1996); and Report of the Appellate Body, "Korea—Taxes on Alcoholic Beverages," WTO Document WT/DS/75/AB/R (January 18, 1999).

## The WTO's Impact on Section 301

Some commentators say that the WTO has curtailed Section 301's use.[121] This is true in the sense that the United States now brings most claims directly to the WTO, without first initiating a formal Section 301 investigation.[122] However, the claim is overstated because it assumes Section 301 is simply a unilateral U.S. legal procedure, as opposed to a larger process of public-private collaboration whose purpose is to gather facts and steadily ratchet up pressure on foreign governments in the shadow of international trade law. According to a former chair of the Section 301 committee, the existence of the WTO in many ways "simplified" the use of Section 301 as a process.[123] Even as a formal procedure, from 1995 to 1998 the USTR initiated twenty-four Section 301 investigations, exceeding the annual average during Section 301's prior history.[124] Although the number of formal Section 301 investigations has dropped since January 1999, the United States often has initiated WTO claims at the time of publicizing its Section 301 and Special 301 annual reports.[125] While there was no formal investigation under Section 301 in these cases, the USTR informally determined whether the United States had a strong legal claim before publishing the trade barrier in the annual report and launching the WTO complaint.

The United States also uses Section 301 to determine, in collaboration with private industry, the amount and type of sanction to apply where a WTO member fails to comply with an adopted WTO judicial decision. The USTR formally publishes a call for comments on its proposal to withdraw trade concessions in retaliation against a WTO member's

121. See, for example, Gero and Lannan (1995, p. 95): "Thus the DSU seriously erodes the credibility of unilateral retaliation under Section 301." Compare Hudec (1996, p. 12): "More than one WTO delegate opined that, by agreeing to the Understanding, the United States agreed to eliminate the WTO illegal trade practices of Section 301." Hudec notes, however, "This was not what the U.S. delegates were telling the Congress."

122. See Trachtman (2003, pp. 27–28), noting the reduced number of WTO cases initiated by the USTR that did not first entail a formal Section 301 investigation.

123. Williamson, interview, May 17, 1999.

124. Before 1995, there were ninety-six "301" actions initiated over a twenty-year period. See "Section 301 Table of Cases," at www.ustr.gov/enforcement/tradelaw.shtml (October 2001).

125. The August 1999 table of cases reports only one additional 301 action in 1999. See "Section 301 Table of Cases." For a current list of Section 301 cases, see USTR, "301 Alert," at www.ita.doc.gov/td/industry/otea/301alert/retallist.html (December 2001).

noncompliance with a ruling.[126] The USTR has collaborated with commercial interests in U.S. retaliations against the EC in the bananas and meat hormones cases, and in its preparation for retaliation following its successful case against Canada's dairy subsidies.

Overall, countries' acceptance of a more legalized WTO dispute settlement system has both facilitated and constrained Section 301's use. On the one hand, given the increased scope of the WTO's coverage and the automatic nature of its legal procedures, the USTR's decision whether to challenge a trade barrier is easier. The USTR is somewhat less concerned about determining an "exit option" in cases involving a WTO violation, since the USTR can file a WTO complaint that cannot be blocked.[127] If successful, and the foreign country complies with the WTO decision, the process concludes. If the foreign country refuses to comply with the WTO decision, the United States may retaliate through a withdrawal of equivalent trade concessions. The United States would not face the prospect of counterretaliation, other than reciprocation through the initiation of a WTO dispute on another matter.[128] To some, "The WTO has now become the preferred locus for 301 retaliations."[129] The WTO has made the threat to invoke international trade law more credible.

On the other hand, the WTO system has constrained the use of Section 301 unilateral actions by the United States. This constraint became apparent in 1995, the year of the WTO's formation, when the United States challenged Japanese practices in the automotive parts market. The USTR had self-initiated a Section 301 complaint in 1994 concerning alleged Japanese restrictive practices in this sector and announced sanctions worth $5.9 billion dollars if Japan did not agree to change its practices and commit to binding purchases of U.S. auto parts. Japan challenged the USTR's threat of unilateral sanctions before the WTO's Dispute Settlement Body. So constrained, the United States negotiated an agreement with nonbinding numerical targets, which commentators

126. See USTR, "301 Alert." A USTR official confirms how the USTR works with private consultants hired by industry in determining the amount and targeting of U.S. retaliations. USTR official, interview, October 18, 2001.

127. Nonetheless, some cases have been too politically sensitive to bring as a full WTO complaint. See chapter 4, note 37 (regarding the EC's challenge to Helms-Burton).

128. For example, a foreign country could bring a WTO complaint against the United States in reciprocation of a U.S. complaint, as the EC arguably did in its complaint against U.S. tax subsidies through U.S. "foreign sales corporations," following U.S. complaints against the EC's banana licensing regime and the EC's ban on hormone-treated beef.

129. Lawrence (2003, p. 16).

widely interpreted as a U.S. capitulation.[130] Kodak's Section 301 case, filed in 1995, confirmed the WTO's constraint on unilateral action against Japan. When Japan refused to yield to U.S. pressure to liberalize its photographic film sector and agree to facilitate an increase in Kodak's market share, the USTR took the case to the WTO, where it lost a panel decision in 1998.[131]

In November 1998, the EC, supported by Japan and sixteen other WTO members as third parties, challenged the legality of Section 301 before the WTO on the grounds that Section 301 mandated unilateral action, regardless of WTO dispute settlement requirements. In a controversial 350-page decision, the WTO panel found that certain provisions of the Section 301 statute constituted a "prima facie" violation of WTO obligations, but nonetheless upheld Section 301's compliance with WTO rules on account of the U.S. government's "undertakings" not to take action under Section 301before exhausting WTO procedures. The panel concluded that "should [the undertakings] be repudiated or in any other way removed by the US Administration or another branch of the US Government, the findings of conformity contained in these conclusions would no longer be warranted."[132] Although the WTO panel conditionally upheld the statute's legality, it deftly placed the United States on notice of the WTO's constraints on the statute's unilateral deployment. The USTR did not have to ask Congress to amend Section 301 on account of a WTO ruling, but only so long as the USTR did not apply Section 301 in violation of WTO procedural requirements.

Nonetheless, the WTO's constraint on U.S. unilateral trade measures is more limited than some commentators recognize. From a practical perspective, the United States still may take many forms of unilateral action against WTO members and not trigger WTO sanctions, since it can often exercise leverage in arguable compliance with WTO rules. As trade lawyer Richard Cunningham remarks, the United States could threaten "suspension or denial of various U.S. Government patents, [regulatory]

130. See "U.S. Threatens Duties on Luxury Cars Worth $5.9 Billion in Japan 301 Dispute," *International Trade Reporter (BNA)*, May 17, 1995, p. 849. For an overview of the case, see Abels (1996, p. 468).

131. Report of the Panel, "Japan—Measures Affecting Consumer Photographic Film and Paper," WTO Document WT/DS44/R (March 31, 1998).

132. See Report of the Panel, "United States—Sections 301–310 of the Trade Act of 1974," WTO Document WT/DS152/R (issued December 22, 1999, adopted January 27, 2000), para. 8.1. For an overview and analysis of the case, see Chang (2000), p. 1157.

approvals (FDA, for example), [and] licenses (e.g., FCC)." Similarly, an "offending country's eligibility for U.S. benefits—[including] foreign aid, Export-Import Bank financing, Overseas Private Investment Corporation or duty-free treatment under the Generalized System of Preferences—could be withdrawn or limited."[133] Washington trade lawyers readily devise and recommend such measures on behalf of their U.S. clients.

Intellectual property firms and agricultural trade associations, in particular, have used the Special 301 process and the annual renewal process of the U.S. General System of Preferences (GSP) program to lobby the USTR to remove developing countries' special tariff preferences. Under its GSP program, the United States grants reduced tariff rates for developing country imports, subject to U.S.-prescribed conditions. When Congress renewed the GSP program in 1984, it added new requirements for the protection of U.S. intellectual property. Not surprisingly, studies show that successful use of the Section 301 process has been "more likely with a GSP beneficiary," in large part because developing countries are more subject to U.S. coercion.[134] Under the WTO, U.S. industry still actively uses the GSP program as leverage. To give an example, U.S. industry argued in 1999 that Armenia, the Dominican Republic, Ukraine, Kazakhstan, Uzbekistan, and Moldova were not adequately protecting intellectual property rights. At an annual GSP review hearing before a U.S. interagency committee, the Dominican Republic ambassador "pledged to work with U.S. industry stakeholders, including IIPA, to ensure that intellectual property rights are protected and enforced."[135] Similarly, the USTR threatened to withdraw GSP benefits from the Philippines in its successful renegotiation of the Philippines' pork and poultry quotas in 1998.[136]

Intellectual property firms have not hesitated to lobby for other forms of pressure as well. In the Argentinian pharmaceutical case, members of the U.S. intellectual property industry suggested that the U.S. Food and Drug Administration ban the importation of Argentinian beef on the grounds that it is not free of foot-and-mouth disease. They thereby hoped

133. See Cunningham (1998, p. 281).

134. See Sykes (1992, p. 313). Also Sell (1998, p. 135), concerning use of Special 301 as leverage. For an overview of the GSP system, see Bhala and Kennedy (1998, pp. 444–69).

135. See Rosella Brevetti, "Interagency Committee Weighs Industry Complaints against Six Countries," *International Trade Reporter (BNA)*, May 18, 2000, p. 780.

136. Confirmed by a former member of the USTR, telephone interview, April 25, 2003, concerning the case WT/DS74.

to coerce Argentina to change its patent law before being obligated to do so under the TRIPS Agreement's transition rules. As one industry representative noted, "This would have gotten Argentina where it hurts."[137] The U.S. pharmaceutical companies nonetheless successfully prompted the USTR to withdraw 50 percent of Argentina's GSP benefits worth US$ 260 million.[138]

Between January 1995 and October 15, 2001, the USTR initiated eleven Section 301 investigations concerning "unreasonable practices" that do not violate WTO obligations, and settled seven of these to its alleged satisfaction.[139] In March 2001, the USTR initiated a new Section 301 investigation of the intellectual property laws and practices of Ukraine, found that Ukraine's policies were "unreasonable," suspended its GSP benefits, and announced additional trade sanctions valued at US$ 75 million a year.[140] The copyright trade association's representative confirms that threats to remove GSP benefits have been "significant and effective, particularly against small countries."[141]

Overall, although a legalized WTO system has somewhat reduced unilateral exercise of U.S. market power, it has simultaneously triggered exploitation by the United States of its comparative advantage in public and private lawyering. The constraints on unilateral political pressure in a category of cases is offset by the expanding scope of obligations covered by WTO rules, such as those involving trade in services and trade in products relying on intellectual property rights. A former USTR official now in law practice agrees that "TRIPS, GATS, standards and telecoms have generated a huge amount of work" for the Washington trade bar.[142] Of the twenty-four Section 301 complaints initiated from 1995 through 1998, six involved patents or copyrights and three involved the film, broadcasting, and magazine industries.[143] The United States initiated

137. Pharmaceutical trade lobbyist, telephone interview, May 20, 1999.

138. See John Maggs, "U.S. Is Set to Penalize Argentina for Piracy," *Journal of Commerce*, January 6, 1997, p. 1A. Also Schmertz and Meier (1997, p. 34).

139. See Cunningham and Emerson (2001, pp. 20–21).

140. See USTR (2002, p. 207).

141. IIPA interview.

142. A member of the Washington firm Hogan & Hartson, telephone interview, May 19, 1999.

143. The five primary Section 301 patent and copyright claims were (1) "Portugal's Practices Regarding Term of Patent Protection (301-103)," self-initiated by the USTR on April 30, 1996; (2) "India's Practices Regarding Patent Protection for Pharmaceuticals and Agricultural Chemicals (301-106)," self-initiated by the USTR on April 30, 1996; (3) "Pakistan's Practices Regarding Patent Protection for Pharmaceuticals and Agricultural

three WTO intellectual property–related complaints in 1999 and two more in May 2000, bringing to fourteen the number of such WTO complaints filed by the United States during the WTO's first five and a half years.[144] Although only two complaints have involved services, the number of services claims could grow in the future.[145] With these and other claims, the USTR may decide, on a case-by-case basis, whether to immediately file a WTO complaint or to use a formal Section 301 investigation to slowly ratchet up pressure.

Section 301's time deadlines arguably served a greater purpose before the World Trade Organization was formed, in large part because the prior GATT dispute settlement system offered no guaranteed time deadlines of its own. However, the WTO's Dispute Settlement Understanding now contains deadlines that also can be used as leverage points. For example, Article 4 of the Dispute Settlement Understanding provides that a party may request the establishment of a panel if "consultations fail to settle a dispute within 60 days." Under Article 12, the panel is to render its decision within "six months." Under Article 17, the Appellate Body is to issue its decision within "sixty days" of an appeal. Because of the WTO system's internal deadlines, the USTR may forgo a formal Section 301 investigation and directly request consultations before the WTO Dispute Settlement Body. The six cases that the United States brought to the WTO in May 1999, following the publication of the matters in the

---

Chemicals (301-104)," self-initiated by the USTR on April 30, 1996; (4) "Honduran Protection of Intellectual Property Rights (301-116)," self-initiated by the USTR on October 31, 1997; and (5) "Intellectual Property Laws and Practices of the Government of Paraguay (301-117)," self-initiated by the USTR on February 17, 1998. The sixth case, "Indonesian Practices Re: Promotion of Motor Vehicle Sector (301-109)," self-initiated by the USTR on October 8, 1996, also involved an intellectual property claim under article 64 of the TRIPS Agreement, but this claim was peripheral to the matter and did not succeed in the subsequent WTO case. In addition, there were a number of cases brought on behalf of entertainment and media industries, such as "Turkey's Practices Regarding the Imposition of a Discriminatory Tax on Box Office Revenues (301-105)," filed June 12, 1996, and "Canadian Communications Practices (301-98)," filed by Country Music Television on December 23, 1994, with the USTR initiating an investigation on February 6, 1995, and "Canadian Practices Affecting Periodicals (301-103)," self-initiated by the USTR on April 30, 1996.

144. See USTR (2001, p. 211; and 2000, p. 291).

145. On August 17, 2000, the United States brought its first WTO telecommunications services complaint against Mexico, following a review of Mexico's practices under Section 1377, the version of Section 301 for telecommunications matters. See USTR (2001, pp. 215–17). Three earlier services-related claims were filed in 1995, but each concerned the EC's banana licensing regime, alleging violations of GATS.

annual Special 301 and Super 301 reports, skipped formal Section 301 investigations.

A more effective WTO dispute settlement system has reduced the importance of Section 301's unilateral retaliatory aspects. However, the public-private fact-gathering, prioritizing, and strategizing that the Section 301 procedure entails remain. The public-private collaborative process now is deployed more informally in the background of WTO complaints and of settlement negotiations conducted in the WTO law's shadow.

## The Complementary Power of Ideas

U.S. public-private partnerships employ carrots as well as sticks to influence foreign government policies. In the intellectual property field, the carrot offered to a developing country is that recognizing and enforcing intellectual property rights will attract foreign direct investment, foster technology-intensive domestic investment, and ultimately improve its economic performance and national welfare by more closely integrating the country into the global economy. PhRMA maintains that aggressive U.S. pressure on developing countries to enhance pharmaceutical protection, despite their protests, is "benefitting them economically as well, as in terms of quality of their healthcare."[146] The wielded stick is that a developing country will face aggressive U.S. legal claims—or possibly other measures—if it does not comply with its WTO obligations.[147]

U.S. firms exploit ideas about the benefits of free trade in goods and services and the benefits of strong intellectual property protection to complement threats of WTO procedures and trade sanctions. Firms attempt to persuade foreign governments that a change in policy is in the foreign country's self-interest. This technique, coupled with threats to withdraw market access, was deployed by the United States to persuade developing countries to sign the TRIPS and GATS Agreements: As Susan Sell, of

146. See, for example, Bale, "Pharmaceutical Research."

147. See, for example, "U.S. Threatens Argentina with Complaint under TRIPs Agreement," *International Trade Reporter (BNA)*, October 20, 1999, p. 1712, recounting PhRMA's urging of the USTR to take action, and the hard-line stance that the USTR has taken. Also "Firms Likely to Urge U.S., EU to File WTO Case against Bulgaria over TRIPs," *International Trade Reporter (BNA)*, October. 15, 1997, p. 1749, describing private firms' lobbying effort against Bulgaria when it attempted to extend its transition period by being classified as a developing country, and reporting industry representatives' insistence that immediate TRIPS implementation be a requirement for WTO accession.

George Washington University, notes, "It was not merely [U.S. corporate actors'] relative economic power that led to their economic success [with the TRIPS Agreement], but their command of IP expertise, their ideas, their information, and their skills in translating complex issues into political discourse."[148] Similarly, political scientists William Drake and Kalypso Nicolaidis have documented how industry worked with U.S. trade representatives and an epistemic network of academics and other "experts" to build the perception that services also constitute traded products that should be covered by trade rules. The International Chamber of Commerce, the U.S. Council for International Business, the Coalition of Services Industries, and "other industry alliances" were active participants in this endeavor.[149] Gradually, these public-private networks were able to break down developing country resistance to the incorporation of services into the international trade regime so that the WTO General Agreement on Trade in Services could be concluded.

U.S. public-private partnerships exploit ideas that advance their material interests as complements to more coercive legal and extralegal actions. Most economists believe that the TRIPS and GATS Agreements should lead to a net flow of funds from developing countries to the United States and to U.S. corporate interests.[150] Following the WTO's creation, U.S. industry continued to work with U.S. public officials to "educate" foreign governments about the benefits of complying with these and other WTO obligations. Industry successfully lobbied the USTR and Congress to allocate funds for educational efforts abroad, often nominally sponsored by international organizations such as the WTO or, in the case of intellectual property rights, the World Intellectual Property Organization (WIPO).[151] The United States has regularly sent representatives from the U.S. pharmaceutical and copyright industries to Geneva as

148. See Sell (1999, pp. 192, also 190). Sell (1998, p. 36) also noted, however, that although U.S. private actors successfully pressured U.S. politicians to take up their cause, and although developing countries accepted the TRIPS Agreement, developing countries "have resisted implementing and enforcing the new policies."

149. Drake and Nicolaidis (1992, pp. 38, 46, 50–51, 56, 61, 66).

150. See, for example, Maskus (2000, p. 142), noting an estimate of "static risk transfers . . . of some $5.8 billion per year" to the United States, and "a net outward transfer of around $1.2 billion per year" for Brazil. Also Deardorff (1990, p. 507): "Patent protection is almost certain to redistribute welfare away from developing countries." For a study of the impact of the TRIPS Agreement on India, see, for example, Watal (2000, p. 733), noting "that prices are likely to increase and welfare likely to decrease" in India.

151. Representative of IIPA, telephone interview, May 17, 1999.

WIPO "faculty" to educate developing country representatives about intellectual property matters.[152] And the U.S. government offers developing countries "technical assistance programs" for the creation of "effective enforcement regimes," the most common being "the review of draft [developing country] legislation" for the recognition and enforcement of intellectual property rights, invariably in connection with a country's efforts toward "joining the WTO."[153]

Finally, U.S. public-private partnerships can shape the jurisprudential application of WTO law to the United States's advantage. The WTO legal system is leaning toward a U.S. common law, fact-intensive, case-by-case adversarial approach. In the words of trade law scholar Raj Bhala, it has moved "away from the old-fashioned continental-style approach to international dispute resolution and towards the Americanization of adjudicatory mechanisms. The fact that the WTO's Appellate Body increasingly functions not simply like a court, as distinct from an arbitral tribunal, but like an American court, is one aspect of this more general trend in the global economy of the new millennium."[154] A more fact-intensive approach could put public representatives and private law firms experienced with common law traditions at a slight advantage. Pieter-Jan Kuijper, director of the Commission's foreign affairs section of the Legal Service and former director of the WTO's Legal Affairs division, confirms the Commission's concern, at least early on, that the United States is exercising undue influence in the development of WTO case law, so that WTO jurisprudence might be borrowing inappropriately from U.S. legal concepts.[155]

152. Members of IIPA and PhRMA, telephone interviews, May 17 and 20, 1999.

153. See Cheek (2001, p. 305).

154. Bhala (1999), pp. 847–49.

155. Pieter-Jan Kuijper, interview in Brussels, June 22, 1999, noting legal concepts of reasonableness, agency discretion, and provisional measures. The traditional dominance of U.S. law schools in educating and thereby shaping the perceptions of international trade lawyers also could ineluctably shape WTO jurisprudence. Courses in international trade law have been more frequently taught in the United States, partly in response to the larger U.S. market for international trade lawyers. A significant number of lawyers at the WTO secretariat, as well as trade lawyers in the Commission and in the Brussels bar, have studied trade law in the United States. Those who studied with John Jackson while he was at the University of Michigan Law School, and now at Georgetown, jokingly refer to themselves as the "Michigan" or "Jackson mafia." Stated in numerous interviews in Brussels and Geneva from 1999 to 2002. At the margins, it is not surprising that U.S. legal concepts and interpretive approaches creep into WTO jurisprudence.

## Constraints on the Role of Private Interests

Despite the relative success of U.S. public-private networks in WTO litigation and settlement negotiations, there are important limits to U.S. public-private cooperation, leading to tension between government officials and firm representatives and their lawyers. USTR officials find that some firms, and particularly their lawyers, can be overbearing and exacerbate the tension.[156] The fundamental cause of this tension is that the USTR represents the national interest, not the firm's interest. In particular, the USTR must consider that the United States may subsequently be on the defensive in a similar case. The USTR must be careful not to apply the relevant WTO agreements in a manner that could subsequently be used against the United States and upset other U.S. constituents. Thus, when USTR officials collaborate with a firm's outside legal counsel, they may engage in a battle of the briefs, with private counsel trying to insert statements binding U.S. policy, and the USTR stripping them out. In defending the FSC tax case against the EC challenge, for instance, private counsel had two goals: first, to win the case; second, to have the U.S. Treasury Department bind itself to rule interpretations favorable to the private sector.[157]

The USTR is particularly concerned about antidumping, countervailing duty, and safeguards cases, given that the United States has been the largest user of these import relief measures. The WTO 2001 Annual Report indicates that between July 1, 1999, and June 30, 2000, the United States had 300 antidumping measures in place, followed by the EC with 190.[158] Similarly, "Between 1980 and 1999, the [U.S. International Trade Administration] initiated 315 countervailing duty cases."[159]

However, an increasing number of WTO members are applying new antidumping and other import relief laws that can prejudice U.S. exporting firms. As of December 31, 2001, ninety-seven WTO members announced that they had enacted antidumping legislation, much of which is new legislation.[160] During the first five and a half years of the WTO

156. A former USTR lawyer, telephone interview, May 14, 1999.

157. USTR official, interview in Washington, D.C., October 18, 2001, dubbing this pas-de-deux a "form of ballet."

158. WTO (2001, p. 32). Similarly, the OECD lists over 300 U.S. antidumping suits from 1997 to 1998; see Hoeller, Girouard, and Colecchia (1998, p. 25).

159. Molyneux (2001, pp. 112).

160. WTO (2002, p.72). WTO (2000, pp. 21, 47) notes that "there were 523 initiations of antidumping investigations in 1998, 15% more than in the previous year. . . . During the period 1 January to 30 June 1999, there were 275 requests for initiation of anti-dumping investigations."

(through June 2000), U.S. exports were subject to eighty-one antidumping investigations in seventeen countries, resulting in fifty-one antidumping measures. The Cato Institute reported that the United States "was the third most popular target of antidumping measures worldwide—trailing only China and Japan" during this period, and that the number of antidumping measures in force against the United States rose 41 percent during the period 1996–2000 compared with 1990–1995.[161]

The United States, however, cannot challenge these third-country measures as strongly as prejudiced U.S. industries would like, because it does not wish to undermine its own antidumping and import relief procedures. As of February 2003, thirty of the first sixty-two WTO complaints involving antidumping or countervailing duty laws were brought against the United States.[162] In addition, eleven safeguard complaints were brought against U.S. safeguard laws, counting the eight complaints against the Bush administration's huge safeguard on steel products in March 2002 as only one complaint. There was no sign of a slowdown. These proliferating challenges to U.S. trade remedy laws generated vehement protest in the U.S. Congress.

In consequence, when the USTR challenges a foreign government's import relief actions, it is much less aggressive than would be a prejudiced commercial firm. For example, the USTR took a less incisive stance in challenging a Mexican antidumping measure against the U.S. sugar industry in order to retain greater discretion for U.S. administration of its laws. According to a USTR official, the United States did not press a "killer issue" in the WTO case because of opposition from the U.S. International Trade Commission that hears U.S. domestic antidumping suits.[163] Similarly, when a WTO panel held that an Australian firm must

161. See Lindsey and Ikenson (2001), also at www.freetrade.org/pubs/pas/tpa-014es.html (October 2001).

162. During the first nine months of 2001 alone, WTO members filed seven requests for consultations and panel formations with respect to U.S. antidumping and countervailing duty laws and measures. See, for example, "U.S. Peppered with WTO Complaints, Criticizes Prior Rulings," *Inside U.S. Trade*, August 24, 2001, p. 6, noting five new WTO challenges, including one against the "Byrd amendment," which provides for the distribution of "the proceeds from antidumping and countervailing duties to U.S. industry petitioners," three EC challenges to U.S. import restraints on steel, and a Canadian challenge to a U.S. provision that "delays the refunding of antidumping and countervailing duties."

163. A former official of the USTR, interview in Washington, D.C., October 18, 2001. The "killer issue" allegedly involved the definition of a "like product" for purposes of antidumping law. The U.S. International Trade Commission wished to retain maximum discretion.

return a WTO-illegal subsidy to the Australian government, the United States reacted unfavorably, maintaining that the panel's remedy went "beyond that sought by the United States."[164] Whereas the U.S. leather industry approved of the panel's remedy, the United States was concerned about the decision's impact on claims against U.S. practices, such as its preferential tax system for "foreign sales corporations." The United States eventually lost the "foreign sales corporations" case, which involved US$4 billion in annual tax subsidies. The U.S. government did not wish to have to demand U.S. corporations to pay back US$4 billion in annual subsidies because of the United States's own WTO-illegal provision. The U.S. beneficiaries of the subsidy would not be pleased, and they certainly would let Congress know their views. The United States thus settled the leather subsidies case outside of the WTO dispute settlement system in a manner less favorable to the U.S. automotive leather industry. Collier Shannon, the Washington, D.C., firm that represented the industry, itself had internal conflicts of interest, since one major partner, Paul Rosenthal, represented the U.S. steel industry, which certainly did not "appreciate" an aggressive challenge to government relief from foreign competition.[165] "If we take a position out of convenience in one case," remarked USTR General Counsel Peter Davidson, "we have to be prepared to have it shoved back in our face next time."[166]

For WTO issues such as intellectual property protection, one might think that U.S. industry and government positions always would align since the United States would always be a claimant. Yet the United States has been a defendant in copyright cases too. For example, the EC successfully challenged a provision of U.S. copyright law that exempts the restaurant and bar industry from paying royalties.[167] While the U.S. copy-

164. See Daniel Pruzin, "U.S. Puts Off Retaliation Decision in Australian Car Leather Complaint," *International Trade Reporter (BNA)*, March 23, 2000, p. 469, noting how "even the United States expressed misgivings, declaring that it did not entirely agree with the decision and that the panel's remedy 'goes beyond that sought by the Untied States.'" Compare "Barshefsky Pledges to Reach Out on FSC after Appellate Body Decision," *Inside U.S. Trade*, February 11, 2000, p. 5.

165. A Washington insider, interview, October 18, 2001. He was not suggesting that the firm had a conflict from a "legal" perspective, but that its clients had conflicting interests in the ruling.

166. Quoted in Jenna Greene, "U.S. Trade Laws in Cross Hairs of WTO Member Nations," *Legal Times*, November 7, 2001.

167. See Daniel Pruzin, "Dispute Panel Affirms U.S. Amendment on Music Licensing Violates WTO Rules," *International Trade Reporter (BNA)*, May 11, 2000, p. 730. For a history of the legislation and the tensions between industry interests in the case, see Helfer (2000, p. 93).

right industry hoped that the U.S. government would lose the case and even provided some assistance to the EC, the U.S. restaurant and bar industries and their allies in Congress who enacted the exemption demanded that the USTR vigorously defend it. When the United States lost the case, it did not revise the law but rather entered into a financial arrangement with the EC.[168] Thus when bringing copyright claims against third countries under the TRIPS Agreement, the USTR must assess the implications for the copyright laws of the United States itself before formulating arguments. Even in copyright cases, U.S. firms may want the USTR to take a tougher position than the USTR will advance.

U.S. trade litigation strategies also take into account U.S. domestic politics. The United States withdrew its threat of a WTO claim against South Africa in response to pressures from AIDS activists on Vice President Gore's presidential campaign. In June 2001, the Bush administration withdrew a U.S. claim against compulsory licensing provisions under Brazil's patent law in the context of widespread protest against the U.S. action from advocacy groups claiming that the United States places corporate interests before life-and-death medical concerns.[169] U.S. Trade Representative Robert Zoellick apparently did not wish "to give opponents of trade liberalization a red-hot issue that appeared to give credence to the idea of the WTO interfering with poor countries' health policies."[170] While the U.S. pharmaceutical industry publicly supported the

168. In the "U.S.-Copyright" case, there was an arbitration under DSU Art. 25 to determine the level of compensation. The United States agreed to pay this compensation, which is to be distributed to EC collecting societies. See "Award of the Arbitrators on E.C. Complaint Concerning United States—Section 110(5) of the U.S. Copyright Act, Recourse to Arbitration under Article 25 of the DSU," WTO Document WT/DS160/ARB25/1 (November 9, 2001).

169. See, for example, Daniel Pruzin and Gary. G. Yerkey "United States Drops WTO Complaint against Brazil over HIV/AIDS Patent Law," *International Trade Reporter (BNA)*, June 28, 2001, p. 1002; and Daniel Pruzin, "U.S. Responds to Criticisms of Brazilian Patent Law Compliant," *International Trade Reporter (BNA)*, February 8, 2001, p. 238. Oxfam backed Brazil's efforts in a policy paper that maintained that the U.S. complaint was an assault on public health. See "Drug Companies vs. Brazil: The Threat to Public Health," at www.oxfam.org.uk/policy/papers/ctcbraz.htm (August 2001). Similarly, fifty-two countries of a fifty-three member United Nations Commission endorsed Brazil's AIDS policy and backed a resolution sponsored by Brazil that called on all states to promote access to AIDS drugs. See "UN Rights Body Backs Brazil on AIDS Drugs," p. 9, at www.news24.com/News24/Health/Aids_Focus/0,1113,2-14,659_1014970,00.html (August 2001).

170. See "U.S., Brazil End WTO Case on Patents, Split on Bilateral Process," *Inside U.S. Trade*, June 29, 2001, pp. 1–2.

U.S. decision, it "feared that the U.S. decision to back down . . . would send a signal to developing countries all over the world that it could not withstand the political heat that comes with aggressively pursuing TRIPS violations, especially with respect to medicines."[171] The pharmaceutical industry's fears were confirmed when USTR Robert Zoellick abandoned it with little consultation in agreeing to the "Doha declaration" regarding WTO enforcement of pharmaceutical patents.[172]

Most important, U.S. national security and foreign policy still affect U.S. strategies before the WTO. The impact of security policy has significantly increased since the attacks of September 11, 2001, that leveled the twin towers of the World Trade Center. Immediately afterward, USTR officials implied that the United States could tailor its stance toward countries on trade issues to obtain those countries' support in the U.S. fight against terrorist networks and the countries that harbor them. As USTR Robert Zoellick stated, "We need an economic strategy that complements our security strategy."[173] With a U.S.-led attack on Iraq looming, the Bush administration postponed filing a WTO complaint against the EC's de facto moratorium on the approval of genetically modified seeds because, in the words of one administration official, "there is no point in testing Europeans on food while they are being tested on Iraq."[174]

These limits to public-private collaboration demonstrate that U.S. trade litigation does not consist of a clientele relationship, but rather ad hoc public-private partnerships formed when diverse interests coincide. Even when they collaborate in WTO trade litigation, public and private interests are not perfectly synchronous. As in most partnerships, there are tensions. Nonetheless, the legalization of the WTO's dispute settlement system spurs U.S. public authorities and private industry to work together as partners to advance their separate, but reciprocal, interests.

171. See, for example, "U.S., Brazil End WTO Case."

172. E-mail from Washington insider, June 27, 2002. See also Gary Yerkey and Daniel Pruzin, "Agreement on TRIPS/Public Health Reached at WTO Ministerial in Doha," *International Trade Reporter (BNA)*, November 15, 2001, p. 1817, noting that "representatives with the pharmaceutical industry were less than enthusiastic," and that Swiss officials, also representing pharmaceutical interests, "expressed fury at being excluded."

173. Zoellick is quoted in the article "Looking Hopeful," *Economist*, September 22, 2001, p. 61.

174. Elizabeth Becker, "U.S. Delays Suing Europe over Ban on Modified Food," *New York Times*, February 4, 2003, p. 6. The United States initiated the WTO complaint after it declared victory in its invasion of Iraq and in its ouster of Sadaam Hussein's regime.

# 4 Is the EC Moving toward a U.S. Partnership Model?

The counterpart of the Office of the United States Trade Representative in Europe is the Trade Directorate-General of the European Commission. Like the USTR, the Commission often depends for its success in international trade litigation on information provided to it by affected firms and industries. Mutually advantageous European public-private partnerships have emerged from this interaction. Organized commercial interests have benefited through potential expansion into foreign markets and enhanced access to, and influence over, the EC institution responsible for negotiating with foreign governments on trade matters. The European Commission has benefited from private industry resources to support its negotiation and litigation of European trade claims. The Commission thereby has enhanced its stature among member states and powerful commercial constituents within the EC, as well as among foreign governments, including the United States.[1] In international trade negotiations, the European Commission has assumed a more dynamic leadership role.

1. As David Coen (1997, p. 104) writes, "The Commission will continue to develop its relationship with business to reinforce the

However, EC public-private partnerships operate quite differently from those in the United States. The EC's more convoluted policymaking process and more fragmented market slow the development of EC public-private trade networks. Directly or indirectly, the European Commission seeks approval of its trade policy initiatives by the EC's fifteen member states, often by consensus. Individual member states can impede the Commission's endeavors. Moreover, many European firms remain predominantly nation-based, even though European market integration has progressed significantly. European firms traditionally have had fewer contacts with the Commission in Brussels than U.S. firms have with officials in Washington. At times, the Commission has proactively sought contact with private firms, lobbying firms to lobby it.

Because the Commission plays a dominant role in forging EC public-private partnerships, this chapter focuses on its strategies. The reasons for the distinctive approaches of the United States and the EC are taken up in chapter 5. Although Commission-dominated public-private partnerships differ from those in the United States, they too have been quite successful in making use of the WTO system, particularly since 1997 when the Commission's new Market Access Strategy began to bear fruit. Although U.S. and EC political structures diverge, their trade litigation strategies have achieved comparable results.

## The EC's Shift to a Market Access Strategy

Between the time the EC was created in 1958 and the WTO in 1995, EC trade policy was relatively defensive. EC officials had to respond to domestic demands for protection on the one hand, and to trade liberalization proposals advanced by the United States to dismantle EC barriers, on the other. The original proposal for establishing a liberal trade regime

Commission's position in relation to nation states." Coen also concludes that "the Commission benefits from improved input into the national policy making process, the establishment of a wider constituency of pan-European firms, and greater policy-making legitimacy." Former U.S. assistant secretary of commerce Franklin Vargo notes, "We are dealing with the EU as a political institution on a large scale." See Vargo, "Issues in U.S.-European Union Trade: European Privacy Legislation and Biotechnology/Food Safety Policy," Testimony before the House Committee on International Relations, Federal News Service (May 7, 1998), referring to the New Transatlantic Agenda signed between the United States and European Union in December 1995. For an overview of the history of U.S.-EU economic relations from World War II through the 1990s, see Pollack and Shaffer (2001b).

under GATT was driven by the United States, not war-torn Europe. At the close of World War II, the United States pressed for a more liberal trade regime based on negotiations of reciprocally reduced tariffs. U.S. leaders such as Secretary of State Cordell Hull maintained that a liberal international regime was needed to avoid repetition of the protectionist policies of the 1930s, which they believed had contributed to economic retrenchment and nationalist tensions that facilitated the rise of the Nazi Party and helped kindle the century's second world war.[2] American leaders believed that liberal economic policies would help rejuvenate Europe and thereby also stem communist expansion from the Soviet east.[3]

The United States continued to play a leading role in the negotiation of seven rounds of multilateral trade negotiations, culminating in the completion of the Uruguay Round and the creation of the World Trade Organization. During the Uruguay Round negotiations, EC negotiators often found themselves responding to U.S. proposals rather than taking the initiative. Although member states broadly supported EC positions in the services and TRIPS negotiations, they differed sharply on agricultural and textile policies, the northern European states generally being more liberal-oriented and members from the south more protectionist.[4] The resulting delay and caution were anathema to productive initiatives. As Hugo Paemen, the European Commission's lead negotiator during the Uruguay Round observed: "Tensions between the Commission and Council over how the latter should exercise this control function created problems at important stages in the negotiations, inhibiting the Commission's ability to be flexible and proactive."[5] At one point, Prime Minister Alain Juppe of France attempted to undercut the Commission's authority by publicly lashing out at the EC's trade commissioner, Sir Leon Brittan: "We do not trust you, Monsieur Brittan, and we will never trust you."[6]

2. See Dam (1970); and Destler (1995, pp. 5–6). Also Goldstein (1993, pp. 137–63): "The national mood created a policy window, allowing those critical of high-tariff policy [such as Cordell Hull and other free-traders] to restructure tariff-making institutions to facilitate tariff reform. The shock of the Great Depression then created an opportunity for political entrepreneurs."

3. See Featherstone and Ginsberg (1993); and Schwok (1991).

4. Woolcock and Hodges (1996, p. 321). Compare Young (2001, p. 21): the concern that the EC has been constrained "from acting coherently and effectively in international trade negotiations . . . is exaggerated."

5. See Paemen and Bensch (1995); and Woolcock and Hodges (1996, p. 321).

6. See Lionel Barber and others, "U.S. Stands Ground on Farm Pact: Statement as France Renews Threats to Veto GATT Deal," *Financial Times*, September 23, 1993, p. 26; and "Except Us," *Economist*, October 16, 1999.

Once the WTO was established, the United States was quick to employ the organization's more legalized dispute settlement system, while the EC was initially on the defensive. Working in conjunction with private enterprises and trade associations, the United States initiated a series of high-profile cases against the EC, challenging long-standing, politically sensitive EC barriers to the importation of bananas and beef.[7] The United States brought eight of the first fifteen WTO complaints resulting in panel decisions. The EC, on the other hand, was challenger only twice (and those were cases also brought by the United States against Japan's alcohol taxes and Indonesia's national car regime).[8]

The EC's role was soon to change, as the European Commission felt pressured to show initiative. In February 1996, the European Commission announced a new Market Access Strategy designed to target more resources toward opening export markets. In essence, the strategy aims to comprehensively identify foreign barriers to EC exports, prioritize them, and press foreign governments to eliminate them. Sir Leon Brittan, the EC's liberal trade commissioner, officially announced the Market Access Strategy not before an audience of member state bureaucrats, but at a business symposium for executives from major EC exporting companies. There he declared a "D-Day for European Trade Policy," promising, "We are going onto the offensive, using our trade powers forcefully but legitimately to open new markets around the world."[9] These publicized remarks marked a sea change from the EC's more prudent, inward-looking, reactive trade policy of the past. Europe was again in conquest of new markets, this time not with guns and war ships, but with electronic databanks and legal briefs.

The process of bringing a trade claim begins with the awareness of an injury, which is then linked to a third-party violation of a right.[10] To

7. See Request for Consultations by Guatemala, Honduras, Mexico, and the United States, "European Communities—Regime for the Importation, Sale and Distribution of Bananas," WTO Document WT/DS16/1 (October 4, 1995); and Request for Consultations by the United States, "European Communities—Measures Concerning Meat and Meat Products (Hormones)," WTO Document WT/DS26/1 (January 31, 1996).

8. See WTO Secretariat, "Update of WTO Dispute Settlement Cases," WTO Document WT/DS/OV/10, (updated as of January 17, 2003); and appendix tables 1 and 3.

9. Directorate-General I Press Conference. See "EU Launches New Market Strategy," *Eurocom Monthly Bulletin*, December 1996, available at www.eurunion.org/news/eurecom/1996/ecom1296.htm (July 2001).

10. In the domestic sociolegal literature, these stages are referred to as naming, blaming, and claiming (that is, perceiving an injury, identifying a culpable party, and bringing a claim against that party). See Felstiner, Abel, and Sarat (1980–81, p. 631).

develop EC awareness of potential claims, Commissioner Brittan established within the Trade Directorate-General a Market Access Unit whose primary role was to interact with EC business interests concerning the trade problems that they faced. The unit created an immense database listing foreign trade barriers by sector and country. The list grew from 350 identified trade barriers in early 1996 to 800 in early 1997, and more than 1,200 in 1998.[11] Businesses could notify barriers through direct contact with the Market Access Unit or indirectly through a sector-specific or country desk within the Commission, through a member state official, through a member state foreign embassy, or through one of the EU's 126 foreign missions. Use of the site rose exponentially, from an average of 30,000 contacts per day in early 1996 to more than 150,000 daily contacts in 1998. The Commission estimated that businesses or their trade associations reported over 90 percent of the identified trade barriers.[12]

From a cynic's perspective, organizing a database is a perfect project for bureaucrats—or, in this case, that multilingual breed, Eurocrats. It is not policy; it is not a solution to business problems; but it is lots of paper—the database, if printed, was over 400,000 pages.[13] Although the U.S. Department of Commerce also created a database, U.S. firms disparaged it, as did many interviewed for this study at the USTR and the Department of Commerce.[14] Well-organized U.S. businesses that face a trade barrier go straight to those who aggressively negotiate on their behalf, the USTR trade negotiators. For them, computer databases can be left for the preparers of government reports.

11. The Market Access database is available on the Internet at http://mkaccdb.eu.int. The data were obtained in a telephone interview with Dorian Prince, former head of the Market Access Unit, on March 5, 1998, and confirmed in a subsequent interview with him on June 28, 1999, in Brussels (hereinafter, respectively, Prince interview, 1998; and Prince interview, 1999). See also Sir Leon Brittan, opening address to the second symposium on the Market Access Strategy, "The EU's Market Access Strategy: One Year On" (November 4, 1997). The database has been revised back to a list of about 850 trade barriers. The reduction results from the Commission's combining some items, eliminating unimportant ones, and resolving others. Alistair Stewart, head of the Market Access Unit, telephone interview, January 16, 2002.

12. Prince interviews, 1998 and 1999. Although the unit could not precisely track which of the 2,200 trade barriers were referred to it electronically, it estimated the number to be about 40 percent.

13. Prince interviews, 1998 and 1999.

14. Interviews with U.S. trade association, May 17, 1999; USTR officials, May 14, 1999; and Commerce official, May 24, 1999. The Commission reports, however, that other officials in the U.S. Department of Commerce speak approvingly of the database and wish that they had available such a developed tool. Stewart interview, 2002.

Interviewed EC business representatives, on the contrary, speak favorably of the Commission's database.[15] The database has served a collateral purpose in Europe not required in the United States. By publicizing its export-oriented strategy through the database, the Commission hoped to forge new links between the private sector and the Trade Directorate-General that otherwise were underdeveloped or did not exist. In the United States, businesses were already approaching the USTR when they faced trade barriers. The Commission lacked this luxury. While the USTR responded to onslaughts of private sector lobbying reinforced by congressional phone calls and committee grillings, the Commission had to contact firms to contact it. Were Brittan's D-Day not to be a British Dunkirk, the Commission had to rally European enterprises to create the public-private networks necessary for trade law's successful application. The Commission hired consultants to provide detailed sectoral and intrasectoral reports on trade barriers, hosted well-publicized informational fora on trade policy (which it urged business executives to attend), distributed glossy brochures, and otherwise solicited European businesses to work with it on EC trade matters.

Given the USTR's unilateral use of Section 301—particularly in the heyday of the 1980s—to muscle foreign countries to import U.S. products, U.S. firms knew that the USTR fought for their export interests. European firms had no such faith. In fact, the more liberal trade-oriented countries in Europe, such as Germany, the Netherlands, and the United Kingdom, opposed the EC's early version of Section 301, the New Commercial Policy Instrument (NCPI), and worked to impede its effective implementation. In the early NCPI case brought by the Dutch company AKZO against U.S. Section 337 of the Tariff Act of 1930, which barred imports on intellectual property grounds, the Dutch government opposed and tried to obstruct the EC's bringing of the GATT case.[16] The Dutch and other export-oriented European member states feared that permitting private firms to bring NCPI cases could trigger a mercantilist unraveling of the liberal trade regime, not its enforcement.

15. Numerous trade associations in Brussels, interviews, June 1999.

16. Members of the Brussels trade bar and a former member of the Commission's Legal Service in Brussels, interviews, June 22, 1999. For the NCPI case, see *Official Journal of the European Communities* 1986 C25/20. For the GATT case, see "United States—Section 337 of the Tariff Act of 1930," 1989 WL 587604 (GATT January 16, 1989).

Brittan's Trade Directorate-General significantly altered the EC's outlook on the offensive use of the WTO dispute settlement system. Commission units now systematically investigate barriers to EC trading interests, using the database as an organizational resource. An EC interagency group, the Market Access Action Group, consisting of representatives from different directorates-general, directorates, units, and desks within the Commission, periodically meets to assign responsibility for investigating trade barriers and to prioritize them.[17] In the investigation, the Commission determines whether the trade barrier exists, whether it constitutes a violation of a WTO agreement or a bilateral or regional one, and the extent of its economic impact on the EC. The EC also has been more active than any other WTO member in negotiating bilateral free trade agreements, multiplying the EC's trading rights against third countries.[18]

Yet, even more than its USTR counterpart, the Commission is understaffed.[19] As of May 2003, the Commission's WTO dispute settlement unit in its Trade Directorate-General still employed only twelve officials.[20] Thus to implement the Market Access Strategy, the Commission attempted to forge better direct working links with EC private enterprises and trade associations. The Commission requires private sector input, especially regarding a case's factual background, if it is to successfully

17. Prince interview, 1998. The Commission investigation typically will be conducted by the Market Access Unit in an Article 133 proceeding (described in the next section), although other units in DG Trade could take primary responsibility. Safeguards and subsidy cases, for example, involve the safeguards and subsidy units in DG Trade. In a TBR case (described later), the TBR unit conducts the investigation. The interagency group met less frequently in 2001–02 (about every two months) than it did in the late 1990s (almost every week), since more business was conducted by e-mail. Stewart interview, 2002.

18. The EC listed these agreements on its website. See "EC Regional Trade Agreements," at www.europa.eu.int/comm/trade/pdf/ecrtagr.pdf (May 2001). See also Gary Yerkey, "Business Execs Call on U.S. to Retake Leadership on Trade, Citing European Gains," *International Trade Reporter (BNA)*, February 15, 2001, pp. 260–61, noting number of free-trade pacts the EU signed since the conclusion of the Uruguay Round. The WTO 2001 Annual Report notes the EC was involved in the highest number of regional trade agreements.

19. Greenwood (2000, p. 80), writes, "Taken as a whole, the Commission has become dependent upon specialist input from outside interests. The European Commission is so small that there might be just one official with responsibility for the affairs of an entire business domain. It has therefore become dependent upon input from specialist outside interests, sometimes to the extent that European business interest groups write Commission reports."

20. E-mail message from a member of the WTO unit in DG Trade, May 12, 2003.

litigate or threaten litigation before the WTO. Many EC business associations have responded, albeit more slowly than in the United States. As Tim Jackson of the Scotch Whisky Association states,

> We must . . . be ready to assist the Commission (which sadly does not have unlimited resources to pursue such matters) often at very short notice when a WTO case is under way. For example, during the Japan case we had to commission market research to help the Commission refute some of Japan's initial submission. . . . It is a "partnership" exercise with other industry colleagues, respective Governments and the Commission.[21]

Jackson noted that the association was also "assisting the Commission by gathering market information/research for their Korea and Chile cases," which also resulted in successful outcomes for the Commission and the European spirits industry.[22]

As a result of these Commission investigations and public-private collaborations, the Commission requested more consultations before the WTO Dispute Settlement Body between 1997 and 2003 than any other WTO member, including the United States. The first three transatlantic disputes that resulted in WTO-adopted reports were all brought by the United States against the EC: the bananas case, the meat hormones case, and a case concerning tariff rates for computer equipment. From 1997 to 1999, however, the tide began to change. During this period, the Commission initiated thirty-six new WTO complaints (resulting in seventeen panel reports), compared with thirty-five U.S.-initiated complaints (resulting in eleven panel reports).

From January 2000 through January 2003, the EC dominated the use of the WTO dispute settlement system against the United States. The EC was the complainant in nineteen of the twenty-three WTO judicial

21. Remarks of Tim Jackson, head of the Scotch Whisky Association (SWA), at a conference in Geneva, May 1997, distributed at conference (on file with author). Confirmed by a USTR official, interview, May 19, 1999; and by a member of the Legal Service of the European Commission, interview, June 22, 1999, noting the trade association provided statistics, pictures of bars, and advertisements. See also "U.S., Europe, Canada Protest Delays in Amending Japan's Liquor Tax Structure," *International Trade Reporter (BNA)*, November 27, 1996, p. 1814, citing the Scotch Whisky Association's direct negotiations with Japanese politicians and government officials.

22. Jackson, 1997 interview; USTR official, 1999 interview; appendix table 3.

Table 4-1. *Adopted Panel and Appellate Body Reports Involving U.S. and EC Complaints*

| *Date of adoption* | *Party* | *As complainant* | *As defendant* |
|---|---|---|---|
| Jan 95–Dec 99 | U.S. | 14 | 5 |
| Jan 95–Dec 99 | EC | 4 | 5[a] |
| Jan 00–Jan 03 | U.S. | 5 | 21 |
| Jan 00–Jan 03 | EC | 19 | 3 |

a. The separate reports on U.S. and Canadian complaints against the EC's meat hormone regulations are treated as a single report. Similarly, the multiple banana cases are counted only once. Otherwise, this figure for the EC as a defendant would be higher.

decisions adopted during this period that were triggered by either a U.S. or EC complaint (table 4-1). The United States was complainant in only five of these twenty-three cases (once as co-complainant with the EC). During this same three-year period, the United States was defendant in twenty-one WTO judicial decisions (losing fifteen of them), of which the EC was complainant in eleven (winning eight). In contrast, the EC was a defendant only three times during this period, and the United States brought none of these complaints. From January 2000 through January 2003, the Commission brought nine of its thirteen WTO complaints against the United States, primarily attacking U.S. antidumping, antisubsidy and safeguard laws and measures. In contrast, the United States brought only three of its nine complaints against the EC. One of these was settled when the United States capitulated against the EC's successful WTO challenge of a U.S. safeguard on wheat gluten. Another was a weak reaction to the EC's challenge of the Bush administration's huge safeguard on steel products.[23]

The EC's successful challenge of U.S. export tax subsidies for "foreign sales corporations" (FSCs) helps explain this dramatic switch in the use of WTO dispute settlement. The EC stung the United States with its FSC complaint in November 1997, which it won before the Appellate Body in February 2000. When the United States failed to comply with the decision, the WTO authorized the EC to sanction the United States by withdrawing

23. "U.S. Drops Restrictions on Imports of Wheat Gluten, Offers Support for Industry," *International Trade Reporter (BNA)*, June 7, 2001, p. 890, noting that the EC agreed to terminate its measures on U.S. corn gluten once the United States terminated its WTO-illegal safeguard on EC wheat gluten. On the steel safeguard cases, see DS260 and DS248 in appendix tables 2 and 4.

trade concessions in an amount of US$4.043 billion dollars per year.[24] Were the EC to implement the sanctions, it would shut out multiple U.S. exports from the lucrative EC market. As one Washington trade lawyer remarked, "The way to understand the FSC case for the EU is not about getting $4 billion, but to emasculate U.S. trade policy and force the United States to deal with the EU in a bilateral relationship."[25] The Commission desired to show member states and European industries that it could effectively defend their interests abroad. The early flurry of U.S. cases against the EC helped spur it to do so.

## Alternative EC Tracks for Challenging Foreign Trade Barriers

The Commission may initiate a WTO complaint against a foreign trade barrier on behalf of a European commercial interest through one of two EC procedures: the traditional Article 133 process or the newer Trade Barrier Regulation (TBR). Pursuant to Article 133 of the European treaty, EC member state representatives meet with Commission trade officials on a weekly basis to monitor the Commission's implementation of EC trade policy. Before the Commission launches most WTO cases, it obtains informal member state approval through a committee of member state representatives. Under the TBR, European private enterprises may directly petition the Commission to investigate foreign trade barriers and represent their interests before the WTO in a manner analogous to that provided in U.S. Section 301. As part of its Market Access Strategy, the European Commission has promoted business use of the TBR. The two processes are described next, followed by an assessment of their relative use and effectiveness for advancing European public and private interests

24. The WTO panel acted as arbitrator in determining the amount pursuant to Article 22.6 of the WTO Settlement Understanding, rendering its decision in August 2002. See Dan Pruzin, "WTO Gives EU Green Light in Sanctions against United States over FSCs," *International Trade Reporter (BNA)*, September 5, 2002, p. 1484; and "European Commission News Release on Request to WTO Compliance Panel for Imposition of Sanctions in U.S., FSC Dispute, with Indicative Product List," *International Trade Reporter (BNA)*, November 23, 2000, p. 1792. The $4.043 billion amount "is based on the value of the subsidy granted by the US under the FSC scheme which the WTO found to be illegal earlier this year." See DS108 in appendix table 3.

25. Interview, Washington, D.C., October 18, 2001.

in WTO litigation and negotiations in the WTO's shadow. Table 4-2 provides an overview of the principal actors in the Article 133 and TBR processes.

### *Article 133 Process: Inside the Labyrinth*

The EC system for implementing trade policy is more convoluted than that of the United States because of the EC's quasi-federal, quasi-intergovernmental political structure. European member states have tried to increase their leverage over the shaping and application of global trade rules by pooling their resources and speaking with a single voice through the European Commission. At the same time, the member states are wary of granting too much authority to the Commission, which, in advancing some member state interests, could harm their own. The Commission's legal stance in a WTO complaint can implicate not only multiple European export interests but also multiple member state internal regulations, as well as EC regulations.

The traditional means for the EC to initiate trade complaints in GATT (and now the WTO) is through what is known as the Article 133 process, in reference to the EC treaty article governing EC trade policy.[26] Before assessing how the Commission and private enterprises work this process, however, it is important to review briefly the relations between the Commission and EC member state governments under the Article 133 procedure. Whereas much has been written on the relative roles and powers of the member states and Commission under Article 133 in the negotiation and approval of trade agreements, this chapter concentrates on how the Commission and European businesses deploy the Article 133 process to advance their interests through public-private networks operating in the shadow of WTO law.[27]

Under Article 133, the Council of the European Union, which consists of one representative from each of the fifteen member states, is to make

26. The provision governing EC authority over trade policy was initially numbered Article 113 of the Treaty Establishing the European Community of 1958. The Treaty of Amsterdam, ratified in May 1999, amended this treaty by adding new provisions and eliminating outdated ones. In the process, the articles of the treaty were renumbered. Article 113 became Article 133.

27. See, for example, Meunier and Nikolaidis (1999); Meunier (2000); Van den Bossche (1997, p. 23), addressing "the competence and conduct of the European Community in international economic relations"; Emiliou and O'Keeffe (1996); Maresceau (1993); and Macleod, Hendry, and Hyett (1996).

Table 4-2. *Actors and Their Roles in Article 133 and TBR Procedures*

| *Article 133* | | *Trade Barrier Regulation* | |
|---|---|---|---|
| *Actor* | *Actor's role* | *Actor* | *Actor's role* |
| Council | Formal decisionmaker for "implementation" of EC trade policy, though has not become involved in trade disputes. Council is to decide matters by QMV. | Council | Never been involved in a TBR decision. Council can revise a Commission TBR decision by QMV (the reverse of voting under Article 133). However, if the EC is to take trade countermeasures authorized by the WTO, then Council to decide by QMV. |
| COREPER | Informal decisionmaker beneath Council. Rarely involved. Heard Helms-Burton matter, but did not refer it to the Council. | COREPER | Same role, but never involved in a TBR decision. |
| Article 133 Committee, consists of one representative per member state | It is to "consult" with Commission over conduct of "negotiations." The *titulaires* meet once a month and the "deputies" meet weekly in Brussels concerning trade matters. | TBR committee, consists of one representative per member state | TBR committee is an "advisory committee." Any member state on the committee that objects to a Commission decision can refer the matter to the Council. |
| European Commission: DG Trade, divided into units for GATT, GATS, WTO dispute settlement, | Maintains market access database. Interacts with private firms. Agenda setter in the Article 133 Committee. Submits "proposals" for trade | European Commission: DG Trade, TBR unit | After consultation with the TBR committee, Commission can initiate "examination" of the complaint, and conduct an investigation. It is |

| | | | |
|---|---|---|---|
| market access, trade defense instruments, and so on | "negotiations" to the Council and "consults" with the Article 133 Committee. Maintains it has de jure authority to initiate WTO trade claims, and clearly has de facto authority. Works with Legal Service in WTO litigation. | | to "report" to the TBR committee within five to seven months. The procedure can be terminated or suspended. Commission decisions shall apply after ten days unless a member state refers matter to the Council. TBR unit assists Legal Service if matter litigated before the WTO. |
| Trade Commissioner | Final decisionmaker for filing of a WTO complaint | Trade commissioner | Final decisionmaker for filing of a WTO complaint. |
| Legal Service of the Commission | Primary litigator for the EC before WTO panels. | Legal Service of the Commission | Primary litigator for the EC before WTO panels. |
| Private businesses and trade associations | Can lobby, and provide information to, the Commission and member state officials for the EC to defend their interests and bring a case to the WTO. | Private businesses and trade associations | Individual enterprise can file a complaint to the Commission's TBR unit claiming a violation of a multilateral trade agreement. Also can file a complaint "on behalf of a Community industry" that has suffered injury from violation of a bilateral trade agreement. |
| Private lawyers | Can advise firms on potential WTO complaints. Can provide assistance to Commission in WTO litigation. Legal Service may hire a private law firm to assist it with a WTO case. | Private lawyers | Increasingly advise firms and trade associations on TBR complaints. Can provide assistance to Commission in WTO litigation. Legal Service may hire a private law firm to assist it with a WTO case. |

all decisions for "implementing" the EC's "common commercial policy" in response to proposals submitted by the European Commission.[28] The Council operates through sectoral variants, although external commercial policy is typically handled through the General Affairs Council, which consists of the foreign affairs ministers of the fifteen member states.[29] The Commission, which represents EC member states on trade matters that fall within the EC's competence, is instructed to conduct commercial negotiations with other countries and organizations in consultation with a committee of member state representatives, known as the "Article 133 Committee," again in reference to the treaty article. In practice, however, the Article 133 Committee has by and large deferred implementation of EC trade policy to the Commission, which, in turn, has provided European enterprises with a central contact in Brussels, facilitating the formation of EC public-private partnerships.

Although formally the General Affairs Council is to make all decisions on "implementing" the EC's external commercial policy, its authority is (at best) ambiguous, particularly in regard to the bringing of WTO trade complaints. First, since Article 133 refers to "negotiations" of trade agreements and not litigation, the Commission maintains that it is solely competent to decide whether to bring a trade complaint in implementation of the agreements.[30] The EC treaty, however, is silent on this point, and the member states could amend it to clearly place these powers in the Council were the Commission to ignore member state views. Consequently, to

28. Under Article 133, "(2) The Commission shall submit proposals to the Council for *implementing* the common commercial policy. (3) Where agreements with one or more States or international organizations need to be negotiated, the Commission shall make recommendations to the Council, which shall authorize the Commission to open the necessary *negotiations*. . . . The Commission shall conduct these negotiations in *consultation* with *a special committee* appointed by the Council to assist the Commission in this task and within the framework of such directives as the Council may issue to it. (4) In exercising the powers conferred upon it by this Article, the Council shall act by qualified majority vote" (emphasis added). "Treaty of Nice Amending the Treaty on European Union, the Treaties Establishing the European Communities and Certain Related Acts," *Official Journal of the European Communities*, ser. C, no. 080, March 3, 2001, p. 43.

29. The General Affairs Council is sometimes referred to as the Foreign Affairs Council, and informally as the "senior" Council. The two most important sectoral variants of the Council are the Agricultural and Ecofin (economic and finance) Councils. For an overview of the Council and its sectoral variants, see Hayes-Renshaw and Wallace (1997, pp. 14–15, 29–33); and Hix (1999, pp. 63–68). For ease of reference, I refer generically to the Council.

30. A member of the Commission's DG Trade, interview, Brussels, June 13, 2001, pointing to the Commission's powers as guardian of the treaty pursuant to Article 211 of the treaty (formerly Article 155). See also Woolcock (2000, pp. 387–88); and Bronckers and McNelis (2001, pp. 458–59).

maintain good relations with the Council, the Commission always obtains de facto approval of at least a "qualified majority" of the Article 133 Committee before initiating a WTO complaint.[31] As an official in the Commission's Trade Directorate-General states, the Commission uses the Article 133 Committee "as a sounding board" to ensure that it is "on the right track."[32] (Although the Commission filed a third-party submission before a WTO panel without the support of a qualified majority, the submission was an exception and did not involve the EC as a complainant.)[33] Second, the General Affairs Council only meets about once a month to discuss selected matters of political importance and rarely discusses matters brought before the Article 133 Committee regarding the implementation of trade agreements. The Council thus has delegated most of the Council's powers over trade matters (whatever they may be) to the Article 133 Committee, which, in turn, has deferred to the Commission.

The Article 133 Committee, which also consists of one representative from each member state, originally was created to "consult" with the European Commission in an advisory capacity about the Commission's implementation of Council decisions.[34] The Committee exercises authority informally, however. The Committee almost never takes a vote in its meetings, although votes are usually not necessary, since decisions are typically made by consensus. If no member state formally objects, the chair of the Article 133 meeting simply notes whether sufficient votes support the measure and if so, concludes the meeting by confirming the

31. Decisions on Article 133 matters are, technically, to be made by the Council by "qualified majority vote" (QMV). Under the EC system, votes on decisions to be taken by QMV are weighted per country, so that larger countries such as Germany have more votes than smaller ones. Article 205 of the EC treaty, as amended, sets forth the number of votes each member state holds on the Council, and the number of votes required to adopt an act by QMV. Under the system, in 2003 sixty-one out of a total of eighty-seven votes were required to pass an act by QMV following a Commission proposal. When the EC's membership expands, the voting calculations were to change as provided in the Treaty of Nice.

32. Interview in Brussels, June 16, 2001.

33. The Commission filed a third-party submission in support of Canada's and Brazil's claims before WTO panels against each other's aircraft subsidies, even though member states were divided because suppliers of airline parts from certain member states benefited from the subsidies, while others were harmed. Confirmed by a member state representative to the Article 133 Committee, interview, Brussels, June 23, 1999, and by a Commission official in DG Trade, interview, Brussels, June 24, 1999.

34. For an overview of the Article 133 Committee, see Hayes-Renshaw and Wallace (1997, pp. 86–90). There are informal "subgroups" of the Article 133 Committee involving services, automobiles, steel, and mutual recognition agreements. Commission Official in DG Trade, interview, June 16, 2001.

decision made.[35] Depending on one's view of the Commission's authority to initiate trade complaints, the Committee either authorizes the Commission to proceed with the action that the Commission proposes, or the member states merely express their agreement with the Commission's independent decision.

In theory, if a member state objects to a matter, the Commission should refer the matter to COREPER (the EC's Committee of Permanent Representatives), the body immediately below the Council.[36] If COREPER likewise is unable to resolve the matter by consensus, it should refer the matter to the Council, which would then make a decision by a qualified majority vote. However, the Article 133 Committee practically never refers the decision whether to initiate a WTO trade complaint to COREPER. In fact, according to Commission and member state representatives in Brussels, the Article 133 Committee has referred only one EC complaint before the WTO to COREPER, and that was the politically charged complaint over U.S. (Helms-Burton) legislation involving potential U.S. extraterritorial sanctions against European foreign investors in Cuba.[37] Neither committee members nor the Commission wish to transfer decisionmaking authority on trade matters from themselves, who are trade specialists, to the Council, which consists of foreign affairs ministers. Foreign affairs representatives sitting on the Council are the member state analogues to the U.S. Secretary of State, while the *titulaires* on the Article 133 Committee are the highest member-state representatives on trade matters, although in Europe they do not hold cabinet-level positions.[38] Since most authority over the implementation of EC trade policy resides in the Commission, the actual analogue to the USTR is a member of the Commission, currently the trade commissioner, Pascal Lamy.

35. Michael Johnson, a former Article 133 representative from the United Kingdom, telephone interview, March 5, 1998. See also Johnson (1998). The chair of the meeting is a representative of the member state that holds the presidency of the Council at the time. The presidency rotates every six months among the fifteen member states. In 2002–04 it will have been held, in order, by Spain, Denmark, Greece, Italy, Ireland, and the Netherlands.

36. The term in French is the *Comité des Représentants Permanents*, or COREPER. For an overview of COREPER, see Hayes-Renshaw and Wallace (1997, pp. 72–84).

37. Commission and member state representatives, interviews, Brussels, June 23, 1999, and June 16, 2001.

38. Member state representative to Article 133 Committee and a former high-level member of DG Trade, interview, Brussels, June 25, 1999, and telephone interview, April 25, 2003. See also Hayes-Renshaw and Wallace (1997, p. 90); the permanent representatives in COREPER also "are senior officials from the national ministries of foreign affairs, with the rank of ambassador" (p. 74).

The member state trade officials on the Article 133 Committee do not play the primary role in implementing EC trade policy, including whether to initiate a WTO complaint. The Commission does. First, not even the highest-ranked members of the Article 133 Committee, the *titulaires*, directly oversee most EC actions, since they meet only once a month in Brussels. Only particularly sensitive matters are referred to these monthly meetings, which the director-general of DG trade, currently Mogens Peter Carl, attends. For example, the EC's WTO challenge of U.S. tax provisions for foreign sales corporations was approved by the *titulaires*. Generally, however, the lower-ranked "deputies," who meet almost every Friday in Brussels, informally authorize the initiation of WTO proceedings and other EC trade measures, although they follow instructions from their superiors.[39]

Second, the deputies typically defer to Commission representatives, who set the agenda for Article 133 Committee meetings. The Commission determines whether to raise a matter for the committee's attention, when to raise it, and how to raise it. The Commission submits almost all agenda matters, position papers and written proposals, although member state representatives can also refer matters through the Council presidency.[40] The deputies indirectly authorize EC actions, including the filing of a WTO complaint, by not opposing a proposal or position paper that the Commission submits. The Commission's trade commissioner makes the final decision as to whether to initiate a WTO complaint.[41]

As an example of Commission predominance, when I was in Brussels, a Commission official handed me a copy of a Council circular in which the Council expressed its support for the Commission's Market Access Strategy and noted the achievements to date. Yet it turned out that a Commission official had initiated and drafted the circular in order to

39. Commission official in DG Trade, interview, Brussels, June 16, 2001. See also Johnson (1998). The *titulaires* typically meet in Brussels the last Friday of the month, unless a special meeting is called on an extraordinary matter. Otherwise, lower-level "deputies" from the member states, together with representatives from the member states' permanent missions in Brussels, meet each Friday in Brussels. The deputies also attend the monthly meeting of the *titulaires*. All national representatives are assisted by members of the Council's permanent secretariat in Brussels, which provides administrative assistance for Article 133 Committee meetings.

40. Commission official in DG Trade, interview, June 16, 2001. The committee agenda shown to me in Brussels, for example, contained one matter referred by a member state and twelve by the Commission. I was informed that this was representative of a typical Article 133 Committee agenda.

41. Member of Lamy's cabinet, interview, Brussels, June 18, 2001. The decision is not made by the College of Commissioners, consisting of twenty members in 2003.

obtain the Council's formal support. When I presented the document to a member state representative, he merely confirmed that it had gone by his desk and that he believed that he had skimmed it. His role had been reduced to monitoring the Commission's multiple endeavors. Similarly, the Commission has de facto authority in antidumping decisions, where the Council typically "rubber stamps" Commission determinations.[42]

Max Weber's remarks on bureaucratic authority are apt here: "Bureaucratic organizations, or the holders of power who make use of them, have the tendency to increase their power still further by the knowledge growing out of experience in the service. For they acquire through the conduct of office a special knowledge of facts and have available a store of documentary material peculiar to themselves."[43] When issues proliferate, a bureaucracy's grasp of the underlying facts and specialized understanding of law augment its authority. Member states may predominate in the determination of the EC's political positions in trade negotiations, with the Commission acting as a "promotional broker" and an "agent" with some discretion in the negotiations.[44] The Commission predominates, however, in the deployment of trade law, whether by initiating trade complaints or conducting settlement negotiations in the law's shadow. The Commission prevails because it has acquired greater expertise in handling the technicalities and increasing demands of WTO law. Only the Commission investigates, defends, and challenges trade barriers before the WTO's Dispute Settlement Body, and thus member state representatives lack the Commission's acquired knowledge. In the words of one member state representative to the Article 133 Committee, national representatives typically defer to the Commission as "the professor."[45] Another member state representative describes Commission officials as "specialists because they argue WTO cases"; since member states "no longer have these types of specialists," they give the Commission "greater deference," that is to say, greater decisionmaking power.[46] With the enlargement of the EC to twenty-five member states in 2004, the Commission's expertise and authority on trade matters compared with that of member state officials should further increase.

42. See Ostry (1990, p. 47), citing Bellis (1989, pp. 67–68).

43. See Weber (1947, p. 339).

44. See Meunier and Nikolaidis (2000; also 1999, p. 477). On the notion of the Commission as a "promotional broker" compared with a technocrat, see Rometsch and Wessels (1994, pp. 208–10).

45. Interview, Brussels, June 25, 1999.

46. Interview, Brussels, June 23, 1999.

Where necessary, the Commission works behind the scenes with member state representatives to forge consensus on a matter before formally presenting it to the Article 133 Committee. Failing consensus, the Commission attempts to ensure that its recommendation is supported by at least a "qualified majority" of member states, in which case the matter is still not referred to COREPER or the Council for the institutional reasons just noted. As one Commission official boasted, "Eventually, we get them."[47] Although member state divisions can arise over the treatment of WTO disputes, Commission officials less frequently have to act as promotional brokers to bridge member state divisions.

Many member state representatives, especially those from more liberal-oriented northern states, do not mind "being gotten" by the Commission. They realize that delay and irresolution hamper EC trade policy, especially in relations with the United States. As one northern representative to the Article 133 Committee stated, "EC trade policy works by permission of the French." That is, if other member states interfere too much with the Commission's work, the "French win" because the Commission's initiatives toward trade liberalization are slowed.[48] A French representative to the Article 133 Committee notes, however, that the French do not object to the de facto delegation of decisionmaking to the Commission for the bringing of trade claims, provided that the Commission is successful. Member states challenge the Commission's authority primarily in negotiations over the removal of EC trade barriers, not in legal actions against foreign ones.

Because of the centralization of EC trade policy, European businesses can work more effectively with a main contact within the Commission on international trade matters, either bypassing national authorities or (more typically) working in coordination with them. Businesses thereby may play more active roles, despite Article 133's reputation as a state-centric procedure, and despite the fact that Article 133 meetings take place behind closed doors without private parties present. Guided by a Commission representative, sophisticated businesses can ensure sufficient support within the Article 133 Committee prior to the Commission's submission of a proposal. Where needed, they can coordinate positions with businesses in other member states so that each respectively contacts its representative for endorsement. If a matter is raised at an Article 133

47. Commission official in DG Trade, interview, Brussels, June 21, 1999.

48. Member state representative to Article 133 Committee, interview, Brussels, June 23, 1999.

Committee meeting, the meeting may merely ratify a decision that has already been made.

For example, although the United Kingdom's Scotch Whisky Association played the leading role in the Japan, Korea, and Chile alcohol cases, it also worked with the European-wide trade association CEPS (the European Confederation of Producers of Spirits) and CEPS's constituent members. These included French cognac producers who contacted French representatives. The process, says a representative of the Scotch Whisky Association, "involved preparing, researching and communicating our case effectively on a persistent basis, for a very long period of time, to our respective Governments and to the Commission."[49] While some member states "rolled their eyeballs" at the number of EC cases brought in support of the U.K. spirits industry, the cases nonetheless went forward.[50] "Government affairs," maintains a senior European lobbyist, boils down to "the three I's": "information," "image" and "influence."[51]

Although there is some ambiguity regarding the European Commission's authority for the implementation of EC trade policy, the Commission clearly plays the dominant role, albeit subject to member state pressures and constraints. The consolidation of trade authority in a single European institution facilitates greater business input in EC trade disputes. Businesses can work behind the scenes with EC officials to more effectively challenge foreign barriers to their exports. The WTO's legalized structure and the Commission's Market Access Strategy so induce them. As European businesses learn to profit from the WTO dispute settlement system, they attempt to use the reputedly state-centric Article 133 mechanism more frequently.

## *Europe's Reply to U.S. Section 301*

European businesses have a more direct track to solicit Commission representation of their interests: the Trade Barrier Regulation, enacted in December 1994 in anticipation of the WTO's formation.[52] The TBR

49. See remarks of Tim Jackson, SWA, May 1997.

50. The quotation is from a member state representative to the Article 133 Committee. Interview, Brussels, June 23, 1999.

51. See Caine (2000), citing Christopher Boyd, senior vice president of environment and government affairs of LaFarge SA, a global manufacturer of construction products.

52. The Trade Barrier Regulation's formal name is "Council Regulation 3286/94 of 22 December 1994 (Laying down Community Procedures in the Field of the Common Commercial Policy in Order to Ensure the Exercise of the Community's Rights under International Trade Rules, in Particular Those Established under the Auspices of the World

grants individual enterprises legal rights to petition the Commission to investigate trade matters and bring WTO claims on their behalf. The TBR replaced an earlier analogous regulation that European businesses largely ignored, the New Commercial Policy Instrument.[53] Unlike the NCPI, the Trade Barrier Regulation permits individual businesses to petition the Commission to initiate a WTO complaint, so that they do not require the support of an entire "Community industry." The TBR also relaxed the proof of injury requirement to that of a "material *impact* on . . . a sector or economic *activity* . . . of the Community or a *region*" (emphasis added), in contrast to the NCPI's requirement of "injury" to a "Community industry."[54]

The Council enacted the NCPI in 1984 in response to U.S. actions taken under Section 301 against European steel and agricultural interests. The French government promoted the NCPI as a counter to U.S. Section 301.[55] European businesses were not enticed. They filed only seven NCPI petitions during its ten-year history. The Commission rejected two of the seven on the ground that the complainants failed to present sufficient evidence of an "illicit commercial practice."[56] Member states interfered with others, as in the Dutch company AKZO's complaint against the discriminatory nature of U.S. intellectual property rules as applied to imports.

Because the NCPI was ineffective, the French pressed for a new regulation with more flexible procedural requirements. Northern liberal-oriented member states, such as Germany, the Netherlands, and the United Kingdom, initially objected, fearing that the regulations would be used for protectionist purposes.[57] The Trade Barrier Regulation nonetheless was enacted, ultimately by consensus, as part of an internal EC package

---

Trade Organization)," *Official Journal of the European Communities*, ser. L, no. 349, December 31, 1994, pp. 0071–0078 (hereinafter TBR). See also website concerning the TBR maintained by the Commission: www.europa.eu.int/comm/trade/policy/traderegul/index_en.htm (August 2, 2003).

53. The NCPI's formal name was "Council Regulation 2641/84 of 17 September 1984 (on the Strengthening of the Common Commercial Policy with Regard in Particular to Protection against Illicit Commercial Practices)," *Official Journal of the European Communities*, ser. L, no. 252, September 20, 1984, pp. 1–6 (hereinafter NCPI).

54. Compare TBR, Article 4, and NCPI, Articles 2 and 3.

55. See Bronckers (1984, p. 719).

56. The two rejected complaints were brought in 1989 by FEDIOL (the European Seed Crushers' and Oil Processors Federation), concerning Argentine export restrictions on soya beans; and in 1991 by SmithKline and French Laboratories, concerning Jordan's allegedly insufficient patent protection.

57. See Molyneux (2001, pp. 236, 242).

pursuant to which the French supported the signing of the Uruguay Round Agreements, including the Agreement on Agriculture, in return for passage of the TBR and guaranteed EC support of French agriculture.[58] Since its inception, the Commission has only deployed the TBR offensively to challenge foreign trade barriers, and not defensively.[59] As a result, all EC member states now support the TBR's use.[60]

The TBR grants a business the right to force the Commission to act. In practice, however, just as under U.S. Section 301, European businesses must depend on public officials to represent their interests before foreign governments and WTO panels. Businesses realize that antagonism is self-defeating. In consequence, there have been no legal challenges to Commission decisions under the TBR to date. There was one formal challenge to the Commission under the NCPI, but the European Court of Justice held that the Commission correctly found that the Argentine practices at issue did not violate GATT.[61]

Businesses thus collaborate with the Commission in applying the TBR, forming ad hoc public-private networks, as in the United States. Businesses choose which mechanism to use—TBR or the Article 133 route—in consultation with, and in response to, the Commission's advice. When Volkswagen complained to the Commission about a problem that it encountered with a Colombian sales tax on automobiles, the Commission advised it to file a TBR complaint. Volkswagen's attorneys twice came to the Commission with drafts on which Commission officials made suggestions for improvement, before Volkswagen finalized its submission.[62]

Businesses sometimes have deferred almost entirely to the Commission as to whether to proceed under the TBR or Article 133 process. When the

58. See Devuyst (1995, pp. 449–67), also noting the use of sectoral side payments to the Portuguese textile industry to secure the assent of a reticent Portuguese government for the conclusion of the Uruguay Round.

59. See Molyneux (2001, p. 244). The TBR challenge to the Brazilian Export Financing program, however, concerned the impact of Brazilian export subsidies on the EC as well as foreign markets. The EC filed a third-party submission in the WTO complaint brought by Canada.

60. Member state representatives to the Article 133 Committee from Germany and the United Kingdom, as well as members of the Commission's TBR unit, interviews, Brussels, June 1999.

61. See *Fédération de l'Industrie de l'Huilerie de la CEE (FEDIOL)* v. *Commission,* Case 70/87 (1989), ECR 1781. See also Bronckers and McNelis (2001, p. 449).

62. Commission official in the TBR unit, interview, Brussels, June 13, 2001. See also "Colombia—Discriminatory Taxes on Automobiles," O.J. C236/05 (2000).

Italian silk federation, Federtessile, filed an early TBR complaint against U.S. application of rules of origin to Italian silk products, Federtessile had not even heard of the TBR until the Commission, in search of successful test cases, mentioned it.[63] The United States was requiring that the silk products be labeled "made in China," which was where the fabrics were woven, and not Italy, where they were dyed and finished.[64] The "China" label undermined the fabrics' quality claims and subjected them to quantitative quotas applied to Chinese textiles. Such a labeling did not bode well for selling Italian silk products at luxury goods prices in the U.S. market.

In the TBR complaint procedure, Federtessile was represented by no outside or in-house counsel. Rather, the Italian silk federation depended entirely on the Commission to prepare its complaint and lead it through the TBR procedure. The federation supplied the Commission with all relevant factual information for purposes of the Commission's investigation, the WTO filing, consultations, and ultimate settlement with the United States. The public-private partnership, formed at the Commission's instigation, was a success for both parties. U.S. rules of origin eventually were modified to the Italian silk industry's satisfaction, following Congress's passage of the Miscellaneous Trade and Technical Corrections Act of 1999.[65] The Italian silk industry sang the Commission's praises. The Commission, in turn, touted the silk case as a great

63. Mr. Tettamanti, a representative of Federtessile based outside of Milan, Italy, telephone interview, February 19, 1998.

64. See "Commission Decision of Feb. 18, 1997, on the Initiation of International Consultation and Dispute Settlement Procedure Concerning Changes to United States Rules of Origin for Textile Products Resulting in the Non-conferral of Community Origin on Certain Products Processed in the European Community," *Official Journal of the European Communities*, ser. L, no. 62, March 4, 1997, p. 43. In legal terms, the U.S. test should be whether the products underwent a "substantial transformation" in Italy. The United States initially ruled that they had not.

65. Days before formal WTO consultations were scheduled to begin, the United States agreed with the EC to change the application of U.S. rules of origin to the silk products. See "U.S. and EU Reach Framework for Settling Rule of Origin Spat," *International Trade Reporter (BNA)*, July 23, 1997, p. 1275. However, the industry subsequently challenged U.S. implementation of the settlement, which led to the filing of a new EC complaint against the United States before the WTO on November 19, 1998. See Daniel Pruzin and Rossella Brevetti, "EU again Seeks WTO Consultations over U.S. Rules of Origin for Textiles," *International Trade Reporter (BNA)*, December 2, 1998, p. 1999. The dispute finally was settled to the industry's satisfaction, following Congress's action. See P.L. 106-36 §2423 (1999); and Paula L. Green, "Label Rules Relaxed for Importers of Silk," *Journal of Commerce*, September 24, 1999, p. 12. See also DS85 and DS151 in appendix table 4.

success. The Commission now could better promote business use of the Trade Barrier Regulation.[66]

Similarly, COTANCE, which represents hundreds of small leather tanners, brought TBR complaints against Argentine and Japanese market access barriers. It did so, however, following a Commission-financed consultant's report concerning trade barriers confronting the leather industry.[67] Again, the leather industry was dependent on the Commission's entrepreneurship. The steel trade association Eurofer also initiated TBR complaints against the U.S. Antidumping Act of 1916 and against Brazil's import licensing system. Eurofer was founded in 1976 under the Commission's initiative and still remains close to the Commission.[68]

TBR cases, nonetheless, require producer input since they are often factually intensive. Cases involving foreign administrative practices require ongoing EC public-private monitoring in an attempt to check abuses. The TBR case concerning Argentine import practices for textiles revolved around Argentine customs valuations of a broad array of products at higher amounts than their sales price.[69] The TBR procedure facilitated the needed public-private collaboration.

The TBR is more than a legal procedure. It is a conduit that links the public and the private. Members of the TBR unit refer to businesses as their "customers," customers that, like any good entrepreneur, they seek.[70] The TBR encourages businesses to bypass their national representatives and peak trade associations and to forge ongoing relationships with units within the Commission to monitor and challenge foreign trade practices. Of the first twenty TBR cases, none were brought by peak trade associations, six were brought by sectoral associations, and fourteen by intrasectoral associations or individuals firms.[71] Since the TBR's inception,

66. See, for example, Michael Smith, "U.S. Accepts EU's 'Made in Europe' Label," *Financial Times,* August 8, 1997, p. 6: "The Commission said it was optimistic about other cases in the TBR system."

67. Representative of leather trade association COTANCE, interview, Brussels, June 22, 1999. Confirmed in Prince interview, 1999.

68. See Hayes (1993, p. 140). Eurofer is the European Confederation of Iron and Steel Industries.

69. Commission official in TBR unit, interview, Brussels, June 13, 2001.

70. For example, when I called a Commission official in the TBR unit and mentioned that I had just set up an interview with a representative from COTANCE, the leather trade association in Brussels that had filed two TBR complaints, the Commission official replied, "Oh, so you are talking to one of our customers" (Brussels, June 21, 1999).

71. De Bièvre (2003).

private business and Commission officials have worked increasingly together, with the result that the Commission now needs to spend less time publicizing the instrument.

The TBR procedure has also sparked the interest of private legal counsel in Brussels. The legalistic nature and greater transparency of TBR procedures, compared with the Article 133 process, explains why lawyers have written extensively about it, even though the Article 133 procedure is used more frequently. Private lawyers help promote the TBR's use through promotional brochures and articles that they circulate to potential clients. These lawyers often work for Brussels affiliates of U.S. law firms, such as Wilmer, Cutler & Pickering, Hogan & Hartson, and Coudert Brothers.[72] They, too, have incentives to publicize the TBR instrument and have had some success in this regard. Commission officials report that businesses work more frequently with outside legal counsel on TBR complaints.[73]

### *Shrinking Differences between the Trade Barrier Regulation and U.S. Section 301*

A number of legal scholars and practitioners have compared the Trade Barrier Regulation and its predecessor to U.S. Section 301. Most consider the TBR to be the less powerful instrument.[74] They point to two primary constraints: (1) The TBR's narrower scope and (2) its weaker enforcement measures. However, the WTO system has reduced the significance of both constraints, as attested by the increased number of TBR complaints during the late 1990s, and their market-opening outcomes.

On its face, U.S. Section 301 provides a broader scope of coverage than does the TBR, especially since Section 301 can be used as a unilateral

72. See, for example, Bronckers (1984), now working for Wilmer, Cutler & Pickering; Molyneux (1999), while working for Hogan & Hartson; Vander Schueren and Luff (1996), Vander Schueren is a partner at Coudert Brothers, Brussels; and Zonnekeyen (1995, p. 143), who has worked for a number of Brussels law firms, including Baker & McKenzie. While practicing EC lawyers have written a number of articles on the NCPI and the TBR, they have not written anything on the Article 133 process.

73. Petros Sourmelis, official in the TBR unit, interview, Brussels, June 13, 2001.

74. See Bronckers (1984); Mavroidis and Zdouc (1998, p. 407); and Zoller (1985, p. 227). See also Steinberg (1999, p. 219): "The Community's formal vehicle for engaging in third-country negotiations, the Trade Barriers Regulation, offers a slow and rarely used procedure." Also Johnson (1998) and telephone interview, February 1998. In the interview, Johnson, a former U.K. representative to the Article 133 Committee, referred to the TBR as "mere window dressing" and affirmed that the Article 133 process is the only one that matters in the EC.

instrument. Section 301 addresses not only all WTO matters, including new WTO issues such as intellectual property protection and trade in services, but also non-WTO matters such as competition law, the protection of investor and labor rights, and intellectual property requirements that are more stringent than those set forth in the TRIPS agreement. The TBR, in contrast, was designed to facilitate the EC's bringing of "WTO complaints on behalf of affected EC enterprises," and not unilateral action against practices that the EC simply does not like.

Moreover, the TBR should not have covered all WTO matters. In its Opinion 1/94, the European Court of Justice held that EC member states (and thus not the Commission under the TBR) retained competence over most intellectual property and services matters under the GATS and TRIPS agreements.[75] Following the Court's decision, EC Trade Commissioner Brittan affirmed that the TBR's scope would be "restricted to: (a) areas of exclusive Community competence (trade in goods and in services not implying movement of persons), and (b) individual issues falling within the Community's competence in the areas of shared competence."[76] In consequence, the TBR arguably should not have applied to, or should have required unanimous member state consent for, most services and intellectual property matters.

In practice, however, the Commission's TBR unit broadly applied the court's opinion so as to maximize its authority to bring intellectual property and services claims. The Commission's TBR unit first maintained that all intellectual property claims that have "an impact on trade in goods" are covered by the TBR.[77] Then, when a TBR claim against a provision of

75. The European Court of Justice's Opinion 1/94 (World Trade Organization), *European Court Reports*, 1994, p. I-5267, November 15, 1994, held that, under Article 133 (as then applicable), the member states retained exclusive or shared competence over most matters covered by the WTO TRIPS and GATS agreements. Regarding trade in services, the court held that the EC institutions had exclusive competence only where the provision of the service does not involve any movement of persons or a foreign commercial presence (paras. 43–45) or involves an area in which the EC has achieved complete harmonization internally or has otherwise expressly conferred negotiating powers on Community institutions (paras. 95–97). Regarding intellectual property matters, the court held that EC institutions had exclusive competence only over the prohibition of "the release into free circulation of counterfeit goods" (paras. 55–56), unless full harmonization has been accomplished internally (paras. 102–03). See Meunier and Nikolaidis (1999, p. 477, and 2000, pp. 335–39).

76. Commission Press Release IP: 94-1125, Rapid (November 30, 1994), extract of a speech by Sir Leon Brittan.

77. See the Commission's *Guide to the Community's Trade Barrier Regulation: Opening New Trade Opportunities for European Business*. See also Molyneux (2001, p. 257).

U.S. copyright law did not affect trade in goods, the TBR unit advanced a separate rationale for its competence. The legal provision curtailed the payment of royalties by bars and restaurants for the use of sound recordings. This U.S. measure, said the Commission, fell within the EC's exclusive competence because it regulated a cross-border "licensing service" that did not implicate a movement of persons.[78] No member state challenged the Commission's action before the Court of Justice because it was not in any member state's interest to do so, especially given the position of Europe's intellectual property industry.[79] As a result, five of the first nineteen TBR complaints involved intellectual property issues, even though the claims may have lain outside of the Commission's exclusive powers. The claims ranged from a European pharmaceutical industry complaint against Korean patent law, an Irish music rights organization's complaint against U.S. copyright law, and complaints of French cognac producers, French winemakers, and Italian producers of Prosciutto di Parma against failures of Brazil and Canada to protect their geographical indications ("*appellations d'origin*").[80] In addition, the Commission continues to administer a sixth intellectual property claim originally filed in

78. See "Notice of Initiation of an Examination Procedure Concerning an Obstacle to Trade, within the Meaning of Council Regulation (EC) No 3286/94, Consisting of Trade Practices Maintained by the United States of America in Relation to Cross-Border Music Licensing," *Official Journal of the European Communities*, ser. C, no. 177, November 6, 1997, para. 3.

79. The complaint was supported by copyright interests throughout the EC. The Commission took into account the "unanimous support given by the General Assembly of Gesac [Groupment Européen des Sociétés d'Auteurs et Compositeurs] to IMRO's complaint." See "Notice of Initiation of an Examination Procedure Concerning an Obstacle to Trade, within the Meaning of Council Regulation (EC) No 3286/94, Consisting of Trade Practices Maintained by the United States of America in Relation to Cross-Border Music Music Licensing," *Official Journal of the European Communities*, ser. C, no. 177, June 11, 1997, pp. 5–6.

80. For the TBR complaint filed by the consortium of Parma ham producers ("Consorzio del Prosciutto di Parma"), see "Notice of Initiation of an Examination Concerning an Obstacle to Trade, within the Meaning of Regulation (EC) No 3286/94, Consisting of Trade Practices Maintained by Canada in Relation to the Imports of Prosciutto di Parma," *Official Journal of European Communities*, ser. C, no. 176/4, June 22, 1999, pp. 6–8. For the cognac case, see "Notice of Initiation of an Examination Procedure Concerning an Obstacle to Trade, within the Meaning of Council Regulation (EC) No. 3286/94, Consisting of Trade Obstacles Maintained by Brazil Concerning Trade in Cognac," *Official Journal of the European Communities*, ser. C, no. 103/3, 1997, pp. 1–2. For the wine case, see "Report on Examination under TBR Procedure," Conseil Interprofessionel de Bordeaux ("CIVB")—Canada, Ref. 078/03, February 12, 2003, at www.europa.eu.int/comm/trade/policy/traderegul/civb.pdf (March 2003).

1991 by the International Federation of the Phonographic Industry (IFPI) concerning Thailand's enforcement of copyrights. Even under the former NCPI, four of the seven private petitions involved intellectual property matters.[81]

The Treaty of Nice changed this legal situation when it came into effect on February 1, 2003. The Nice treaty amended Article 133 to provide for the EC's exclusive competence over "the negotiation and conclusion of agreements in the fields of trade in services and the commercial aspects of intellectual property," subject to certain exceptions, such as for "trade in cultural and audiovisual services."[82] As a result, the EC member states effectively ratified the Commission's broad assertion of competence by amending the EC treaty.

Second, Section 301 should provide for more effective pressure than the TBR, since Section 301 authorizes the USTR to take unilateral action in retaliation against foreign trade barriers, even where no international legal obligation has been violated. Under the TBR, in contrast, an EC enterprise may only submit a complaint where there is a "right of action established under international trade rules."[83] The Commission must investigate the complaint, and if it concurs that the EC's rights have been violated, then it must submit any claim before the relevant international tribunal (that is, before the WTO).[84] The USTR's initiation of a Section 301 proceeding thus historically posed a greater threat to a foreign government.

The WTO's binding dispute settlement system, however, has constrained the United States's unilateral use of Section 301 and concomitantly enhanced the EC's threat of an international trade action, especially since China and Taiwan (referred to as Chinese Taipei) joined the WTO in November 2001. The EC thus wields greater leverage in threatening to bring an international trade claim than it had in the past, so that foreign

81. See Bronckers and McNelis (2001, p. 431).

82. "Treaty of Nice Amending the Treaty on European Union, the Treaties Establishing the European Communities and Certain Related Acts," *Official Journal of the European Communities*, ser. C, no. 80/15-16, March 10, 2001. In the Treaty of Nice, the member states agreed to modify Article 133 to provide, in paragraph 5, that these matters would be covered (although also subject to exclusions for trade in "educational services, and social and human health services," as well as "agreements in the field of transport").

83. See TBR, Article 4. Article 2 defines "international trade rules" as "primarily those established under the auspices of the WTO and laid down in the Annexes to the WTO Agreement, but they can also be those laid down in any other agreement to which the Community is a party and which sets out rules applicable to trade between the Community and third countries."

84. See TBR, Article 12.2.

parties are more likely to settle a TBR complaint. Although the Commission began no TBR cases during the TBR's first twenty-one months, it initiated seventeen TBR investigations between October 1996 and April 1, 2001, three times the number brought under the NCPI over ten years. Thirteen of these TBR claims involved practices in North and South America: three concerned the United States, five Brazil, two Argentina, and one each Canada, Colombia, and Chile. From 1997 to 1999, the Commission filed seven WTO complaints resulting from TBR investigations, including the EC's challenges against the U.S. Antidumping Act of 1916, a provision of U.S. copyright law, U.S. rules of origin, Argentine and Japanese trade barriers affecting the leather industry, and Brazilian import licensing practices for textiles. This figure is comparable to the number of U.S. Section 301 complaints filed during its heyday. By December 1999, the EC had also settled three TBR complaints without having to litigate them before a WTO panel—the U.S. rules of origin case, a case involving Brazil's import licensing regime for steel products, and the Thai sound recordings case.[85] Three other complaints—the Argentine leather case and U.S. copyright and antidumping cases—led to WTO panel decisions in which the EC prevailed. By June 2001, four more TBR complaints had been settled, one involving Chile's treatment of EC fishing vessels,[86] and another concerning Brazil's treatment of French cognac.[87] In short, the differences between the TBR and Section 301 have become more formal than substantive.

Finally, the EC has signed more bilateral trade agreements than any other WTO member. Although the TBR permits individual enterprises to

85. See Van Eeckhaute (1999, pp. 210, 212), concerning the U.S. and Thai cases; and Maclean (1999, p. 91), concerning the Brazilian case.

86. The EC requested the formation of a WTO panel in the Chilean swordfish case. See "EU Requests Swordfish Panel against Chile," *Bridges*, November–December 2000, p. 9. The EC settled the case the day before the panel was to be formed. Commission official in TBR unit, interview, Brussels, June 13, 2001. The settlement allowed EC fishing boats limited access to Chilean ports as part of a scientific evaluation of swordfish stocks in the Southeast Pacific. The EC and Chile also agreed to establish a multilateral framework for the conservation and management of swordfish. See Daniel Pruzin, "EU and Chile Announce Settlement of Swordfish Dispute, Suspend WTO Case," *International Trade Reporter (BNA)*, February 1, 2001, p. 204. See also DS193 in appendix table 4.

87. The French association of cognac producers, the Bureau National Interprofessionnel du Cognac (BNIC), alleged, among other matters, that Brazil had failed to protect its geographical indication in breach of the WTO TRIPS agreement. BNIC claimed that Brazil permits local producers to sell an alcoholic beverage under the name of *conhague*. BNIC also maintained that its spirits are subject to a discriminatory tax rate in violation of Article III.2 of GATT 1994. See Broncker and McNelis (2001, pp. 471–72).

bring complaints under bilateral trade agreements only "on behalf of a Community industry," the Commission has interpreted the provision liberally.[88] The Commission heard, for example, French cognac producers' complaint of Brazil's treatment of their *appellation d'origin* under a "1992 Framework Co-operation Agreement between the Community and Brazil," among other grounds.[89] The Commission also drafted amendments to the TBR that (if ever adopted) would formally extend the TBR's coverage to individual firm complaints under EC bilateral agreements, which increasingly include binding dispute settlement.[90]

## Use of Article 133 and TBR Procedures to Date

Although the TBR has gained acceptance, the EC uses the Article 133 process far more frequently. The EC brought twenty-seven of its first twenty-eight WTO complaints through the Article 133 procedure. From June 9, 1998, to October 14, 1999, the use of the TBR increased, with the EC bringing six of seventeen of its WTO complaints pursuant to the TBR, three of which were against the United States.[91] Seeing that the TBR could be deployed successfully, European firms began to file more cases, and to play a more active role in the proceedings. This shift toward enhanced public-private coordination in Europe in turn prompted greater use of the less transparent Article 133 procedure, as private enterprises

88. Under Article 4 of the TBR, complaints from Community enterprises "only are admissible if the obstacle to trade alleged therein is the subject of a right of action established under international trade rules laid down in a multilateral or plurilateral trade agreement." This restriction does not apply to complaints brought "on behalf of a Community industry" or by a member state. TBR, Article 3.

89. See the Commission's case overview, at www.europa.eu.int/comm/trade/policy/traderegul/bra_cog.htm (March 2003).

90. The Commission proposed such a revision as part of the Amsterdam treaty, but has since shelved the proposal. Stewart interview, 2002.

91. By January 1999, the percentage of TBR claims as a proportion of all EC claims referred to the WTO Dispute Settlement System had risen to about 20 percent. See Sir Leon Brittan, "Removing Barriers to Trade: The EU's Market Access Strategy," speech to the Brussels Chamber of Commerce, Brussels, January 28, 1999. Two of the six WTO complaints brought via the TBR, however, involved the same matter, "U.S. rules of origin for silk products," which was settled successfully for the EC. The other four TBR matters were "Japan—Imports of Finished Leather"; "United States—Anti-Dumping Act of 1916"; "Argentina—Exports of Hides"; and "United States—Licensing of Musical Works." For an overview, see Van Eeckhaute (1999, pp. 199, 212). The EC won both cases against the United States and the case against Argentina before the WTO. It is still in consultations with Japan. See "Le Règlement sur les Obstacles au Commerce," *Economie: Les Echanges*, March 16–23, 2001, p. 10–11 (on file with author).

increasingly work with the Commission and member states behind the scenes to rally support for their claims. Just as U.S. firms work closely with the USTR without needing to file a Section 301 petition, so European firms work with the Commission without filing a TBR complaint.

EC enterprises face a maze of national and EC supranational councils, committees, directorates-general, directorates, units, and sectoral and country desks when they ask public officials to act on their behalf. They typically rely on someone within the European Commission, possibly in conjunction with a national authority, to guide them through the process and thus rely less on private counsel than do U.S. businesses. The Brussels trade bar has played a less active role than its Washington, D.C., counterpart in helping firms to challenge foreign trade barriers, although outside law firms have become more active in Brussels in recent years.[92]

Firms may prefer certain aspects of the TBR procedure to the Article 133 process. First, the different voting rules under the TBR can somewhat enhance the leverage of Commission-business partnerships against reticent EC member states. Under the TBR, the Commission's decision to file a WTO complaint can be overturned only by a qualified majority vote of the Council, whereas a Commission proposal under Article 133 requires qualified majority approval.[93] This flip in voting requirements renders member states' ability to forestall a Commission TBR proposal more difficult, although the TBR unit is by no means autonomous. Firms thus can bring a TBR complaint where they feel that a member state could block an Article 133 decision. The German company Dornier Luftfahrt, for example, had been unsuccessful in obtaining the Article 133 Committee's authorization for the Commission to initiate a WTO complaint against Brazilian subsidies granted to its competitor Embraer. EC suppliers to the Brazilian company located in other member states indirectly benefited from the subsidies and lobbied their member states to oppose any EC action. These member states, however, were unable to block the Commission's initiation of a TBR investigation, which ultimately led the EC to

92. See Bronckers and McNelis (2001, pp. 460–61).

93. See TBR, Articles 13.2 and 14. The Commission is only required to keep the Article 133 Committee abreast of developments in TBR procedures in order for it to "consider any wider implications for the common commercial policy." TBR, Article 7.2. Where the EC brings a case before the WTO and the WTO member in question fails to comply with a WTO ruling against it and the Commission is authorized by the WTO Dispute Settlement Body to implement retaliatory measures, then the decision to implement such measures is subject to a decision by the Council by a qualified majority vote, in accordance with Article 133 of the treaty. See TBR, Article 13.3.

file a third-party submission in support of Canada's WTO complaint against the Brazilian subsidies. Dornier Luftfahrt was positioned to benefit from the EC's support of Canada's successful lawsuit.[94]

Most important, the technical nature of TBR work provides the Commission and firms with somewhat greater discretion, so long as issues do not become politicized. Because of the TBR's technical nature, member states tend to assign lower-ranked officials to the TBR committee (the Article 133 Committee's counterpart for TBR matters).[95] Member state representatives find TBR committee work less exciting because it involves fact-intensive litigation files on potential WTO claims, sometimes of relatively small economic impact. For them, the files comprise too many facts, too much law, and not enough policy or diplomacy. This is a province for lawyers, not the high politics of diplomatic encounter. The Commission and private complainants thus are granted somewhat more leeway to develop TBR cases and to determine negotiation and litigation strategies. Even though the Article 133 process typically works fluidly, the more Commission-friendly rules and technical nature of TBR procedures can influence a firm's expectations and behavior.

Second, the TBR may offer some advantages to smaller enterprises or large firms with relatively less important commercial claims. One of the goals of the EC's Market Access Strategy is to provide smaller businesses that lack established Brussels contacts with better access to Commission officials. The Commission's Market Access Unit developed its database, in part, so that it could be in better contact with small and medium-sized businesses through the Internet.[96] The Commission reports some success, claiming that companies employing fewer than 400 people are the most frequent users of its market access database.[97]

Working with small and medium-sized businesses is relatively more important in Europe because these enterprises constitute a larger percentage of Europe's gross domestic product and exports than they do in the United States. As European Commissioner Erkki Liikanen states, "We must remember that more than 95% of enterprises are SMEs. Over 90% of European enterprises are micro enterprises with fewer than

94. See Van Eeckhaute (1999, p. 211); and Bronckers and McNelis (2001, p. 457).

95. Member state representative to the Article 133 Committee, interview, Brussels, June 23, 1999.

96. Prince interview, 1998.

97. Prince interviews, 1998 and 1999, claiming that over 55 percent of daily queries concerning the database come from such companies.

10 employees. SMEs employ 66% of the workforce in the private sector."[98] The TBR grants these enterprises the legal right to have the European Commission investigate an issue on their behalf, provide them with all nonconfidential information available, conduct a hearing at which arguments may be presented, and publish the relevant decision in the EC's *Official Journal*. The TBR prescribes a timetable to assure enterprises that a decision will be made within a relatively certain time period, at least as compared with the Article 133 process.[99] The Commission's decision is even subject to review by the European Court of Justice. Although businesses work with the Commission as a partner, not as an adversary, the law forms a framework for business-Commission relations that can strengthen businesses' leverage.

The Commission's TBR unit maintains that its technical, law-oriented procedures reduce the pressure on it to balance a member state's political interests against a small enterprise's trade problems. Leather tanners, silk fabric finishers, and producers of Parma ham, for example, are not politically powerful industries. They are predominantly small, family-owned enterprises located in northern Italy that lack close contacts with Italian officials in Rome.[100] The TBR increases the likelihood that EC representatives will address their trading problems, and they have correspondingly benefited. In the Italian silk case, the silk producers were not supported by EURATEX, the Europe-wide textile trade association, because some of EURATEX's members benefited from more stringent U.S. rules of origin. European weavers profited from U.S. labeling rules that required more production processes to be completed in Europe for a product to receive a European label. Yet the Italian silk producers prevailed through

98. Remarks of Erkki Liikanen, commissioner for Enterprise and Information Society, "Economic Policy and Enterprise Culture," October 14, 1999, at a conference organized by UNICE (Union of Industrial and Employers' Confederations of Europe, the peak organization in the EU representing employers), at www.europa.eu.int/rapid/start (March 2003). The relative importance of SME exports was emphasized by Dorian Prince, former head of the Market Access Unit. Prince interview, 1999.

99. Commission officials state that the procedure generally takes six to seven months. Commission official in the TBR unit, interview, Brussels, June 29, 1999. Private lawyers still press for more speed and greater certainty. As Brussels attorneys Marco Bronckers and Natalie McNelis (2001, p. 446) write, "Unfortunately, the deliberations of the Commission and the Member States following the conclusion of the internal examination are not subject to any time-limit," so that "cases routinely take far longer" than the intended "five to seven month time-limit."

100. Prince interview, 1999.

use of the TBR mechanism.[101] Similarly, the TBR complaint of the Irish Music Rights Organisation (IMRO) against provisions of U.S. copyright law involved only a relatively minor amount of royalties for a trade association on the periphery of the EC. Yet the EC successfully defended IMRO's interests before the WTO, and the United States agreed to pay financial compensation that the EC will channel back to IMRO's members. Some business associations maintain that the TBR unit is more responsive to their trade concerns than members of the Article 133 Committee and other units within the Commission.[102]

Third, as with the use of Section 301 in the United States, Commission-business partnerships may deploy the more transparent TBR procedure as a tool to increase pressure on foreign governments without starting a formal WTO complaint. As the TBR scores initial successes and becomes better known, the Commission believes that the bringing of a TBR complaint can induce foreign governments, especially less powerful ones, to negotiate and modify practices. Over time, the Commission and private firms have learned to use the TBR more tactically.[103] The Commission can use the TBR procedure to notify foreign governments that if they do not implement WTO requirements, a WTO complaint will follow. The TBR report thereby serves as a shadow WTO complaint and an incentive for settlement without the embarrassment of losing a WTO case.

The Commission, working with private industry, deploys the TBR more as a "problem-solving device" than a means to litigate outcomes: "European industry is advised, first and foremost, to use the TBR as a means to persuade the EU's trading partners to settle disputes quickly and amicably."[104] A Commission official in the TBR unit calls the TBR "an instrument of suasion" and refers to changes made in Korean and Brazilian customs administration practices in response to TBR investigations and negotiations in their shadow.[105] The European Federation of Shipbuilders, he notes, brought a TBR complaint against Korean ship-

101. Member of TBR unit, telephone interview, February 1998.

102. Tettamanti of Federtessile, interview, February 19, 1998.

103. Petros Sourmelis, official in the TBR unit, interview, Brussels, June 13, 2001.

104. See Bronckers and McNelis (2001, p. 453). Confirmed by Commission official in the TBR unit, interview, Brussels, June 13, 2001.

105. Commission official in the TBR unit, interview, Brussels, June 13, 2001. The EC filed a WTO complaint against Brazil on October 14, 1999, and then reached an agreement with Brazil that Brazil would not apply its nonautomatic import licensing system to the EC products in question. The Commission continues to monitor Brazil's practices.

building subsidies in the hope of negotiating a reduction in their amount, as opposed to a full-blown WTO litigation, since some EC member states also subsidize their shipping industries.[106] Similarly, Volkswagen brought a TBR complaint concerning tax practices in Colombia in the hope of exercising more "leverage" in negotiating a tax reduction.[107]

The Commission also may commence a TBR investigation merely to notify the third country that it is monitoring the country's regulatory behavior. IFPI, an association of sound-recording companies, continues to monitor Thailand's enforcement of copyrights in conjunction with the TBR unit's administration of a complaint filed in 1991.[108] The association and Commission can use the TBR process as leverage to keep pressure on Thailand to crack down on copyright infringers, under the threat that a WTO complaint could follow.

Most businesses, especially larger ones, nonetheless have continued to prefer the Article 133 process for a number of reasons. For one thing, it can avoid the delay of a TBR procedure, which takes at least six or seven months before the Commission will take a claim to the WTO. For another, it avoids disclosing arguments to foreign governments, giving them less time to prepare a defense in a complex WTO proceeding. Perhaps most important, the Article 133 process permits businesses to remain more anonymous, while Commission representatives negotiate the removal of foreign barriers on their behalf. Although a trade association can file a TBR complaint in order to avoid naming an individual enterprise, a foreign regulator could still perceive the enterprise as being aggressive or hostile. The TBR, in this sense, can be viewed as a formalization of effective public-private partnerships that operate less transparently within the Article 133 process. Large and well-organized nation-based firms can rely in particular on the support of their national representatives in the less-transparent Article 133 process.

Overall, large multinational businesses and those that are members of national or EC trade associations with offices in Brussels are best positioned to work the system, whether under Article 133 or the TBR. The Scotch Whisky Association, whose members constitute one of the United Kingdom's largest export sectors, is renowned for successfully working

106. Commission official in the TBR unit, interview, Brussels, June 13, 2001. The EC filed a WTO complaint regarding this matter on October 21, 2002.

107. Commission official in the TBR unit, interview, Brussels, June 13, 2001.

108. See Van Eeckhaute (1999, p. 211).

with the Commission to pry open foreign markets.[109] The industry's initial success in the 1996 Japan–Alcoholic Beverages case, concerning alleged tax discrimination in favor of Japanese producers of *shochu*, spurred it to work with the Commission in the EC's successful WTO complaints against South Korean and Chilean tax practices that favored their local beverages, *soju* and *pisco*. When Chile modified its internal tax regime in light of the Japan–Alcoholic Beverages decision, the EC brought a new complaint, alleging that the modified law still violated the antidiscrimination rules of GATT Article III. After the Appellate Body found against it, Chile lowered its taxes on all distilled spirits to the same level applied to *pisco*.[110] A sophisticated repeat player, the Scotch Whisky Association likewise has worked with the Commission on the WTO terms of accession of China, Taiwan, and Russia, among others.[111] Other members of the European Confederation of Producers of Spirits (CEPS) also have deployed the EC's trade instruments. French associations of cognac producers and Bordeaux winemakers brought TBR complaints, respectively, against Brazil's and Canada's nonrecognition of the "cognac," "Bordeaux," and "Medoc" geographical indications.[112]

109. The spirits sector represents a major EC export interest, which the association maintains is "among [the] top 5 export sectors . . . , with EU spirits exports totaling 4 billion ECU" in 1996. Remarks by Tim Jackson, SWA, May 1997. See also "EU Urged to Act Tough on Spirit Tariff Reforms," *European Reporter*, October 2, 1999. According to Dorian Prince, scotch whisky has been the United Kingdom's top export earner. Prince interview, 1999.

110. See Rosella Brevetti, "Chile Modifies Distilled Spirits Taxes to Comply with Adverse WTO Ruling," *International Trade Reporter (BNA)*, February 1, 2001, pp. 204–05. The EC first brought a complaint against Chile's alleged discriminatory taxation of imported spirits on June 4, 1997. The Appellate Body report was adopted by the WTO Dispute Settlement Body on January 12, 2000.

111. See Remarks by Tim Jackson, SWA, May 1997: "We also take the opportunity of WTO Accession to work closely with the Commission on the forthcoming accessions, particularly, China, Russia and Taiwan to ensure that distilled spirits import tariffs in these markets are reduced, ideally to zero, and non-tariff barriers, especially internal tax discrimination, are eliminated." The Scotch Whisky Association director added, "During the Uruguay round, CEPS [the Confédération Européenne des Producteurs de Spiritueux] worked with the Commission from an early stage to ensure that tariffs were eliminated on brown spirits in Canada, the United States and Japan."

112. On the cognac case against Brazil, see "Trade Obstacles Maintained by Brazil Concerning Trade in Cognac," *Official Journal*. On the Bordeaux case against Canada, see *Conseil Interprofessionnel du Vin de Bordeaux* ("CIVB"). See also the Commission's overview of the case, at www.europa.eu.int/comm/trade/policy/traderegul/can_bor.htm (March 2003), noting "that the Commission is currently in the process of negotiating a bilateral agreement with Canada on trade in wine and spirits. This agreement would foresee the definitive elimination of the names listed as 'generic' in Canada, including 'Bordeaux,' 'Médoc' and 'Medoc.'"

## Summary

The EC's decisionmaking process for bringing trade claims does not simply consist of European member states and the European Commission negotiating over potentially divergent national and EC interests. Rather, it is a dynamic, ad hoc, hybrid, multitiered process in which private interests are deeply implicated. It is multitiered because private interests can network behind the scenes simultaneously at the national and supranational levels with member state and Commission representatives in order to profit from the removal of foreign trade barriers. It is ad hoc because private businesses coordinate their positions among themselves and form partnerships with EC public officials on an ad hoc basis. It is a hybrid process because it is neither purely intergovernmental nor purely private, but rather involves public-private networks operating in the shadow of international trade law.

As in the United States, EC trade policy has been centralized in a specialized trade agency, the Commission's Trade Directorate-General. This specialized agency, in turn, works with other bureaucratic agencies, in this case the Commission's Legal Service and other directorates-general, such as Agriculture. The Commission's Trade Directorate-General also is subject to member state oversight, just as the USTR is closely monitored by the U.S. Congress. In both cases, these political bodies respond to commercial constituent pressures, although the pressures are much more intensive in the United States. In Europe, the Commission has had to play a more proactive role in generating public-private coordination so as to effectively deploy WTO law. Chapter 5 explains why.

# 5 *Why a More Aggressive U.S. Approach?*

The United States and European Community have similar trade goals. They both strive to enhance their firms' access to foreign markets, while defending their internal regulatory prerogatives. The effectiveness of their strategies is likewise comparable. During the WTO's first eight years, the United States brought seventy WTO complaints, which resulted in nineteen panel decisions, while the EC brought fifty-eight WTO complaints, which resulted in twenty-three panel decisions. Each has been relatively successful in gaining foreign concessions for its export interests Appendix tables 1 to 4 provide summaries of these U.S. and EC complaints and their outcomes.

At the same time, U.S. and EC methods for challenging trade barriers differ significantly. Although the public database compiled by the EC's Market Access Unit resembles U.S. compilations of "Super 301" and "Special 301" "priority" foreign trade practices, it is not accompanied by the buildup and litigation threats surrounding the publication of U.S. reports. Rather, the EC retains the database for internal investigative purposes before privately approaching a foreign government concerning a barrier's removal.[1] Similarly, although the EC issues an annual report on U.S. trade barriers, it does not attempt to use the report as a lever to force open the U.S. market. The EC's report is not published with fanfare on a set date at which time new WTO complaints are announced. Rather, the EC report's primary objective is to neutralize U.S. threats in bilateral consultations by referring to a published list of U.S. trade barriers and by subjecting the United States to its own tactics.[2]

In addition, EC authorities often appear more deferential than the United States to developing country interests, such as those of former EC colonies. Both the United States and the EC brought WTO complaints against India's use of quotas invoked on balance of payments grounds, but the EC settled with India to gradually phase out its quotas within four years, while the United States continued to litigate.[3] Similarly, an EC pharmaceutical lobbyist confirms that the United States took a more aggressive stance concerning South Africa's enforcement of pharmaceutical patent rights than did the EC.[4] The EC also was more flexible than the United States in negotiations over implementation of the Doha declaration on access to medicines for developing countries.[5] European authorities often pursue similar trade objectives, but their relative autonomy from private sector pressure permits them to adopt different methods.

The more aggressive U.S. market access strategy reflects the more aggressive role of U.S. private interests in trade policy. This chapter examines the political, historical, economic, and cultural reasons for the more

1. Alistair Stewart, head of the Market Access Unit, telephone interview, January 16, 2002. While the Commission notifies the foreign government before adding a trade barrier to its database and may use that opportunity to have the barrier removed, the primary reason for its notice is to ensure the accuracy of the barrier's description before publication, further investigation and, where appropriate, reference to the EC's member state representatives. The Commission's Market Access Unit's ongoing compilation of trade barriers more closely resembles the U.S. Department of Commerce's Market Access and Compliance Service. See www.mac.doc.gov (March 2003).

2. Commission official at U.S. desk in DG Trade, interview, Brussels, June 25, 1999.

3. India continued to limit imports to protect its balance of payments even though it had long had a surplus of currency reserves, as confirmed by representatives from the International Monetary Fund. Compare DS190 and DS196 in appendix tables 1 and 4.

4. EC trade association on patent matters, interview, Brussels, June 28, 1999.

5. See, for example, "WTO Stumbles over Doha Agenda Hurdles as Deal Unravels on TRIPS/Medicines, S&D," *International Trade Reporter (BNA)*, January 2, 2003, pp. 6–7.

proactive role of business within the United States in international trade disputes. These differences can be broken down into four categories:

POLITICAL STRUCTURE. In the U.S. political process, Congress plays a more active role: it exhorts the USTR to support specific industry and company interests. In the EC's more convoluted political process, by contrast, member states demand that EC officials exercise greater caution when challenging foreign trade barriers, especially where the challenge could implicate conflicting member state interests. Businesses respond to these divergent political opportunities.

BUSINESS-GOVERNMENT RELATIONS. U.S. private firms are more comfortable and experienced with lobbying at the federal level, especially with regard to external trade matters. EC businesses' less aggressive approach to lobbying arises not only from the less conducive EC political system but also from Europe's more corporatist traditions of government-business relations and from the EC's shorter historical legacy. U.S. firms operate within a more unified U.S. market structure, whereas many European firms retain a national focus so that lobbying in Brussels seems somewhat more remote.

USE OF LAWYERS AND ADVERSARIAL LITIGATION. U.S. private firms are more likely to employ private law firms to work with trade officials in international trade litigation. This tendency is rooted in U.S. "adversarial legalist" traditions and U.S. firms' greater distrust of government. EC firms, in contrast, tend to be more wary of litigation and to work more discretely with government in the defense of their interests.

ADMINISTRATIVE CULTURE. U.S. trade officials tend to be more responsive to private lobbying on account of U.S. political-cultural expectations, which are nurtured and facilitated by Washington's "revolving-door" administrative culture. EC trade officials, on the other hand, are more likely to be career civil servants in Brussels and thus to develop somewhat greater administrative discretion. They work in an administrative culture that attempts to allay national concerns over favoritism toward firms from rival EC member states.

## Impact of Political Structure

U.S. and EC political processes work in opposite directions toward their common goals. Because the USTR is pressed by Congress to support specific industry and company interests, U.S. firms maintain greater leverage over U.S. trade policy. As addressed in chapter 3, U.S. firms, together with their executives and large shareholders, help finance congressional and presidential political campaigns. Members of the House of Representatives, whose small districts often depend on company-specific or industry-specific employment, are particularly vulnerable to pressure from individual firms. Their two-year terms subject them to almost constant campaigning. Congress created the USTR to respond to private interests and their congressional defenders in "watchdog" committees: the trade subcommittees of the Senate Finance and the House Ways and Means Committees. These committees call the USTR before them to testify and explain its actions. If unsatisfied with USTR policy, Congress retains the power to pass legislation forcing the USTR to act, to withhold or withdraw trade negotiating authority, to block ratification of signed agreements, to limit budgetary allocations, or to hold other legislation hostage.

The decentralized political power structure of the United States and its less-unified political parties help explain the enhanced role of interest groups.[6] As political scientist Clyde Wilcox concludes, "If political scientists were charged to design a national legislature to maximize interest group influence, they would be hard pressed to improve on the American Congress."[7] Members of the U.S. Congress are freer to "behave like local representatives rather than members of a national organization bearing collective responsibility for government."[8]

To enlist private sector political support for U.S. trade policy, the USTR has created sector-specific business advisory councils and committees on trade.[9] Appointments to these committees often favor campaign

6. See Loomis and Cigler (1998, pp. 5–6), noting U.S. constitutional guarantees of free speech and association, decentralized political power structure, less-unified political parties, and American cultural values as explanations for the enhanced role of interest groups.

7. Wilcox (1998, p. 89), noting the "many points of access to the U.S. Congress" and the "incentives to listen to interest groups." See also Molyneux (2001, p. 60): "Among the developed nations, the United States is unique due to the fact that the legislature plays a major role in the development and enunciation of international trade policy."

8. "Politics Brief," *Economist*, July 24, 1999, p. 51.

9. See, for example, Abbott (1996, p. 971).

donors to whom elected officials feel beholden. As reported after the fall 2002 election, "The White House rewarded major supporters of Republican candidates in the 2002 midterm elections with seats on a trade advisory committee that meets regularly with the U.S. Trade Representative and provides input to the president regarding trade agreements."[10] The White House released "all Clinton administration appointees." The new list included such major campaign givers as the chief executives and presidents of Weyerhaeuser, the National Cattlemen's Beef Association, eBay, the National Association of Manufacturers, Hanna Steel Corporation, IBM, SC Johnson, Toys R Us, the Carlyle Group, and Victoria's Secret.[11]

The European political process, on the other hand, can slow the development of close Commission–private sector partnerships in trade litigation. First, there is much less parliamentary pressure on European trade officials to act on behalf of specific industries. At the EC level, the European Parliament holds little power over external trade matters. The European Commission and Council only consult the European Parliament on trade policy pursuant to informal procedures.[12] Although the role of the European Parliament in EC politics is increasing and the Commission is consulting it more in matters of trade, the EC treaty grants the European Parliament no constitutional or legal authority over trade policy. Thus firms and trade associations rarely lobby the European Parliament over the bringing of trade complaints against foreign trade barriers.[13] Moreover, even if the European Parliament were to attain some authority over EC trade policy and firms were to lobby European parliamentary representatives, EC parliamentarians are less affected by local

10. "White House Rewards Donors with Slots on Key Advisory Committee," *Inside U.S. Trade*, December 13, 2002, p. 1.

11."White House Rewards Donors," p. 16, reporting, for example, that executives from the National Cattlemen's Beef Association gave $298,878 to Republican candidates compared with $52,200 to Democratic candidates, and that executives from Weyerhaeuser gave $244,750 to Republican candidates compared with $74,250 to Democratic candidates, citing Federal Election Commission reports.

12. The European Commission and Council have agreed to consult with the European Parliament pursuant to the Luns-Westerterp and other informal procedures. See Molyneux (2001, pp. 208–10): "Formally . . . the European Parliament plays a very limited role . . . [although it has] developed informal procedures to allow it to keep a dialogue on trade matters with the other Community institutions." Also Woolcock (2000, p. 380): "The indirect role of the EP contrasts with the role of the U.S. Congress." Confirmed by Commission official, interview, Brussels, June 13, 2001.

13. Commission official in DG Trade, interview, Brussels, June 16, 2001.

industry and company concerns than their counterparts in the U.S. Congress. For one thing, EC parliamentarians are elected every five years. For another, they are elected by proportionate representation from party lists, not by individual election in separate electoral districts containing dominant local firms.[14]

As for the member states, European executive branches largely control trade policy and are not subject to much parliamentary pressure. Under member state parliamentary systems, parliamentarians vote on a party line or risk a vote of no-confidence. A vote of no-confidence would trigger a new parliamentary election, putting their seats at risk.[15] When parliamentarians are elected through a list system, as opposed to individually, they are even less exposed to company pressure, which is the case in most member states.[16] Because member state executive departments determine trade policy, they are better able to balance competing constituent interests from across the nation. In addition, in many member states, the lead executive agency remains the foreign affairs ministry, which tends to favor foreign policy concerns over firms' specific commercial interests.

Second, the European Commission must balance not only sectoral interests (as must the USTR), but also national ones—those of the fifteen member states. Political scientist Simon Hix thus characterizes the EC policy process as a "consociational model of interest intermediation . . . divided along cultural rather than socioeconomic lines: into the different nation-states of western Europe."[17] Hence Europe is more likely to take a "package approach" to trade negotiations, as opposed to a "sectoral one," which can be "frustrating" for European business.[18] EC member states are wary that a Commission action in one sector important to one European country could adversely affect sectors important to it. In contrast, there is much less interstate conflict over U.S. trade policy. Interstate

14. See Hix (1999, p. 167 ff.). Although there are national variants, the concept of a list system is that "parties nominate lists of candidates in multimember districts, that the voters cast their ballots for one party list or another . . . , and that the seats are allocated to the party lists in proportion to the numbers of votes they have collected." Lijphart (1999, p. 147).

15. See Devuyst (2000, p. 40); and "Politics Brief," *Economist*, p. 51, which notes that a negative vote under a European parliamentary system brings down the government in power, so that "members of Parliament must toe a party line."

16. Lijphart (1999, p. 145).

17. Hix (1999, p. 202).

18. Cowles (2001a, p. 242).

rivalries in the United States are less prevalent because there has long been a single U.S. market.

If a Commission unit were to become too close to a private commercial interest, the unit could be challenged by EC member states with competing commercial interests. Thus "the Commission's preferred strategy is to seek principal forms of dialogue from [pan-European associations]."[19] The Commission's mantra is to serve the "Community interest" or "public interest," not a specific interest of a specific firm from a specific member state.[20] WTO cases must be viewed as "EC cases."[21] Although this situation may be changing, many Commission officials still consider it potentially "dangerous for their careers to be seen fraternizing with industry."[22] Because of member state concerns that an official could favor firms from the official's home country, the Commission faces a more complicated situation than its U.S. counterpart.

European firms, too, face additional obstacles because Commission decisions are subject to indirect control by member states. Firms often must lobby at both the national and European levels, especially where they use the Article 133 procedure. As a leading analyst of European government-business relations writes, "In practice, interests tend to use a combination of routes simultaneously," referring to a "national route" and a "European route."[23] Even where an enterprise successfully lobbies its national representative for assistance, that is only one vote of fifteen. The other member states can delay or block the bringing of a trade complaint. In contrast, the U.S. political process invites greater private participation than is generally available to EC firms.

A case against the United States involving the "Havana Club" trademark, which pitted claims between the French firm Pernod Ricard against its rival Bacardi over ownership of the mark, illustrates the contrast.[24]

19. Greenwood (1997, p. 4).

20. Even though the remark may be self-serving, Cowles (2001a, p. 242) finds support in a Commission official's statement that "DG Trade tends to focus on the 'wider public interest' as opposed to industry concerns *per se* in trade negotiations." The official further remarked that Commission perceptions are based on "what they believe are the larger societal interests—including those of labor, consumer, and environmental groups."

21. DG Trade official, interview, Brussels, June 1999. Confirmed by member of the Brussels bar and former member of the Commission, Brussels, June 28, 2002.

22. DG Trade official, interview, Brussels, June 22, 1999.

23. See Greenwood (1997, p. 11).

24. See Dinan (2003, p. 175), providing overview of the case and noting the "Florida Governor's office . . . intensive lobbying campaign . . . on Bacardi's behalf" resulting in

Pernod Ricard had entered a joint venture with a Cuban state-owned entity to acquire the "Havana Club" trademark, which the Cuban seller had already registered with the U.S. Patent and Trademark Office in 1976. The trademark, however, had been confiscated from the Arechabala family following the Cuban revolution. Barcardi is a major contributor to the Republican Party and a promoter of economic sanctions against Cuba. It helped write and bankroll, for example, the controversial Helms-Burton law, the subject of an earlier U.S.-EC trade dispute. In 1997 Bacardi purchased what it held were the prior rights in the trademark from the Arechabala family. Bacardi then rallied its congressional allies to enact legislation that was specifically targeted to block the Pernod Ricard joint venture from ever enforcing its rights in the trademark in the United States.

When Pernod Ricard asked the Commission to initiate a WTO complaint challenging the U.S. legislation, the Commission had to delay for months, despite France's vigorous support, because Italy objected within the Article 133 Committee. Although Italy finally relented and WTO consultations could begin, the Commission faced further delay and uncertainty. It still had to obtain the committee's approval for the EC's request that a WTO panel be formed. Some member states feared that the United States had offered Italy exemptions from U.S. retaliation against the EC's banana import licensing regime, so as to impede EC action. Eventually, however, the EC brought the case and prevailed in part, winning its claim that the U.S. law violated WTO national treatment and most-favored-nation obligations.[25]

## Business-Government Relations

U.S. firms and trade associations respond to the opportunities offered by the U.S. political system. They more habitually and aggressively lobby

---

political appointees overruling career employees in the U.S. administration. Lobbying story confirmed in teleconference call with former member of the USTR, April 24, 2003. See also Thomas Edsall, "Gov. Bush Reveals Lobby Effort; Documents Show Intervention in Trademark Case of GOP Donor," *Washington Post,* October 18, 2002, p. A12; "Rum, Macaroni and Bad Politics," *Chicago Tribune,* September 2, 2002, p. 20.

25. Member state representative to the Article 133 Committee, interview, Brussels, June 23, 1999. See also Larry Speer, "Battle over Cuban Rum Trademark New Threat to EU-US Relations," *International Trade Reporter (BNA),* February 17, 2000, p. 269; "EU Member States Split on Approval for WTO Panel on Section 211," *Inside U.S. Trade,* March 10, 2000, p. 1; and Dinan (2003).

trade officials in Washington to challenge foreign trade barriers than do their EC counterparts in Brussels. Yet political structure alone does not explain different U.S. and European practices. The longer history of a unified market and federal political system in the United States and the different EC traditions of business-government relations are important factors. Long before the European Community came into being, the United States had a single market, and Washington, D.C., was a center for legislative and agency lobbying.

Although the situation is evolving, many firms continue to primarily look to their national representatives to defend their interests within the EC and abroad because of tradition and institutional inertia.[26] Larger European firms traditionally had close relationships with national governmental representatives, sometimes because they were actually owned by the state, or were considered to be "national champions" (as in France).[27] Even where these firms are members of Brussels-based lobbying associations, their first governmental contact may remain their national representative. In the steel industry, Corus (the entity resulting from the merger of British Steel and the Dutch company Koninklijke Hoogovens) maintains close relations with the British government, and Arcelor (the entity resulting from the merger of French Usinor Sacilor and companies from Spain and Luxmbourg) with the French government. For many companies, these contacts are more important than ties between European trade associations, such as Eurofer, and the European Commission.[28]

As a result, the EC often must balance the interests of competing national industrial interests working through competing national representatives. In the automobile sector, for example, the EC must balance the interests of other European car companies against German car companies that invest and sell to a greater extent in foreign markets. These intraindustry divisions can generate national divisions within the Article 133 Committee. Intra-EC divisions thus arose in the EC's challenges to Brazil's and Canada's domestic content requirements for the automobile sector.[29]

26. See Coen (1997, p. 93), stating that "a system of national representation favoring inertia made it illogical for firms to change existing patterns of behavior."

27. Schmidt (1996).

28. A lawyer for Corus in a private law firm, interview, Washington, October 18, 2001.

29. Action was delayed because of splits among the interests of German versus other European car companies. Interviews in Brussels with ACEA, the European automobile trade association, June 29, 1999; Commission official from Legal Service, June 24 1999; and Commission official in DG Trade, June 21, 1999.

The EC has lacked a basic "pan-European trade association representing the automobile parts industry."[30]

Small and medium-sized enterprises, in particular, are less likely to have close contacts in Brussels. For these firms, lobbying in Brussels is more remote and often involves dealing with officials speaking a nonnative language and displaying nonnative manners and perspectives. Lobbying in Brussels offers them a less obvious payback. As analysts of EC government-business relations observe, "Business associations are more likely to have differentiated territorial structures, the more their members are small rather than large firms, and serve local and regional markets rather than national/international markets."[31]

In addition, much EC legislation takes the form of "framework directives" that may leave varying amounts of discretion for implementation to member states.[32] Those EC firms and industries whose activities remain centered within a single member state thus often continue to contact predominantly national representatives on regulatory matters, despite the growth in EC-initiated legislation. Member states' implementation of the directive occurs through national political and bureaucratic processes. The directive form of legislation has no counterpart in the United States.

Historically, the first EC-wide enterprises were often subsidiaries of American multinationals, not European firms. In the wake of the Marshall Plan, many U.S. corporations invested in large European subsidiaries. Today in Brussels, multinational U.S. firms remain on the lobbying forefront. One member state representative to the Article 133 Committee meetings said he seemed to receive "more calls from U.S. industry than from EU industry."[33] The *Economist* reports that "the most effective lobbying force in town [Brussels] is commonly considered to be the EU Committee of the American Chamber of Commerce."[34]

Corporatist and centralized European traditions of government-business relations also constrain aggressive lobbying by individual

30. See Steinberg and Stokes (1999, p. 218).

31. See Coleman and Montpeti (2000, p. 164).

32. On the directive as a legislative instrument, see Shaw (2000, pp. 244–45). See generally de Witte, Hanf, and Vos (2001), assessing the numerous ways in which flexibility for member states is built into EU law.

33. Interview, Brussels, June 23, 1999.

34. "The Brussels Lobbyist and the Struggle for Ear-Time," *Economist*, August 15, 1998, p. 42. The EU Committee of AmCham represents American multinationals in the EC. See Cowles (1996, p. 33).

European firms. In corporatist systems, as in Germany and Scandinavia, firm interests are aggregated into peak organizations that negotiate with state and labor representatives to reach a consensus.[35] The lead representative of the EC automobile trade association, ACEA, confirms that "in the EC, one is taught to [work] in a spirit of consensus," which "affects firm behavior."[36] In centralized systems, as in France, the state plays a more dominant "top-down" role through its professional civil service.[37] As U.K. political scientists Mark Aspinwall and Justin Greenwood write, "Modern European states . . . have a tradition of strong political parties or administrative elites, insulating them (at least relative to America) from particularist private demands."[38]

Under European corporatist and centralized systems, firms are more accustomed to working with state public officials through hierarchical confederations that combine trade associations from multiple sectors, such as BDI in Germany, MEDEF in France, and UNICE in the EC.[39] Even though lobbying has become more decentralized in Brussels, many European firms continue to lobby through trade associations representing firms throughout Europe on a cross-sectoral or sectoral basis.[40] When lobbying is conducted through "peak" associations, individual firm views

35. Philippe Schmitter (1974, p. 85) presents classic corporatism as a system where actors "are organised into a limited number of singular, compulsory, non-competitive, hierarchically ordered and functionally differentiated categories." This situation is changing, though not yet to the extent of a U.S. decentralized model of lobbying. For an assessment of different forms of capitalism with different traditions of government-business relations, see Hollingsworth, Schmitter, and Streeck (1994); Katzenstein (1976, p. 14), noting the United States is "a country marked by a strong society and a weak state"; and Wilson (2003).

36. ACEA representative, interview, Brussels, June 29, 1999.

37. See Schmidt (1996, p. 47), referring to France's "statist tradition . . . in which government has the power and authority to take unilateral action at the policy formulation stage, without prior consultation with those most interested in the policy."

38. See Aspinwall and Greenwood (1998, p. 1).

39. BDI is the acronym for the Bundesverband der Deutschen Industrie, MEDEF for the Mouvement des Entreprises de France (which superseded the CNPF, or Conseil National du Patronat Français in 1998), and UNICE for Union des Confédérations de l'Industrie et des Employeurs d'Europe (the Union of Industrial and Employers' Confederations of Europe). The CBI, or Confederation of Business Industries, is the peak business trade association in the United Kingdom but is less important for national industry than its German and French counterparts. See Cowles (2001b, pp. 163–65).

40. As Greenwood (2000, p. 77) notes, "There are now over 600 formal European level business associations . . . and approximately 250 firms with representatives offices in Brussels." Greenwood (p. 96) adds that "some two-thirds of Euro groups are federations of national organizations."

are diluted or offset by the countervailing priorities of other firms.[41] When firms' views and interests are divided along national lines—a legacy of traditionally segregated European markets—these peak institutions lose a good deal of their effectiveness.[42] Although these traits are becoming less pronounced (note the increased role of large multinational European firms), individual European enterprises remain less likely to directly lobby and network with the Commission than firms in the United States: "While big business-European Commission relations have developed in other policy areas over the past two decades, this pales in contrast to the century-old relations between continental [national industry associations] and their respective governments."[43]

Even European firms that lobby actively in Brussels on internal market matters lobby less regarding external commercial relations.[44] In particular, they press governmental officials less aggressively to litigate over foreign trade barriers than their U.S. counterparts. Whereas the U.S. government has created a system of private sector councils and committees to advise it on trade policy, "there is no formal structure of advisory committees at the EU level."[45] The result is relatively greater discretion for European public

41. See Greenwood (2000, pp. 81–82): "In order to arrive at 'an opinion,' UNICE has to seek to reflect the broad constituency of its members interests and positions, which are in turn very often the result of compromises made at the national level. To help it arrive at common positions, UNICE uses its network of permanent committee structures, which in turn heightens the tendency for compromise. Thus, the organization is well recognised for providing generalized, 'lowest common denominator' positions which are not always very helpful in providing the institutions with a clear signal to act upon."

42. Aspinwall and Greenwood (1998, p. 2) observe: "At the EU level, territorial interests, rather than functional or ideological ones, have always been predominant."

43. Cowles (2001b, p. 176). See Cowles (2001b, pp. 162–63): "Before the TABD, there was no significant business-government relationship at the European level in external trade matters. . . . The TABD changed this business-government dynamic. With the creation of the TABD, a new business-government relationship emerged in Brussels in common commercial policy." Cowles (p. 171) argues that TABD serves to weaken the traditional national industrial associations by encouraging firms to bypass them and directly contact Commission and national officials. Also De Bièvre (2003).

44. Members of the Commission's Legal Service, interviews, June 22 and 23, 1999. See also Ostry (1990, p. 33), comparing the political economy of business-government relations in the EC in relation to GATT trade liberalization negotiations with that of internal EC market integration: "The divergence between the role of the major European corporations in the two high policy processes could scarcely be more marked. . . . [T]he multinational corporations—through their new organization the European Roundtable . . . —played a fundamentally important and leading role in the strategic formulation of the move to the internal market and have continued to do so as it has proceeded."

45. Woolcock (2000, pp. 380–81). See also Cowles (2001a, p. 241): "European business has not formally organized itself in Brussels to lobby Commission officials on trade issues.

authorities. According to a Danish representative to Article 133 Committee meetings, "Our firms do not come to us with trade problems. They tend to invest to get around a barrier; they don't litigate."[46] Another member of the Article 133 Committee agrees, "We still tend to see trade policy largely as diplomacy."[47] A lobbyist for the chemical industry's trade association concurs: "We Europeans still see ourselves as negotiators. We are not a litigious people."[48] According to a member of the Commission's DG Trade, there appears to be a different mentality among U.S. firms, which view a WTO case as "their case," whereas EC companies tend to consider cases to be the responsibility of public authorities.[49]

Faced with different historical legacies, the Commission has had to encourage firms to help it to more effectively enforce European trading rights. Although federal agencies in the United States also have sponsored the formation of national interest groups to advance federal goals, the Commission feels more pressed to do so in light of the EC's historical, economic, and political contexts. The U.S. Commerce Department, for example, took the initiative in founding the U.S. Chamber of Commerce in 1912 to advance federal agency goals, and government officials in agricultural departments took the lead in creating the American Farm Bureau Federation.[50] However, these U.S. associations became completely independent of the government over time. Similarly, whereas U.S. Section 301 goes back to 1974, the Commission's TBR procedure dates only to 1995.[51]

. . . U.S. industry for example, has direct channels to the Commerce Department and USTR on trade issues through ISACs [Industry Sectoral Advisory Committees]. European industry does not."

46. Interview, Brussels, June 24, 1999.

47. Interview, Brussels, June 25, 1999.

48. Reinhold Quick, lobbyist for CEFIC (the European Chemical Industry Council), interview, Brussels, June 25, 1999.

49. Interview, Brussels, June 24, 1999.

50. On U.S. governmental sponsorship of interest groups generally, see, for example, Loomis and Cigler (1998, pp. 13–15): "In the early twentieth century, relevant government officials in the agriculture and commerce departments encouraged the formation of the American Farm Bureau Federation and the U.S. Chamber of Commerce respectively." See also Lowi (1979, p. 79): "The Department of Commerce . . . took the initiative in founding the U.S. Chamber of Commerce in 1912. Without official endorsement in 1912, the fusion of local chambers into one national business association would more likely never have taken place. Most of the negotiating sessions among local leaders, the National Association of Manufacturers, and others were arranged by, and took place in, the office of the secretary of Commerce and Labor. The final organization charter was written there. . . . The Department of Commerce fostered the trade associations where they already existed and helped organize them where they did not yet exist." On the role of the U.S. Department of Commerce in the formation of the Transatlantic Business Dialogue in the early 1990s, see Cowles (2001b).

The Commission's trade units are now attempting to close the gap. Just as the forging of public-private links in the United States helped change business behavior and expectations toward the international trading system in the 1970s,[52] the TBR and market access database are being employed to spur EC firms to work with the Commission to take more effective action against foreign trade barriers. "The Commission," says Alistair Stewart, a former head of the TBR unit, "would like a new reflex to be developed on [business's] part, and considers that this would be very much in their interest."[53] Successful use of the TBR, Stewart emphasizes, will require "a certain change in attitude in EC companies."[54] A leading trade lawyer in Brussels concurs: "Industry here has to change mentally."[55] To develop this reflex, the Commission has held press conferences, distributed glossy brochures, hired consultants, contacted European trade associations to bring claims, and prepared claims for them.

In contrast, larger U.S. firms tend to employ well-staffed governmental affairs departments to track, strategize, and thereby shape federal legislation and regulatory policy. In 1997 alone, firms spent over $1.4 billion on lobbying in Washington, dwarfing the amount spent in Brussels.[56] These firms do not need to work through the intermediary of member state officials who speak their native tongue. They do not defer lobbying to "peak" organizations in Washington. They form ad hoc associations to address specific trade barriers—such as the Coalition against Australian Leather Subsidies. When they face trade problems, they contact the USTR directly. For them, lobbying is less controversial and more routine, particularly in regard to international trade. As a lobbyist from the U.S. intellectual property industry complains, his European counterparts in business are "less aggressive." They don't like to "rock the boat." A U.S.

51. As noted earlier, the NCPI was enacted in 1984 but was a more constrained and ultimately inefficacious instrument. See chapter 4, note 55.

52. See Destler (1995, pp. 14–15).

53. Stewart (1996, pp. 123, 125). The efforts of the Commission to stimulate greater public-private interaction in the EC is not limited to the trade realm. Greenwood (2000, p. 97) also notes the "entrepreneurial role of the European Commission, in particular, in funding the start up of Euro groups" for EC lobbying generally.

54. Stewart (1996, pp. 123, 125).

55. Interview, Brussels, June 28, 1999.

56. See "Tab for Washington Lobbying: $1.42 Billion," *New York Times*, July 29, 1999, p. A14 (reported by the Center for Responsive Politics, a research group based in Washington, D.C.). Compare Shaiko (1998, p. 15): "Lobbying expenditures for 1996 totaled roughly $1 billion." For a report on lobbying by the U.S. pharmaceutical industry, see, for example, Novak (1993, p. 58).

lobbyist's business is to "stir things up," not smooth things over. "We thrive on confrontation."[57]

Nonetheless, as Europe integrates, European individual firms and branch-specific trade associations work more closely with the Commission in Brussels. Lobbying in Brussels, while rapidly expanding, is largely a phenomenon of the past decade, taking off in the clamor for the single market of "Europe 1992"[58] and the elimination of national veto rights over most legislative matters:[59] "Of the ten biggest 'public-affairs consultancies' in Brussels, five have arrived since 1990."[60] As more European firms operate on an EC-wide basis, and as they are affected by more legislation enacted in Brussels, they allocate more resources to working with EC institutions.[61] European cross-border mergers and acquisitions and the creation of a single European currency, the euro, are accelerating the trend. "From an individual firm's point of view, the rewards from national corporatist bargaining with governmental and labour actors, and even membership of 'national' peak associations of business, have receded as the benefits of private action have increased."[62] Even for French business, "Big businesses . . . now find themselves the privileged interlocutors of the European Commission, and partners rather than supplicants of French ministries in the lobbying efforts of the nation. . . . French government officials who typically frowned on lobbying when

57. U.S. lobbyist, telephone interview over copyright matters, May 17, 1999. Compare interview with Commission official handling copyright matters, Brussels, June 24, 1999, stating that the Commission's strategy is "based on cooperation rather than confrontation."

58. See Van Schendelen (1993, p. 6), concerning the publicity given to the Commission's push for the creation of a "single European market" by 1992, particularly following the 1986 Single European Act. In this effort, 500 legislative measures were passed during a six-and-a-half-year period, significantly harmonizing European legislation. During this period of heightened EC legislative activity, European firms increasingly followed the legislative process in Brussels. See also Coen (1997, pp. 95, 99), concerning "movement towards single-issue groups with a mobile and changing membership" following the Single European Act from the traditional peak European federations, and "trend towards an increasing partnership between firms and the Commission at the European level"; and Coen (1998, p. 75).

59. See Greenwood (1997, p. 53): "The SEA [Single European Act], and later the TEU [Treaty of European Union], considerably extended the constitutional reach of the qualified majority system of voting." The Treaties of Amsterdam and Nice, further modifying the EC treaty and the TEU, extended this trend.

60. "Brussels Lobbyist," *Economist*, p. 42.

61. Cowles has estimated that around 60 percent of all legislation affecting industry in the EC originated in Brussels. See Greenwood (2000, p. 77), citing Cowles.

62. Hix (1999, p. 167 ff.).

it involved the national government, even encouraged it when it involved the EU."[63]

According to a lobbyist for the French multinational firm Lafarge SA, "In Europe, Brussels is becoming much more important than national capitals in terms of our government affairs work. Most of the laws that affect us start their lives in Brussels."[64] As the figures on new TBR cases demonstrate, European firms indeed are developing new reflexes and going to the Commission more frequently with WTO complaints. However, given the EC's decisionmaking structure, firms and associations that have developed close contacts with the Commission must continue to work through member state officials as well, especially on matters involving the Article 133 Committee.

## Use of Private Lawyers and Adversarial Litigation

Having long operated within corporatist and centralized civil law systems, European companies and trade associations (those in the United Kingdom being an exception) have less frequently employed private lawyers on trade matters. Rather, they have let the Commission's civil servants take the lead.[65] Eurofer, the European steel association, admits that it "relies on the Commission for legal services," in contrast to the U.S. steel industry, which hires large teams of lawyers to defend its international trade concerns.[66] When bringing offensive claims against foreign trade barriers under the TBR, European companies and associations have been less likely to hire lawyers to advance their arguments. For many European companies, this has been "the Commission's job."[67] European businesses tend to work more discretely and less legalistically with public officials. The idea of an individual enterprise forcing the government's hand on international economic matters through a legal procedure remains alien to their traditions.

63. See Schmidt (1996, pp. 66, 235).

64. See, for example, Caine (2000), quoting Christopher Boyd.

65. National and European trade associations traditionally worked without the assistance of attorneys. Jacques Bourgeois, former member of the Commission and now member of the EC trade bar, working for the firm Akin, Gump, Strauss, Hauer & Feld based in Washington, D.C., interview, Brussels, June 28, 1999. Confirmed by Commission official, interview, Brussels, June 21, 1999.

66. Representative of Eurofer, interview, Brussels, June 29, 1999.

67. Confirmed by members of the Commission's TBR unit, Brussels, June 22, 1999.

Lawyers in the Commission's Legal Service who bring and defend WTO cases do not receive well-prepared complaints from industry but rather go to EC firms with requests when they need information. When they do, some find that it can be "hard to get answers from EC companies."[68] When the Commission has gone to both U.S. and European firms for information concerning a common foreign trade barrier, U.S. firms have provided more information.[69] Although the Commission's understaffed Legal Service often hires an outside law firm to provide assistance on a WTO matter, the law firm works for, and is paid by, the Commission, not a private enterprise.[70] This Commission-steered outsourcing differs from U.S. public-private partnerships. "Private interests," maintains a Legal Service lawyer, "are not much involved in EU cases. They sometimes are behind the initiation (especially under the TBR), but little involved in the legal and even factual arguments before panels."[71]

As a result, although European enterprises use private counsel more frequently than in the past, there remains far less trade work for the Brussels bar than its Washington, D.C., counterpart.[72] When European enterprises do hire outside counsel, they often engage Washington law firms, or their branches in Brussels, especially in challenges against U.S. regulatory barriers.[73] Daimler Benz and BMW hired the Washington firm Hogan & Hartson to assist them with the 1994 GATT case, U.S.–Corporate Average Fuel Economy. The European shipbuilding industry hired Richard Weiner of Hogan & Hartson's Brussels office to prepare the TBR complaint against Korea's shipbuilding subsidies.[74] And Marco

68. Former Commission official in Legal Service, interview, Brussels, June 21, 1999.

69. Member of the TBR unit, interview, Brussels, June 29, 1999.

70. The Commission pays the firms a lump sum, which can be significantly less than normal fees. Member of the Commission's Legal Service, interview, Brussels, June 25, 1999. Regarding an understaffed Commission more generally, see Nugent (1994, p. 89), calculating a ratio of 0.8 staff in EU institutions per 10,000 European citizens, compared with a staff ratio of 322 per 10,000 citizens at the member state level.

71. E-mail message, March 11, 2003.

72. Member of the Commission's DG Trade, interview, Brussels, June 13, 2001; and EC trade lobbyist, interview, Brussels, June 25, 1999.

73. Similarly, the Commission sometimes has outsourced WTO work to U.S. law firms. For example, when the EC challenged U.S. methodology for determining whether a governmental subsidy was passed on following a privatization, the Commission hired the Washington, D.C., firm of Hogan & Hartson to assist it. Commission official in DG Trade, interview, Brussels, June 24, 1999. Confirmed by Washington trade lawyer, Washington, D.C., October 18, 2001.

74. A former member of the Commission's Legal Service, interview, Brussels, June 21, 1999; and a Commission official in the Trade Directorate-General, interview, Brussels, June 13, 2001.

Bronckers, a Dutch lawyer long experienced in trade cases, moved to the Brussels office of Wilmer, Cutler & Pickering, which also hired former WTO Appellate Body member and Commission director general Claus-Dieter Ehlermann.[75] The Commission, in turn, is more reticent than the USTR in working with firms' private legal counsel. One EC private attorney who formerly held an internship in the Commission's DG Trade goes so far as to say, "The Commission dislikes the involvement of law firms."[76]

Private lawyers' more constrained role in challenging foreign trade barriers replicates the situation in EC import relief cases. Although some European trade associations may employ an internal lawyer who helps monitor antidumping claims, the employee tends to be rather young and inexperienced.[77] Trade lawyers in Brussels lament that they receive fewer antidumping cases from European firms and, even then, cannot demand the fees that Washington lawyers command. When bringing antidumping claims to protect their home market from low-priced imports, European firms often do not hire lawyers. Rather, they file a petition for antidumping relief with the European Commission—after already having obtained the Commission's informal support of the filing—and let the Commission do the work.[78] To the private trade bar's regret, European firms tend to clamp the purse.

In the more adversarial legalist U.S. system, U.S. firms not only budget government affairs departments and retain professional lawyer lobbyists to promote their trading interests. They also hire lawyers to advance their positions in trade litigation. The reason is explained in the work of Bob Kagan at Berkeley's Center for the Study of Law and Society. Kagan

75. Bronckers formerly worked for the Dutch law firms Trenite Van Doorne and Stibbe, Simont, Monahan, Duhot. He was involved in a number of NCPI and TBR cases. For example, Bronckers represented Akzo in its controversial challenge to Section 337 of the U.S. Tariff Act of 1930.

76. E-mail message from Candido Garcia Molyneux at the Brussels office of the Washington law firm Covington & Burling, January 7, 2002.

77. Reinhold Quick, lobbyist for European Chemical Industry Council, interview, Brussels, June 25, 1999. CEFIC is among the most active users of antidumping complaints in the EC, having filed 61 out of a total of 350 EC antidumping actions between 1980 and 2000 (De Bièvre 2003).

78. Brussels lawyer, interview, June 28, 1999. These tendencies were confirmed by lawyers and government officials in Brussels. Antidumping law is extremely technical, involving the calculation of preliminary and final antidumping margins, the definition of the relevant product market, and the determination of whether "material injury" criteria are fulfilled, so that large legal fees potentially can be generated.

demonstrates how American culture tends to be adversarial and legalistic, in large part because of a deep mistrust of governmental power and a fragmented system of government that provides numerous openings for private adversarial challenge.[79] In matters of trade, U.S. companies and trade associations are wary of having U.S. government officials represent their interests. They engage law firms to assist them in WTO complaints, whether the United States is a complainant or defendant. They hire trade law specialists, often former senior members of the USTR, such as Bob Cassidy and Robert Novick at Wilmer, Cutler & Pickering, Alan Wolff at Dewey Ballantine, or Warren Maruyama at Hogan & Hartson. Many of these law firms have become "full service providers," with lobbyists, economists, and other nonlawyers on their staffs. These law firms not only provide assistance in Washington but also send teams to Geneva for a WTO case. One USTR lawyer recalls private lawyers traveling to Geneva on six of the last ten WTO cases he handled.[80] Not surprisingly, the Washington, D.C., trade bar is much larger than its counterpart in Brussels.[81]

## Administrative Culture

U.S. firms hire their own legal counsel even though the USTR assigns more government lawyers to handle WTO litigation than does the Commission. In January 2003, the USTR employed over two dozen lawyers on trade matters.[82] These lawyers were supplemented in individual WTO

79. See Kagan (2000, p. 12). Kagan (p. 3) finds that the U.S. "style" of regulation is "uniquely legalistic, adversarial, and expensive." See also Kagan (1995, pp. 88–118); and Epstein (1998, pp. 12–13). Only about a third of Americans say they trust the federal government, and most others believe politicians do not have their interests at heart, according to analysis by the Pew Research Center for People and the Press.

80. E-mail message, March 10, 2003. In contrast, a lead lawyer at the EC's Legal Service handling WTO matters states, "It has not happened yet that representatives of a private interest have traveled with us to Geneva. But I know of one case when they traveled there on their own!" E-mail message (March 11, 2003).

81. Information obtained from the international trade section of the Washington, D.C., bar and interviews with members of the private bar in Brussels, Belgium, June 28, 1999. Approximately 2,100 lawyers registered themselves in Washington, D.C., as trade lawyers, although this number likely is inflated regarding lawyers' primary activity.

82. E-mail correspondence with a representative from the USTR (January 17, 2003), noting that, as of mid-January 2003, there were twenty-five or twenty-six designated legal positions in the USTR in Washington (of which one or two needed to be filled), complemented by three lawyers in the United States's WTO mission in Geneva, making twenty-eight or twenty-nine (legal) positions in total. In addition, he noted that the USTR is "filled

disputes by those from other U.S. departments, including the Departments of Commerce, Agriculture,[83] Treasury,[84] Office of Patents and Trademarks,[85] and Environmental Protection Agency.[86] Lawyers from the Department of Commerce take the lead in WTO disputes over antidumping matters, under USTR's supervision.[87] In contrast, the EC's Legal Service assigns about ten lawyers to handle WTO disputes, including one person in Geneva, complemented by about six lawyers in DG Trade, although lawyers in DG Trade and other directorates-general also follow WTO matters affecting their missions.[88] Yet both the USTR and the Commission's Legal Service are understaffed. Whereas the Legal Service more frequently outsources cases to law firms that it hires, the USTR more frequently works with law firms employed by private companies. These law firms prepare legal briefs from which the USTR can draw, as desired.

---

with lawyers in non-legal slots" (that is, the number does not include lawyers handling diplomatic negotiations or other matters). In terms of legal positions where lawyers handle WTO cases on a "regular" basis, there were, in addition to the "1–2 vacancies," "roughly 15 'lead counsel,' 2 supervisors, and 3 'local counsel'" in Geneva, although these lawyers' time could be split between WTO litigation and negotiation issues.

83. Lawyers from the U.S. Department of Agriculture assist in all U.S. agricultural cases, such as the EC–Meat Hormones and the EC–Wheat Gluten cases.

84. Lawyers from the U.S. Department of the Treasury assisted in the United States–FSC case brought by the EC against the United States, and the numerous tax cases that the United States brought against the EC. In light of the importance of the FSC case, Kenneth Dam, deputy secretary of the Treasury, made "a 5-minute opening statement and an Assistant Solicitor presented the rest of the case" in the second proceeding before the WTO Appellate Body. E-mail from USTR attorney, January 22, 2003. See Dam (1970, 2001).

85. Lawyers from the U.S. Patent and Trademark Office assist in all patent and trademark cases brought under the TRIPS Agreement.

86. Lawyers from the EPA, for example, assisted in the U.S.–Shrimp-Turtle and the U.S.–Reformulated Gasoline cases.

87. According to a lawyer at the USTR, "The best example of non-USTR lawyers taking 'a' lead is in the antidumping/countervailing duty area, where for some time now we have had Commerce Department lawyers act as lead counsel under the supervision of USTR attorneys. We tried this for the first time in the Korea DRAMS dispute when resources were particularly tight at USTR, but have continued it in the bulk of the cases to date, with greater or lesser involvement by the USTR attorneys depending on the case and the individuals involved." E-mail from USTR attorney, January 22, 2003.

88. Although the attorneys in the EC's Legal Service that handle WTO matters also have other duties, they are less likely to attend negotiations than their USTR counterparts. E-mail message from a lead Legal Service attorney on WTO matters, January 21, 2003. Besides DG Trade, EC lawyers following WTO matters may work in such directorates-general as DG Agriculture, DG Enterprise, DG Internal Market, and DG Consumer Affairs.

The USTR's trade lawyers work more comfortably with law firms hired by private firms and trade associations because it is part of Washington's culture. It is what public officials and private firms expect. USTR officials' careers depend on their responsiveness. When a younger U.S. official does not immediately return a phone call to a business representative with clout, a high-level political appointee will hear of it and ensure that better "public service" is rendered in the future.

Probably the greatest immediate facilitator of public-private trade partnerships is Washington's "revolving door" bureaucratic culture. Lawyers and lobbyists in Washington build up their resumes by dabbling in public life for a few years and then serving— lucratively—private commercial clients. As former USTR Robert Strauss observes, lawyers often go to work for the U.S. government not because they want a public service career, but because "they know that [government work] enables them to move on out in a few years and become associated with a lobbying or law firm [where] their services are in tremendous demand."[89] The career civil servant is rarer in the "revolving door" of Washington's arcades.

Senior agency positions in Washington are filled by political appointees who may remain for a single four-year term, at most. Many USTR personnel formerly worked for, or are otherwise associated with, industry. An appointment to the key USTR post for textile negotiations provides but one example:

> In February, 2002, David Spooner was appointed the special textile negotiator within the USTR's office. Mr. Spooner's background fits the other common profile among government officials working on international trade issues—that of a close association with Congress or a specific industry in the U.S. private sector. Before his appointment . . . , Mr. Spooner was an advisor on textile trade issues for House of Representatives member Sue Myrick, a Republican from North Carolina. Not surprisingly, the U.S. textile industry has a significant presence in Representative Myrick's legislative district and Mr. Spooner's appointment . . . insures that the textile industry has easy access to USTR's office whenever textiles trade matters arise.[90]

89. See Jill Abramson, "The Business of Persuasion Thrives in Nation's Capital," *New York Times*, September 29, 1998, p. A1, quoting Strauss.

90. Charles Irish, a law professor at the University of Wisconsin, "U.S. Trade Policies and Thailand," speech to the Thai Chamber of Commerce, May 22, 2002, Bangkok (on file with author).

Similarly, in October 2002, the USTR hired the director of trade relations at Eastman Kodak to become assistant USTR for intergovernmental affairs and public liaison. What better public-private liaison than an official who formerly held "senior international trade positions at Eastman Kodak, Lucent Technologies and AT&T" and "served" as a business representative on "several USTR trade advisory committees."[91]

Former USTR representatives populate Washington law firms and trade associations and accumulate far more trade law experience than the new recruits of public agencies.[92] Former USTR Charlene Barchefsky, former deputy USTR Jeffrey Lang, and two former USTR general counsel, Robert Cassidy and Robert Novick, are at Wilmer, Cutler & Pickering. Mickey Kantor, Barchefsky's predecessor at USTR, is at Mayer, Brown, Rowe & Maw, and is on the board of directors of Monsanto and Pharmacia. Former USTR Robert Strauss is a chief lobbyist at Akin, Gump, Strauss, Hauer & Feld. Former USTR general counsels Alan Holmer and Judith Bello were designated president and executive vice president of the pharmaceutical trade association PhRMA. Members of the Washington trade bar typically have worked in government and can tailor their presentations accordingly. As one advocate states, to be effective, "you need to think through matters from an official's standpoint and provide him with arguments he can use."[93]

91. In its press release, USTR noted that the new official, Christopher Padilla, had "played a leading role in the coalitions supporting passage of Trade Promotion Authority and permanent normal trade relations with China. Padilla has served on several USTR trade advisory committees since 1996." See "Chris Padilla Named Assistant USTR for Intergovernmental Affairs and Public Liaison," at www.ustr.gov/releases/2002/10/02-95.htm (February 2003).

92. See, for example, "Wilmer, Cutler & Pickering Announces Barchefsky Is Senior International Partner," *International Trade Reporter (BNA)*, August 2, 2001, p. 1241; "Former Deputy USTR Jeffrey Lang to Work for Major Law Firm," *Inside U.S. Trade*, September 18, 1998, p. 12; *PhRMA 1999 Annual Report,* at www.phrma.org/publications/annual99/s_staff.html (March 2000); and "Wheat Coalition Hires Former USTR Mickey Kantor for WTO Talks," *Inside U.S. Trade*, July 23, 1999, p. 21. Former trade officials from the Department of Commerce do the same. Former under secretary of commerce for international trade David Aaron now works for Dorsey & Whitney's D.C. office. See "Aaron to Leave Commerce Department in March for Law Firm," *Inside U.S. Trade*, February 4, 2000, p. 15. Former assistant secretary of commerce Franklin Vargo is now vice president for International Economic Affairs of the National Association of Manufacturers. See Gary Yerkey, "U.S. Companies Launch Bid to Bridge Divide in Congress over Labor, Environment," *International Trade Reporter (BNA)*, February 8, 2001, pp. 225–26.

93. Peter Lichtenbaum of Steptoe & Johnson, interview, October 30, 2001. Lichtenbaum became an assistant secretary at the Department of Commerce in 2003.

Concomitantly, less-experienced attorneys in the USTR office face lobbyists who are both former high-ranked USTR officials and potential future employers. One interviewee at the USTR said that he had been there for four years, held one of the longer tenures at the USTR, and considered himself "an old-timer."[94] The pressure to positively respond to requests and suggestions stems not just from a moral calling to serve the "U.S. public interest" but also, consciously or unconsciously, from an economic incentive to prop one's personal prospects. This revolving door in Washington forges better understanding among public and private representatives. Playing (or desiring to play) both roles enhances each side's willingness, appreciation, and effectiveness in the network.

The USTR, accordingly, more readily supplies firms with information about a trade position or strategy. U.S. lobbyists state that the USTR understands that its role is to represent U.S. enterprises' export interests, or, as one representative bluntly puts it, to "serve us."[95] U.S. firms complain that Commission officials, by contrast, are more "condescending" and less helpful than USTR personnel.[96] A member of the Brussels bar, and former member of the Commission, agrees: the "Commission can be more snobbish toward firms."[97]

Like their U.S. counterparts, European civil servants often share class- and university-based links with business that can promote effective public-private networks.[98] Unlike their counterparts, however, EC officials associate a higher social status with their jobs and tend to be better remunerated.[99] The Commission is organized largely on a French continental model of *fonctionnaires*, or public servants, who tend to graduate at the top of their class from elite universities and receive greater compensation

94. Interview, Washington, D.C., October 18, 2001.

95. Representative of U.S. trade association, interview, May 19, 1999.

96. Representative of U.S. trade association, interview, May 19, 1999. A U.S. lobbyist on intellectual property matters confirms that the U.S. government is much more supportive of his industry than is the European Commission. Representative of U.S. intellectual property association, interview, May 17, 1999.

97. Interview, Brussels, June 28, 1998.

98. See, for example, Molyneux (2001, p. 153), noting "the strong link between the French state and big business" whose leaders are typically top graduates from the same *grandes écoles*.

99. Commission officials, interviews, Brussels, June 21 and 28, 1999, noting higher salaries, higher status, and greater job pleasure of work in the Commission, compared with the USTR, and asserting that it feels better to work for the Commission than for some trade association.

than their U.S. counterparts. Although the exceptions may be increasing, Commission officials are much more likely to pursue life careers as civil servants.[100] This career structure reinforces the Commission's greater insulation from lobbying pressures.[101] The Commission's Legal Service, in particular, tends to work at arm's length from private lawyers hired by business.

Nonetheless, the Commission has attempted to become more responsive to private trading interests, albeit less so than some U.S. and European firms might prefer. Leading officials within the Commission recognize that the Commission needs to coordinate with firms to effectively represent Europe's interests in enforcing trade rules. The Commission's Market Access Strategy and its Trade Barrier Regulation are tools not only to socialize European firms to work with the Commission but also to socialize Commission officials to collaborate with firms and thereby mutually develop the reflexes that facilitate effective public-private networks.

100. See W. John Moore, "The Influence Game," *National Journal,* February 5, 2000, p. 421, noting the departure of Sir Leon Brittan, former EC trade commissioner, who became a consultant to the London-based law firm Herbert Smith, and Hugo Paemen, former Commission negotiator during the Uruguay Round and EU ambassador to the United States, now working for the Washington, D.C., firm Hogan & Hartson. There also are examples of former Commission officials who are now trade lawyers in the Brussels trade bar, such as Jacques Bourgeois, working for Akin, Gump, Strauss, Hauer & Feld, and Alastair Sutton, working for White & Case. Interestingly, in both of these cases, former Commission lawyers are working for the Brussels branches of Washington-based law firms. Nonetheless, although there is some indication that EC civil servants also are moving to private law firms, this tendency is much less common than in the United States. For example, although it is true that Hugo Paemen moved to a Washington law firm, he was forced to leave the Commission because of its mandatory retirement rules. Commission member, interview, Brussels, June 13, 2001.

101. As Claude Barfield (2000, p. 271) writes: "Though the EU system recently may have moved slightly in the direction of a more open U.S. style of decisionmaking, the EU trade bureaucracy still operates with much greater power and insulation from private sector pressure than does its U.S. counterpart."

# 6 *Transatlantic Public-Private Partnerships*

U.S. and European firms and industries often face common barriers to trade, be it in Asia, South America, or elsewhere. When they are not litigating against each other, they are often on the same side challenging third-country import barriers, such as Indonesia's former nepotistic "national" car policy, India's nonrecognition of pharmaceutical and agricultural patents, and Japan's and Korea's differential taxes on hard alcohol. The United States was a co-complainant or third party in eleven of the first twelve EC complaints against other WTO members that resulted in panel decisions.[1] The EC was a co-complainant or third party in nine of the first fifteen U.S. complaints against other WTO members that resulted in panel decisions (see table 6-1).[2] This record raises a number

1. As of January 17, 2003, the United States was a co-complainant in four of these cases and a supportive third party in seven of them. The term supportive "third party" refers to a case in which the United States submits a third-party submission in support of an EC complaint pursuant to Article 10 of the WTO Dispute Settlement Understanding.

2. As of January 17, 2003, the EC was a co-complainant in four of these cases and a supportive third party in five.

of questions. To what extent have public-private networks for the litigation of trade claims by the United States and EC become transatlantic networks? To what extent has transatlantic cooperation, where it has occurred, been at the initiative of trade officials or of private parties? To what extent have domestic private parties formed partnerships with foreign trade authorities to challenge their own domestic regulations?

## Limits to Transatlantic Cooperation between Trade Officials

U.S. and EC trade officials generally do not form transatlantic partnerships to cooperate in the bringing of trade claims against common foreign trade barriers. They rarely collaborate in WTO litigation for the following five primary reasons:

—*Their industries' interests diverge* in specific contexts.

—*Government officials process industries' interests differently* on account of dissimilar U.S. and European political structures or issue-specific political contexts.

—*U.S. and European methods of challenging trade barriers diverge* owing to different approaches to bargaining, as well as *strategic attempts to negotiate preferences* or to free-ride on the other's more aggressive course.

—*The WTO's institutional context* generates transatlantic rivalries and hostility.

—*The lack of continuity of USTR personnel* due to Washington's "revolving door" administrative culture impedes transatlantic agency cooperation.

To look, first, at the economic interests of U.S. and European firms, these interests may converge, but they are never identical. Firms face diverse market challenges and constraints. Where firms invest in a country, they may benefit from a trade barrier and thus lobby government officials not to challenge it. Specific market contexts affect the relative salience of trade barriers, as in the automobile market in Japan: "European and U.S. automakers each want to further open Japan's new car market, but they face different barriers to entry and different constraints on what they feel they can demand of Japan."[3]

Second, the institutional settings and political contexts in which trade officials work affect the manner in which business interests are articulated

*Text continues on page 134*

3. Steinberg (1999, p. 214).

Table 6-1. *U.S. and EC Participation as Complainants, Defendants, and Third Parties in All WTO Cases Resulting in Adopted Panel or Appellate Body Reports, as of January 17, 2003*

| *Report number* | *Title* | *U.S. participation* | *EC participation* |
|---|---|---|---|
| *Adopted Appellate Body report* | | | |
| WT/DS2, 4 | United States—Standards for Reformulated and Conventional Gasoline | Defendant | |
| WT/DS8, 10, 11 | Japan—Taxes on Alcoholic Beverages | Complainant | Complainant |
| WT/DS18 | Australia—Measures Affecting the Importation of Salmon | Third party | Third party |
| WT/DS22 | Brazil—Measures Affecting Desiccated Coconut | Third party | Third party |
| WT/DS24 | United States—Restrictions on Imports of Cotton and Man-Made Fibre Underwear | Defendant | |
| WT/DS26 | European Communities—Measures Affecting Meat and Meat Products (Hormones) | Complainant | Defendant |
| WT/DS27 | European Communities—Importation, Sale, and Distribution of Bananas | Complainant | Defendant |
| WT/DS31 | Canada—Certain Measures Concerning Periodicals | Complainant | |
| WT/DS33 | United States—Measure Affecting Imports of Woven Wool Shirts and Blouses | Defendant | Third party |
| WT/DS34 | Turkey—Restrictions on Imports of Textile and Clothing Products | Third party | |
| WT/DS46 | Brazil—Export Financing Programme for Aircraft | Third party | Third party |
| WT/DS48 | European Communities—Measures Affecting Livestock and Meat (Hormones) | Cf. DS26 | Defendant |
| WT/DS50 | India—Patent Protection for Pharmaceutical and Agricultural Chemical Products | Complainant | Third party |
| WT/DS56 | Argentina—Imports of Footwear, Textiles, Apparel and Other Items | Complainant | Third party |

| Report number | Title | U.S. participation | EC participation |
|---|---|---|---|
| *Adopted Appellate Body report (continued)* | | | |
| WT/DS58 | United States—Import Prohibition of Certain Shrimp and Shrimp Products | Defendant | Third party |
| WT/DS60 | Guatemala—Anti-Dumping Investigation of Portland Cement from Mexico | Third party | |
| WT/DS62, 67, 68 | European Communities—Customs Classification of Computer Equipment | Complainant | Defendant |
| WT/DS69 | European Communities—Measures Affecting Importation of Certain Poultry Products | Third party | Defendant |
| WT/DS70 | Canada—Measures Affecting the Export of Civilian Aircraft | Third party | |
| WT/DS75, 84 | Korea—Taxes on Alcoholic Beverages | Complainant | Complainant |
| WT/DS76 | Japan—Measures Affecting Agricultural Products | Complainant | Third party |
| WT/DS87, 110 | Chile—Taxes on Alcoholic Beverages | Third party | Complainant |
| WT/DS90 | India— Quantitative Restrictions on Agricultural, Textile and Industrial Products | Complainant | Cf. DS 96 |
| WT/DS98 | Korea—Safeguard Measure on Imports of Certain Dairy Products | Third party | Complainant |
| WT/DS103, 113 | Canada—Importation of Milk and the Exportation of Dairy Products | Complainant | |
| WT/DS108 | United States—Tax Treatment for "Foreign Sales Corporations" | Defendant | Complainant |
| WT/DS121 | Argentina—Safeguard Measures on Imports of Footwear | Third party | Complainant |
| WT/DS122 | Thailand—Anti-Dumping Duties on Iron or Non-Alloy Steel and H-Beams from Poland | Third party | Third party |

*(continued)*

Table 6.1 *(continued)*

| *Report number* | *Title* | *U.S. participation* | *EC participation* |
|---|---|---|---|
| *Adopted Appellate Body report (continued)* | | | |
| WT/DS135 | European Communities—Prohibition of Asbestos and Asbestos Products | Third party | Defendant |
| WT/DS136 | United States—Anti-Dumping Act of 1916 | Defendant | Complainant |
| WT/DS138 | United States—Countervailing Duties on Lead and Bismuth Carbon Steel from UK | Defendant | Complainant |
| WT/DS139, 142 | Canada—Certain Measures Affecting the Automotive Industry | Third party | Complainant |
| WT/DS141 | European Communities—Anti-Dumping Duties on Cotton-Type Bed-Linen from India | Third party | Defendant |
| WT/DS146, 175 | India—Measures Affecting the Automotive Sector | Complainant | Complainant |
| WT/DS161, 169 | Korea—Measures Affecting Imports of Fresh, Chilled, and Frozen Beef | Complainant | |
| WT/DS162 | United States—Anti-Dumping Act of 1916 | Defendant | Third party |
| WT/DS165 | United States—Import Measures on Certain Products from the European Communities | Defendant | Complainant |
| WT/DS166 | United States—Safeguard Measure on Wheat Gluten from the European Communities | Defendant | Complainant |
| WT/DS170 | Canada—Patent Protection Term | Complainant | |
| WT/DS176 | United States—Section 211 Omnibus Appropriations Act | Defendant | Complainant |
| WT/DS177, 178 | United States—Safeguard Measure on Lamb from New Zealand | Defendant | Third party |
| WT/DS184 | United States—Anti-Dumping Measures on Hot-Rolled Steel Products from Japan | Defendant | Third party |
| WT/DS192 | United States—Safeguard Measure on Combed Cotton Yarn from Pakistan | Defendant | Third party |

| Report number | Title | U.S. participation | EC participation |
| --- | --- | --- | --- |
| *Adopted Appellate Body report (continued)* | | | |
| WT/DS202 | United States—Safeguard Measures on Circular Welded Carbon Quality Line Pipe | Defendant | Third party |
| WT/DS207 | Chile—Price Band System and Safeguard Measures relating to Agricultural Products | Third party | Third party |
| WT/DS212 | United States—Countervailing Measures on Products from EC | Defendant | Complainant |
| WT/DS213 | United States—Countervailing Duties on Carbon Steel Flat Products from Germany | Defendant | Complainant |
| WT/DS231 | European Communities—Trade Description of Sardines | Third party | Defendant |
| WT/DS217, 234 | United States—Continued Dumping and Subsidy Offset Act of 2000[a] | Defendant | Complainant |
| *Adopted Panel report (not appealed)* | | | |
| WT/DS44 | Japan—Measures Affecting Consumer Photographic Film and Paper | Complainant | Third party |
| WT/DS54, 55, 59, 64 | Indonesia—Certain Measures Affecting the Automobile Industry | Complainant | Complainant |
| WT/DS79 | India—Patent Protection for Pharmaceutical and Agricultural Chemical Products | Third party | Complainant |
| WT/DS99 | United States—Anti-Dumping Duty on DRAMS from Korea | Defendant | |
| WT/DS114 | Canada—Patent Protection of Pharmaceutical Products | Third party | Complainant |
| WT/DS126 | Australia—Subsidies Provided to Producers and Exporters of Automotive Leather | Complainant | |
| WT/DS132 | Mexico—Anti-Dumping Investigation of High-Fructose Corn Syrup from US | Complainant | |

*(continued)*

Table 6.1 *(continued)*

| *Report number* | *Title* | *U.S. participation* | *EC participation* |
|---|---|---|---|
| *Adopted Panel report (not appealed) (continued)* | | | |
| WT/DS152 | United States—Sections 301-310 of the Trade Act of 1974 | Defendant | Complainant |
| WT/DS155 | Argentina—Measures on the Export of Bovine Hides and the Import of Finished Leather | | Complainant |
| WT/DS156 | Guatemala—Anti-dumping Measure regarding Grey Portland Cement from Mexico | Third party | Third party |
| WT/DS160 | United States—Section 110(5) of the US Copyright Act | Defendant | Complainant |
| WT/DS163 | Korea—Measures Affecting Government Procurement | Complainant | Third party |
| WT/DS179 | United States—Anti-Dumping Measures on Stainless Steel from Korea | Defendant | Third party |
| WT/DS189 | Argentina—Definitive Anti-Dumping Measures on Ceramic Floor Tiles from Italy | Third party | Complainant |
| WT/DS194 | United States—Measures Treating Export Restraints As Subsidies | Defendant | Third party |
| WT/DS206 | United States—Anti-Dumping and Countervailing Measures on Steel Plate From India | Defendant | Third party |
| WT/DS211 | Egypt—Definitive Anti-Dumping Measures on Steel Rebar from Turkey | Third party | Third party |
| WT/DS221 | United States—Section 129(c)(1) of the Uruguay Round Agreements Act | Defendant | Third party |
| WT/DS222 | Canada—Export Credits and Loan Guarantees for Regional Aircraft | Third party | Third party |
| WT/DS236 | United States—Determinations with respect to Certain Softwood Lumber from Canada | Defendant | Third party |

| *Subtotal*[b] | *U.S.* Count | *U.S.* Percent (of 69) | *EC* Count | *EC* Percent (of 69) |
|---|---|---|---|---|
| *Adopted Panel and Appellate Body reports* | | | | |
| Defendant | 18 | 26.1 | 8 | 11.6 |
| Complainant | 14 | 20.3 | 16 | 23.2 |
| Third party | 16 | 23.2 | 15 | 21.7 |
| Aggregate (defendant, complainant, or third party) | 48 | 69.6 | 39 | 56.5 |
| *Adopted Panel reports (not appealed)* | | | | |
| Defendant | 8 | 11.6 | 0 | 0.0 |
| Complainant | 5 | 7.2 | 7 | 10.1 |
| Third party | 6 | 8.7 | 10 | 14.5 |
| Aggregate (defendant, complainant, or third party) | 19 | 27.5 | 17 | 24.6 |

| *Total* | *U.S.* Count | *U.S.* Percent (of 69) | *EC* Count | *EC* Percent (of 69) |
|---|---|---|---|---|
| Defendant | 26 | 37.7 | 8 | 11.6 |
| Complainant | 19 | 27.5 | 23 | 33.3 |
| Third party | 22 | 31.9 | 25 | 36.2 |
| Aggregate (defendant, complainant, or third party) | 67 | 97.1[c] | 56 | 81.2 |

Source: WTO Secretariat, *Update of WTO Dispute Settlement Cases,* WT/DS/OV/10 (January 22, 2003).

a. The Appellate Body report for United States—Continued Dumping and Subsidy Offset Act of 2000 (WT/DS217, 234) was circulated prior to January 17, 2003. The Panel and Appellate Body reports for this case were adopted on January 27, 2003.

b. Percentages are based on the number of cases resulting in adopted Panel and/or Appellate Body reports listed on the WTO website as of January 17, 2003 (sixty-nine).

c. Although they were not joined, the Canadian complainant in WT/DS48 and the U.S. complaint in WT/DS26 concerned the same matter. If one were to combine these complaints, then the total number of cases resulting in adopted Panel and/or Appellate Body reports would be reduced to sixty-eight, and the U.S. participation in sixty-seven of those cases would amount to 98.5 percent of the total.

and processed. Congressional and member state interference, in particular, compromises trade officials' capacity to coordinate common positions. The EC's more complex trade policy process can dilute the influence of individual firms and hence generate different EC strategies. Alternatively, U.S. or EC officials may attempt to obtain "domestic political mileage" when they challenge trade barriers, such as those of Japan, Korea, or China, so their articulations of industry interests vary on account of transient U.S. and EC political contexts.[4] Trade officials find it difficult enough to coordinate common positions within U.S. and EC internal interagency and interstate processes. The coordination of agency positions within transgovernmental contexts is all the more challenging.

U.S. and EC officials also might forebear challenging a foreign trade barrier, or might structure their arguments differently, because of a WTO claim's divergent implications for domestic regulatory measures. In bringing a WTO complaint, government representatives must be wary of vulnerable domestic regimes that protect other constituencies. In the Japan–Alcoholic Beverages case, the United States and EC transformed their common challenge of Japan's tax system for spirits into a U.S.-EC dispute over the legal criteria to be applied. In doing so, they parried over an earlier conflict between them concerning U.S. automotive taxes, since the EC could have used the legal interpretation in the case involving Japan for a renewed challenge against an allegedly discriminatory U.S. automobile tax. In 1994 the EC had instituted a GATT challenge against U.S. antipollution taxes on the "corporate average fuel economy" of car fleets. In the case U.S.–Taxes on Corporate Average Fuel Economy (CAFE), a GATT panel upheld the U.S. defense that its taxes were permissible under GATT rules because they were designed with the legitimate "aim" of combating air pollution, even though the taxes were applied only on European cars.[5] In the Japan–Alcoholic Beverages case, the Europeans again argued that a complainant need show only a discriminatory effect, an easier standard to meet, with the United States retorting that a complainant also must prove a discriminatory intent. The additional hurdle of

4. Richard Cunningham, lawyer at Steptoe & Johnson, interview, Washington, D.C., October 18, 2001.

5. The U.S. Congress, lobbied by U.S. car manufacturers, had chosen fuel economy thresholds whereby, in practice, only foreign (and particularly European) luxury vehicles would pay the tax. The GATT case was decided after the Agreement Establishing the WTO was signed but before it was ratified by the U.S. Congress. Some analysts suspect that the GATT panel's reasoning may have been influenced by the U.S. domestic political context.

proof supported by the U.S. government irritated the U.S. spirits industry, which simply wanted the taxes reduced.[6] U.S. authorities, however, were necessarily concerned about the impact of the Japan–Alcoholic Beverages decision were the EC again to challenge the discriminatory impact of U.S. automobile taxes under the new WTO regime.[7]

Similarly, although the United States, prodded by Nike and other U.S. shoe companies, supported the EC's challenge against an Argentine safeguard restraint on footwear imports, it nonetheless supported Argentina's argument that the WTO Agreement on Safeguards had eliminated a previous GATT requirement that an import-induced injury be a "result of unforeseen developments." Because the United States more actively applies safeguard measures against imports, and because the relevant U.S. safeguards statute does not include this requirement, the United States argued that the more detailed 1995 WTO Safeguards Agreement, which was silent on the additional requirement, superseded the more general language of Article XIX of GATT. The EC, in contrast, rarely applies its safeguards statute, preferring to use antidumping and countervailing duty measures for industry protection.[8] The EC thus maintained that the additional GATT condition for safeguards relief remained operative. Despite convergent U.S. and European corporate interests, the United States supported defendant Argentina's contention because of U.S. concern about challenges to U.S. safeguards law. The EC won the argument, as well as the case.[9]

Third, in reflection of their contrasting administrative culture, European officials often protest against confrontational unilateralist U.S.

6. A representative of the U.S. spirits industry trade association, DISCUS, telephone interview, May 19, 1999.

7. The WTO panel and Appellate Body appeared to side with the EC so that the United States both won the Japan–Alcoholic Beverages case (on the merits) and apparently lost it (on the legal reasoning). See Hudec (1998, pp. 629–33).

8. In fact, when the EC implemented a provisional safeguard measure on steel products in March 2002 in response to the Bush administration's huge steel safeguard at that time, this was the first safeguard that the EC had imposed since 1993. Commission trade official, telephone interview, Brussels, June 22, 1999, noting lack of safeguard measures in EC. Jean-Francois Brakeland of DG Trade, telephone interview, May 19, 2003.

9. See Bhala and Gantz (2001, pp. 73–87). GATT Article XIX provides, "If, *as a result of unforeseen developments* and the effect of the obligations incurred by a contracting party under this Agreement, including tariff concessions, any product is being imported into the territory. . . ." The WTO Agreement on Safeguards, which was adopted "to clarify and reinforce the disciplines" of Article XIX, does not contain any language concerning "unforeseen developments."

trade maneuvers. Yet both European and U.S. representatives use their market clout to advance U.S. and EC interests. The United States is simply more transparent in doing so. As a lawyer in the WTO secretariat relates, a U.S. official may unabashedly threaten a developing country publicly, and, if the developing country does not comply with the U.S. demand, carry out the threat. A European official, in contrast, may publicly support developing country interests but discretely stab developing country representatives in the back if the country does not comply with European demands. In pursuing its interests, the EC simply adopts a European style. As Richard Steinberg, who was formerly at the USTR, notes, "Instead of publicly threatening retaliation through tariff increases, the Commission may quietly hint at proposals for directives or decisions that would have market-closing effects. Or the Commission may offer the third country greater market access in Europe, or technical aid, in exchange for concessions."[10]

The United States and EC also deploy divergent approaches to obtain advantages against the other. U.S. and EC officials may strive to negotiate preferential bilateral settlements to trade disputes in order to benefit their own commercial constituents. EC officials, for example, challenged preferential U.S. deals with Canada, Japan, and Korea concerning imports of auto parts, semiconductor chips, and beef.[11] These agreements can appear to be neutral and yet have discriminatory effects. The U.S. Auto Pact with Canada, for instance, provided for duty-free imports of automobiles and parts for firms that meet the criteria of "manufacturer," but the criteria were set so that only U.S. automobile companies benefited.[12] Similarly, a U.S. agreement with Korea covered "high-quality beef," a seemingly neutral term, but the definition of beef effectively included "most U.S. beef" while "excluding most EU beef."[13]

10. See Steinberg (1999, p. 218), also stating, "The European Commission usually opts instead for a less confrontational approach in negotiations with third countries."

11. See, for example, Report of the GATT Panel, "Japan—Trade in Semi-Conductors," May 4, 1988, GATT B.I.S.D., 35th Supplement (1989) (adopted May 4, 1988). See also Steinberg (1999).

12. See Report of the Appellate Body, "Canada—Certain Measures Affecting the Automobile Industry," May 31, 2000, WTO Document WT/DS142/AB/R (issued May 31, 2000, adopted June 19 2000); and Bhala and Gantz (2001, p. 21), concerning the successful WTO complaints of the EC and Japan against the Auto Pact for violating GATT Article I, the most-favored-nation clause.

13. Steinberg (1999, p. 242, n. 20).

Alternatively, the United States or EC may attempt to "free-ride" on the other's aggressive actions. The more passive party thereby benefits from enhanced market access while retaining friendlier relations with the foreign country for other purposes, whether to obtain support on a foreign policy issue or a lucrative government procurement contract for a national firm. The United States criticizes the EC particularly for toadying to developing countries that were former colonies in the hope of cornering their markets for other European commercial interests. In the GATS Uruguay Round negotiations, to give one example, the EC was noted for its "desire . . . to be seen by the Brazilians and Indians as a sympathetic player with overlapping interests."[14] U.S. representatives charge that their European colleagues criticize them for being too aggressive but then complain when the United States gets a better deal for its firms.[15] The Europeans do not hesitate to piggyback on successful U.S. challenges to developing country trade barriers, when they can. U.S. and EC methods may reflect not only divergent cultural approaches to bargaining but also strategic behavior against each other.

Fourth, mercantilist rivalry arises within the WTO institutional context despite the WTO's trade liberal goals.[16] From a mercantilist vantage, exports are good and imports are bad. Exports lead to capital inflows and balance of payment surpluses. Imports lead to capital outflows and balance of payment deficits. Even though economists long have debunked mercantilist policy as reducing both national and global welfare, in interstate bargaining, politics, not economic theory, reigns.[17] As good mercantilists, trade officials strive to win offensive cases and penetrate foreign markets while defending domestic trade restrictions and protecting domestic industries. Representatives from the U.S. Congress and EC member states press their trade czars to aggressively bring, defend, and, above all, win cases against each other. The combative rivalry of "beating" the other side, be it about hormone-raised beef, quotas on banana imports, or trade-related tax policies, constrains collaboration. Some

14. See Drake and Nicolaidis (1992).

15. A USTR representative, telephone interview, May 17, 1999.

16. A central WTO goal is to facilitate "mutually advantageous arrangements directed to the substantial reductions of tariffs and other barriers to trade." "Preamble: Marrakesh Agreement Establishing the World Trade Organization," April 15, 1994, *Legal Instruments—Results of the Uruguay Round*, vol. 1 (1994), 33 I.L.M. 1141 (1994).

17. For a history of economic theory concerning the merits of a free trade policy, see Irwin (1996).

European officials maintain that the EC's successful $4 billion dollar challenge against the U.S. tax regime for "foreign sales corporations" was in large part Trade Commissioner Brittan's revenge against U.S. intransigence in negotiating amicable solutions to the WTO bananas and meat hormones disputes.[18]

Officials from antitrust departments, justice departments, and other agencies find cooperation easier since, in their work, they confront common regulatory problems and rarely must defend domestic regulations against a foreign counterpart's challenge.[19] Trade officials operate in a different context. The United States and EC bring more WTO cases against each other than against any other WTO member. Score cards are notched. Pressure mounts. Scars remain. The members of the USTR office even privately bestow in abstentia an annual award on "the most hated trade negotiator." It is named the "Mogens Award," after Mogens Peter Carl, the head of the Commission's Trade Directorate-General.[20]

Fifth, Washington's revolving door administrative culture promotes public-private partnerships at home while impeding transgovernmental public agency coordination. Although officials in the Commission's Market Access Unit attempted to institutionalize more cooperation with U.S. trade representatives when the WTO was established, they abandoned these efforts when their U.S. counterparts left the USTR for the private sector.[21] From January 1998 to mid-1999, the chair of the U.S. Section 301 committee changed three times, with one official leaving for

18. Former European trade czar Leon Brittan and USTR Charlene Barchefsky allegedly despised each other. Trade officials in the European Commission, interviews, Brussels, June 2001.

19. See, for example, Devuyst (2001, p. 127): "Transatlantic relations in the sphere of competition policy are a perfect example of what Anne-Marie Slaughter has labeled a 'new transatlantic order' with specific and functional regulatory agencies networking with their counterparts and creating a dense web of 'fast, flexible, and effective' relations." Also Pollack and Shaffer (2001c, pp. 297–99): "Governance by transgovernmental networks is limited to specific issue areas, such as competition policy, in which regulators on each side of the Atlantic enjoy considerable de facto or de jure independence from their political masters and are guided by sufficiently similar regulatory laws and cultures."

20. A private trade lawyer, interview, Washington, D.C., October 18, 2001. Confirmed by an official at USTR, interview, Washington, D.C., October 18, 2001. See also Steinberg (1999, p. 221).

21. Dorian Prince, interview, March 5, 1998. Former USTR Robert Strauss also maintained that U.S. trade negotiating strategies have been hampered by the USTR's failure to retain experienced trade personnel. *Trade Agreements Act of 1979,* S. Rept. 96-249-69, 96 Cong. 1 sess. (GPO, July 17, 1979), quoting remarks of Robert Strauss, cited in Destler (1995, p. 16).

the telecommunications giant AT&T and another for a private organization promoting U.S.-African relations.[22] To be sure, U.S. and EC trade officials periodically contact each other concerning their positions on trade barriers and, where helpful, profit from each other's submissions to WTO panels. Yet the lack of continuity at the USTR hampers strategic U.S.-EC coordination of trade policy at the same time that it facilitates the input of private interests in U.S. trade networks.

## Cross-National Public-Private Partnerships

In light of these obstacles to transatlantic cooperation in trade litigation, private firms often take the lead in coordinating transatlantic challenges of foreign trade barriers. As Robert Reich writes, the U.S. multinational corporation often works through a "global web, perhaps headquartered in and receiving much of its financial capital from the US, but with research, design, and production facilities spread over Japan, Europe and North America. . . . Battle lines no longer correspond with national borders."[23] With transatlantic direct investment totaling around $1.38 trillion dollars, and with U.S. subsidiaries in Europe and European subsidiaries in the United States accounting for over one-third of transatlantic trade, large firms have interests that extend well beyond the domestic sphere.[24] By the mid-1990s, the value of trade between the United States and EC, combined with sales of U.S. and EC affiliates in each other's markets, had expanded to over $1.7 trillion.[25] The chemical industry, for example, consists of a limited number of large firms on both sides of the Atlantic with substantial cross-border investments. Of the world's largest five chemical companies, Merck and Du Pont are headquartered in the United States, and BASF, Bayer, and Aventis are headquartered in the EC.[26] These multinationals, with their vast transatlantic networks of subsidiaries,

22. Former USTR officials, telephone interviews, May 14 and 17, 1999.

23. See Reich (1991b, p. 153): "Corporate nationality is becoming irrelevant." Also Reich (1991a, p. 47).

24. See "Facts and Figures on the European Union and United States," at *www.eurunion.org/profile/facts.htm* (August 2002). Also Pollack and Shaffer (2001b, p. 4).

25. See Gardner (1997, p. viii). Also Shaffer (2002, p. 29).

26. "Facts and Figures 2000: The European Chemical Industry in a Worldwide Perspective," at www.cefic.be/activities/eco/FactsFigures/ (October 2001). Foreign direct investment in the chemicals sector in the United States was $122.1 billion in 2000, with about 63 percent (that is, about $77 billion) coming from Europe. Foreign direct investment in the

affiliates, and joint ventures, mutually benefit from the leveling of foreign and domestic commercial barriers.

During the late 1990s, the Transatlantic Business Dialogue (TABD) was the primary business forum for coordinating high-level lobbying of U.S. and EC officials over trade and regulatory policy.[27] TABD brought together the chief executive officers of some of the largest transatlantic multinationals, becoming "at times a 'quadrilateral forum' in which the US and EU governments, regulatory bodies, and businesses sit down to discuss and 'negotiate' regulatory matters."[28] Nonetheless, TABD and other cross-sectoral associations have played a relatively insignificant role in challenging trade barriers under WTO agreements, since challenges involve relatively technical matters affecting specific firms and industries.

Firms coordinate WTO challenges to trade barriers on an intrasectoral or ad hoc basis, rather than through cross-sectoral business associations such as TABD. They typically coordinate efforts with their transatlantic industry counterparts to work with each other's home governments. For example, the association of U.S. spirits producers, DISCUS, worked with the European-based Scotch Whisky Association to coordinate U.S. and EC positions in the Korean alcohol case, following the U.S.-EC conflict in their joint case against Japan. As Tim Jackson of the Scotch Whisky Association maintains, these WTO cases "also involved coordinating

---

chemicals sector in Europe was about $86 billion in 2000, with about 93 percent coming from the United States (that is, about $80 billion). E-mail exchanges with Kevin Swift, senior director, Policy, Economics, and Risk Analysis, American Chemistry Council, December 17, 2001, citing "Bureau of Economic Analysis," p. 92, at www.bea.doc.gov (March 2003).

27. Cowles (2001b). Although TABD was first created through the initiative of the U.S. Department of Commerce and the European Commission, TABD stimulated a "bottom-up, pragmatic approach" to transatlantic trade negotiations by incorporating the views of firms and trade associations on both sides of the Atlantic (pp. 217–21, 226–28). Coordinated transatlantic cross-sectoral lobbying is not limited to TABD. National chambers of commerce work through the International Chamber of Commerce (ICC) on international matters, with the United States Council for International Business (USCIB) being the peak U.S. organization and EUROCHAMBRES being the peak European representative. However, one of the reasons that the Department of Commerce and Commission created TABD was because they believed that these networks were ineffective. The United States, in particular, felt that European firms were insufficiently involved in EC policymaking during the Uruguay Round negotiations (pp. 218, 225).

28. Cowles (2001b, p. 216). However, some insiders find that the TABD's impact is much overrated. A leading trade attorney, interview, Washington, D.C., October 18, 2001. There were also concerns in early 2003 that the Bush administration would not continue to support TABD's efforts, so that TABD could be "phased out." E-mail from Washington insider, March 2, 2003, after speaking with a corporate representative involved in TABD.

with friendly foreign spirits industry groups such as DISCUS in the United States and the ACD in Canada, with the result that both the United States and Canada acted as co-complainants with the European Union."[29]

Where intergovernmental cooperation stalls, firms may bypass their own governments and cultivate direct links with public authorities in other jurisdictions, forming cross-border public-private partnerships. U.S. firms pursue this strategy more aggressively than their European counterparts. Most U.S.-based multinationals and many U.S. trade associations operate government affairs offices in Brussels. They lobby the Commission directly, bypassing the USTR. Commission officials report that representatives from PhRMA, the U.S. pharmaceutical trade association, contact them about as often as PhRMA's European counterpart.[30] Similarly, when Argentina implemented safeguard restrictions against footwear imports, Nike representatives met with Commission officials both to learn how the EC was planning to react and to persuade the Commission that the EC had a strong legal and factual case to pursue.[31] Because the EC more seldom applies safeguard restrictions, the EC could (and, in fact, did) take a stronger position than the United States against the Argentine safeguards. This effort followed Nike's lobbying of the USTR to bring a successful WTO challenge against Argentine import duties on shoe imports.[32] Both the United States and EC brought back-to-back WTO complaints against Argentina even though Nike and the European shoe giant Adidas produced their shoes in Indonesia and China, not in the United States or Europe. The firms also assisted Indonesia with its third-party submission in support of the U.S. and EC complaints.[33] Multinational firms such as Nike form cross-national public-private partnerships if they promise to expand the firm's export sales.

Domestic private firms also may assist foreign governments in challenging domestic regulations that they desire removed. Domestic importers

29. Remarks of Tim Jackson, SWA, May 1997. Also DISCUS, interview concerning collaborative efforts in Korean case, May 19, 1999.

30. A Commission official in DG Trade working on intellectual property matters, interview, June 24, 1999.

31. A Commission official in the Market Access Unit of DG Trade, interview, June 1999. The EC-initiated case was WT/DS121.

32. See "U.S. and EU Lodge Complaint against Argentine Shoe Import Duties," *International Trade Reporter (BNA)*, October 29, 1997, p. 1875. The U.S.-initiated case was WT/DS56.

33. For additional background on the Argentina-safeguards case, see Bhala and Gantz (2001, p. 73); and "U.S. to Back Possible EU Case against Argentine Footwear Duties," *Inside U.S. Trade*, May 1, 1998, p. 11.

of foreign products always benefit from WTO challenges. They sometimes visit Brussels or Washington to help develop a case that they cannot otherwise bring before domestic courts. Similarly, domestic producers may benefit from WTO challenges to domestic legislation that they could not block through the domestic political process. The intellectual property industry, for example, provided assistance in U.S. and EC challenges before the WTO to the other's domestic intellectual property laws. The EC copyright industry benefited when the United States initiated formal WTO consultations against Ireland, Denmark, and Sweden over the adequacy of their copyright protection and enforcement procedures. Without the U.S. challenges, changes in EC member state practice would have been delayed for years.[34] Portugal did not even offer patent protection until the United States asked for formal WTO consultations against it.[35] Similarly, the trade association for the U.S. restaurant and bar industry lobbied Congress successfully for exemptions from paying music royalties, to the detriment of music copyright associations. The European Commission, in challenging the relevant U.S. legislation, met and corresponded with representatives of the U.S. music rights associations BMI and ASCAP. BMI also engaged a U.S. law firm to work with the EC in its case.[36] The European Commission and U.S. private music rights association were not formal network partners, but they had reciprocal—albeit not identical—interests. The U.S. private association held useful information that it provided to the EC for the EC's successful challenge.

Overall, multinational firms and trade associations—not trade officials—have taken the lead in the forging of cross-national partnerships to challenge foreign trade barriers. U.S. and European firms and associations sometimes coordinate transatlantically with each other and then work separately with their respective public representatives. At other times they work directly with foreign officials to bring a legal challenge against a third-country trade barrier, especially where firms have yet to persuade their own government to take up the case. Where a developing country lacks the legal and financial resources to pursue a WTO lawsuit, multinational firms may pay a U.S. or European private law firm to do the legal work for it. U.S. and European businesses and associations also discretely assist foreign governments in bringing WTO complaints against U.S. and European regulations.

34. A Commission official, interview, June 24, 1999.

35. See "U.S., Portugal Settle Dispute over Patent Protection under WTO," *International Trade Reporter (BNA)*, October 9, 1996, p. 1566.

36. A Commission official, interview, Brussels, June 29, 1999.

# 7 *The Social, Political, and Legal Implications*

The development of public-private partnerships in the United States and Europe to address international trade claims is a rational response to a more legalized international trading system. WTO legal rights affect company and industry-specific interests. Details of market shares and legal arguments are the province of business executives and legal advocates, not state—or more remote European Community—diplomats. The more legalized international trading system creates stronger incentives for well-placed private actors to engage public legal processes. To litigate effectively in the WTO system, government officials need the specific information that businesses and their legal representatives can provide. Officials therefore strive to establish better working relations with industry on trade matters. The engagement of private firms, in turn, helps national public officials render international public law more effective—hence the reciprocal relationship between WTO public law and private interest.

## Impact of WTO Law on Private Behavior

The deployment of public-private networks in WTO litigation reflects broader shifts in domestic, as well as international, governance.[1] In a world of increasing numbers and complexity, public officials do not hold the resources to effectively implement public policy without the assistance of private parties. Rather, public and private actors depend on each other's resources. Although this development has been examined primarily in the domestic context, public and private actors have also adapted public-private collaborative governance modes to enforce WTO law and otherwise advance their interests in its shadow.

In place of this collaborative arrangement, with its constraints on both public and private parties, some supporters of liberalized trade would like to see a system that allows private firms to directly invoke international trade law. The WTO system, they say, should be viewed as a new world trade "constitution" that grants trading rights to private parties.[2] Under this vision, the system's driving normative goal should be the defense of private trading rights. Private enterprises would be empowered to enforce international trading rights in the domestic legal systems of all WTO members. They would act as private attorneys general to ensure governments' respect of WTO obligations. They would hold rights analogous to those held by private parties against state legislation under the commerce clause of the U.S. Constitution, and against European member state legislation under Article 28 of the EC Treaty.[3] These advocates would like the United States to go further than representing "clients" before WTO bodies. They would like the United States and EC to promote the international rule of law by granting private actors the right to enforce WTO

1. For Rhodes and others on resource interdependencies, see chapter 2, notes 9–19.

2. See, for example, McGinnis and Movsiean (2000, p. 511); Petersmann (1991, pp. 243, 463), asserting that lawyers should "recognize freedom of trade as a basic individual right"; Brand (1992, pp. 95–102); and Symposium, *Journal of World Trade Law* (1998).

3. Private parties may challenge state laws and regulations that discriminate against interstate commerce in violation of their rights under the commerce clause of the U.S. Constitution. See, for example, *Pike* v. *Bruce Church, Inc.*, 397 U.S. 137, 90 S.Ct. 844 (1970); and *Bibb* v. *Navajo Freight Lines, Inc.*, 359 U.S. 520, 79 S.Ct. 962 (1959). Until the EC treaty was renumbered by the Treaty of Amsterdam, Article 28 was Article 30. The Article prohibits "quantitative restrictions on imports and all measures having equivalent effect." Article 28 has "direct effect" so that it may be invoked by private parties before EC member state courts. The term *direct effect* is used to denote provisions of EC supranational law that have direct legal effect in national law and may be invoked before domestic courts. See Brand (1996, p. 556).

rules in national courts—whether domestic or foreign—without a government intermediary or government interference. Some lawyers suggest that private firms should have standing to bring claims directly to the WTO in Geneva.[4]

At first glance, the world trading order does appear to be purely intergovernmental, since only governments have the right to bring WTO claims before the WTO Dispute Settlement Body and private parties do not have the right to invoke WTO rules before U.S. or European courts. However, the ad hoc networks formed between public authorities and private enterprises permit WTO rules to have an *indirect* effect. The WTO panel that heard the EC's challenge to U.S. Section 301 recognized this fact, referring to "the GATT/WTO legal order" as encompassing a "principle of indirect effect," one that ultimately protects "the economic activities of individuals."[5] The panel maintained that the WTO Dispute Settlement Understanding should be interpreted "in the light of the indirect effect such legislation has on individuals and the market-place, the protection of which is one of the principal objects and purposes of the WTO."[6]

The WTO's more effective dispute settlement system permits public authorities to negotiate trade claims with greater leverage. They often negotiate these claims on behalf of private enterprises within the shadow of the WTO dispute settlement system and its growing case law. The WTO system's legalization enhances certainty. This certainty improves the odds of a profitable outcome. Potential profits stimulate enterprises to more actively engage the process. The system's demands on legal resources increases the leverage of private interests within the resulting public-private networks. In this way, the WTO promotes a model under which private enterprises play an active role in litigation and negotiation over regulatory trade barriers. As Tim Jackson of the Scotch Whisky Association said following the EC's successful WTO challenge of Japan's tax system for hard alcohol, "Importantly a key point for us as an exporting industry is that our 'win' gives us moral and legal leverage over

4. See, for example, Ragosta (2000, pp. 739–84), a prominent Washington, D.C., trade lawyer arguing that the WTO "must provide an opportunity for the real party in interest to participate effectively." Alan Wolff, who litigated for Kodak on behalf of the law firm Dewey Ballantine in Washington, D.C., "advocates deputizing private lawyers for particular cases to strengthen the legal resources of the USTR." Barfield (2001, 203, fn 8, citing Wolff).

5. Report of the Panel, "United States—Section 301" para. 7.78 (not appealed).

6. See Report of the Panel, "U.S.—Section 301," para. 7.86 (applying Article 23 of the DSU). The panel also noted "the appreciable 'chilling effect' on the economic activities of individuals" that coercive national legislation, such as Section 301, can have (para. 7.81).

other offending countries which will now be obliged to take the unpopular steps necessary to ensure a fair taxation system for the spirits sector."[7] In practice, the WTO system becomes much more than an intergovernmental system dominated by diplomats negotiating behind closed doors.

In the process, WTO law also affects the structure of government-business relations. Europe's traditional peak trade associations provide little benefit for the litigation of fact-specific trade complaints. To effectively deploy the WTO legal system, Europe's trade authorities have had to work with intrasectoral, product-specific and specialized trade associations or individual firms. WTO-related judicial processes for providing market access (TBR) or market protection (antidumping) thus "cut large coalitions into smaller pieces."[8] As a consequence, EC businesses, with the support of European public authorities, have adapted U.S. models of interest aggregation in order to exploit WTO rights.

WTO law likewise constrains domestic regulatory practice. Executive officials, legislators, and lobbyists refer to international trade law constraints when contemplating new domestic legislation. So do regulatory officials, administrative law judges, and lawyers when they interpret and apply existing regulations. When an environmental group challenged U.S. State Department regulations that had been revised to comply with the WTO shrimp-turtle ruling, the U.S. government argued that the WTO ruling constituted "the law of nations," and that "an act of Congress ought never to be construed to violate the law of nations, if any other possible construction remains."[9] The majority of the U.S. Court of Appeals of the Federal Circuit upheld the government's interpretation of the congressional statute, while taking note of the WTO litigation.[10] As one EC lawyer adds, trade lawyers are also regulatory lawyers. They use trade law arguments to advance their clients' interests in the domestic regulatory process, when new regulations are contemplated or existing ones applied.[11]

7. Remarks of Tim Jackson, SWA, May 1997.

8. De Bièvre (2003, p. 13).

9. See *Turtle Island Restoration Network* v. *Donald Evans*, 284 F.3d 1282, 1303 (2002) (dissent).

10. *Turtle Island Restoration Network* v. *Donald Evans*, 1289–1290 (majority).

11. As a Brussels lawyer confirms, "Trade issues and trade arguments are very much used in the adoption of (EU) legislation. I have worked a lot in the EU proposed legislation on electronic take back and restrictions of hazardous substances in electronic products where we used a lot of trade arguments to defend US industry's interests. I think that focusing also in the legislative adoption phase changes somewhat the approach. The law firms are no longer specific trade law firms but regulatory law firms." E-mail from Candido Garcia Molyneux, January 7, 2002.

Often the WTO simply constrains national officials from discriminating against foreigners. However, the distinction between what constitutes discrimination and what constitutes nondiscriminatory regulation is not always clear. The procedural issue of how to enforce WTO law has substantive consequences and requires serious reflection. "Litigation," it has been pointed out, "is a form of governance, related to legislation. Control over litigation is a form of governance, and should be informed by these analytical perspectives."[12]

There remains, of course, a series of political screens between the private interest and a WTO claim being brought and enforced. Complainant governments are gatekeepers that retain discretion not to bring a claim, or to settle or withdraw a claim, on account of countervailing interests. Defendant governments, when they do not prevail, can refuse to comply with the WTO ruling in question, frustrating the private interest at stake, as in the EC–Meat Hormones case. WTO panelists also may take into account political factors in rendering controversial decisions, as some believe occurred in the Appellate Body's shrimp-turtle decision. Ironically, the enhanced rule of WTO law also subjects WTO judicial bodies to increased political scrutiny, so that WTO tribunals may tailor their decisions to account for the decision's potential repercussions on the WTO's public standing, especially within powerful WTO members. Nonetheless, the WTO system is significantly more legalized than the former GATT system, thereby providing increased certainty, and thus incentives, to private parties. Although governmental screens still remain between the bringing of a WTO trade complaint and the private interests at stake, those screens have become more porous.

## Implications for Transatlantic and International Relations

How public-private partnerships are deployed to enforce WTO law can have serious implications for the international trading system—for its stability and for its equity. First, to the extent that public authorities do not appropriately manage and steer these networks, litigation over regulatory policy spurred by private interests could exacerbate tensions among WTO members, particularly among those who most often use the WTO dispute settlement system—the United States and EC. WTO judicial decisions that challenge domestic regulatory policy may awaken political opposition to the WTO legal system within the United States and Europe.

12. Trachtman (2003, p. 58).

Successful WTO challenges of politically sensitive policy measures could trigger populist backlash, potentially undermining public officials' ability to manage a liberalized trading order. Second, the extensive resources deployed by public-private networks in the United States and Europe in WTO litigation exacerbates power asymmetries in the use of the WTO legal system to the detriment of developing countries and their constituents. The WTO legal system has become increasingly costly, favoring legally astute U.S. and EC public-private networks with ample resources.

The legalization of international dispute settlement and the associated adoption of public-private partnerships for trade litigation can affect a government's choice of cases, litigation postures, and settlement options, and, in consequence, interstate relations. Anyone versed in the ways of Washington can imagine the tensions between public officials attempting to represent the U.S. public interest in WTO litigation and private interests attempting to advance their own. This tension has intensified because private parties now play a larger role in WTO cases and the government depends increasingly on their participation to prevail.

Some observers may find that the U.S. system of public-private partnerships provides the United States with a significant advantage in WTO litigation, so that the EC "seems to be battling the U.S. with one hand behind its back."[13] Because of the stronger public-private networks deployed in the United States, the USTR appears to receive better-prepared complaints from the private sector.[14] The EC's Legal Service, in contrast, works more on its own because of the relatively less active participation of European industry and the service's own bureaucratic culture. Some EC officials, as well as WTO members facing even more severe resource constraints, may wish to adopt a U.S.-style approach.

Nonetheless, as this book has demonstrated, public-private trade partnerships work relatively effectively on both sides of the Atlantic, even though they operate in different manners. The United States—with its tradition of intensive private sector lobbying, its long experience with Section 301 collaborations, its revolving door administrative culture, and its comparative advantage in lawyering—was the first to adopt close public-private partnerships to prevail in WTO litigation. The United States has taken a more bottom-up approach, spurred by individual firms, trade

13. Comment of one anonymous reviewer of the manuscript, October 2002.

14. This was confirmed by present and former members of the Commission's Legal Service, interviews, Brussels, June 22, 1999.

associations, and their lawyers. The EC, in keeping with its institutional structure and administrative culture, has seen the benefit of such partnerships but has adopted a more top-down approach, with the European Commission acting as entrepreneur and manager. The Commission too needed private sector assistance to effectively use the WTO legal system. In fact, the EC brought nineteen WTO complaints that resulted in WTO panel decisions between January 2000 and January 2003, whereas the United States brought only five complaints resulting in judicial decisions (see appendix tables 1 and 3). These divergent approaches have their advantages and disadvantages, ranging from the countervailing risks of private capture and bureaucratic rigidity, to the contrasting benefits of dynamic public-private collaboration and rational governmental oversight.

These differing approaches can affect the choice of cases. Since industry brings cases to the USTR more than the USTR self-initiates them, the median U.S. claim may be of greater commercial significance for specific firms, as opposed to U.S. exporters in general. In contrast, the European Commission has hired outside professional consultants to report on foreign trade barriers affecting EC industries, and these reports led to a series of EC complaints before the WTO. The Commission, in particular, initiated a number of WTO claims concerning third countries' use of safeguard procedures, some of which may have been of less immediate commercial significance to individual firms, especially since the WTO litigation process largely takes up the three-year grant of safeguard relief.[15] According to Commission officials, these cases were brought on "principle" for "systemic reasons," to ensure the proper implementation of WTO agreements.[16] Ultimately, however, these cases could have greater systemic impact for EC firms as a whole, since countries' implementation of safeguards could be constrained by these WTO judicial precedents. Similarly, the Commission brought its WTO challenges against U.S. Section 301 and U.S. tax subsidies for "foreign sales corporations" not in

15. Under the WTO Agreement on Safeguards, a WTO member may restrict imports as a "safeguard," subject to certain stringent conditions. It can do so for three years without providing any compensation to any WTO member affected by its safeguard.

16. One member of the Commission's Legal Service questioned why these cases, such as those involving the export of raw hides, needed to be brought given the time and cost required for the EC to litigate them compared with the relatively minor economic impact on EC enterprises. Interview, Brussels, June 21, 1999. One reason that the EC brought some cases in the early years of the WTO may be that the Commission was searching for cases to establish itself. Reinhold Quick, interview, Brussels, June 25, 1999.

response to a private firm's bidding, but strategically in order to enhance its leverage in U.S.-EC bilateral relations. Although the EC won the most commercially significant case in the WTO's history—the FSC tax case—the EC brought the complaint by and large to quash what it considered to be overly aggressive U.S. use of the WTO system against EC domestic policy.[17]

U.S. private activism can undermine the USTR's ability to take a broader view of U.S. national interests at the same time that it facilitates the USTR's work. Private lobbying, backed by congressional pressure, constrains the USTR's ability to manage U.S. trade relations with the EC and other WTO members. EC officials believe U.S. positions are often driven by discrete politically connected private interests that interfere with the United States's ability to negotiate mutually acceptable compromises. One EC official, for example, reportedly criticized the United States for having "essentially privatized its trade policy when there is a strong domestic lobby" and developed "a sort of Wilsonian sense of outrage" over trade violations.[18] In the bananas case, some say "the US turned up the volume on bananas so high that any compromise—such as one proposed within the WTO—became impossible."[19] European firms and trade associations also hold these views.[20] Some U.S. officials concur that a "lawyer culture" dominates U.S. trade policy, and that "trade problems are handled on a case by case basis without setting priorities."[21] The U.S. political system simply offers fewer structural incentives for political officials to forgo the demands of powerful commercial interests on trade matters.

Certainly, the Commission also is subject to private pressure in trade disputes, complemented by member state demands. In such cases, U.S. and EC officials can assume belligerent public stances against the other to appease domestic politicians and constituencies, thereby exacerbating transatlantic tensions.[22] On the whole, however, without a U.S. Congress on its back, the Commission has more flexibility to settle disputes, as is

17. Nonetheless, affected EC enterprises, such as Airbus Industries, certainly follow the case and settlement negotiations with great interest. A member of the Commission, interview, June 21, 1999.

18. Peterson (2001, p. 50), confirmed by a member state representative attending Article 133 Committee meetings, interview, Brussels, June 25, 1999.

19. Peterson (2001, pp. 45, 62).

20. Members of EC trade associations for the chemical, automobile, and pharmaceutical sectors, interviews, Brussels, June 25, 28, and 29, 1999.

21. Frost (1997, p. 34), citing a former Clinton administration official.

22. See Peterson (2001, p. 56).

apparent from its willingness to refrain from implementing the $4 billion in sanctions authorized in the FSC case. The United States, by contrast, issued immediate threats and sanctions in the bananas litigation.

Private pressure on public officials in WTO disputes can affect one of the WTO dispute settlement system's central goals—that of providing a peaceful and objective multilateral way to settle trade conflicts.[23] Where public authorities are unable to steer public-private networks because private interests are able to pressure trade representatives through political lobbying, WTO litigation can undermine diplomatic efforts to reach balanced amicable settlements. The WTO dispute settlement system should not be too closely analogized to domestic judicial processes in which private parties engage adversarial lawyers to defend interests and courts render judgments enforceable by the state's police powers. Rather, the WTO remains an international institution that provides a forum for governments to negotiate trade concessions and agreements, to monitor compliance, and to resolve conflicts through, and with the assistance of, a more legalized dispute settlement process. Impairment of this broader goal of conflict resolution could have repercussions for the global trading order. The domestic political fallout from transatlantic trade conflicts over discrete matters, such as taxes, bananas or genetically modified foods, could stir up greater opposition to the WTO and its legalized dispute settlement system in both the United States and Europe.

There are signs of growing discomfort with WTO dispute settlement procedures in the U.S. Congress, as the United States has lost a series of WTO cases concerning U.S. trade remedy laws. Senator Max Baucus of Montana, a former chair of the Senate Finance Committee, has labeled WTO tribunals "kangaroo courts," lambasting them for having "attacked and weakened . . . our laws" by "exceeding their authority."[24] His Senate colleague Jay Rockefeller from West Virginia has exclaimed, "These WTO tribunals have violated their mandate not to increase or reduce the rights and obligations of WTO Members; have imposed their preferences and interpretations, and those of a biased WTO Secretariat, on the United States and on other WTO Members; and have issued decisions with no basis in the legal texts they supposedly were interpreting."[25] The vociferousness of these challenges does not bode well.

23. I thank Bob Hudec for helping draw out this point from his review of the manuscript.
24. *Congressional Record*, online ed., May 14, 2002, p. S4308-26.
25. *Congressional Record*, online ed., May 23, 2002, p. S4800.

If the United States and EC aggressively deploy the WTO legal system on the offensive and, instead of adhering to its decisions when they lose as defendants, initiate retaliatory legal complaints, then the system could collapse. As the world's predominant economic powers, the United States and EC determine much of the structure and maintenance of the global trading order.[26] To date, they have been at the forefront of multilateral trade liberalization endeavors and, ultimately, of the trading system's management and stability. If these powers become disenchanted with a legalized WTO system, the system's prospects will dim. Scholars and public officials need be conscious not only of a privatized system's capacity for enhancing the effectiveness of international trading rights but also of its destructive potential.

Nonetheless, although private input in U.S.-EC trade disputes could be better managed, it should not be blamed for placing U.S.-EC relations in jeopardy. Large numbers of U.S. and EC trade claims against each other are a byproduct of the volume and scope of transatlantic trade, and the normal defense of constituent interests in a legalized setting. Even though politicians and trade officials on one side of the Atlantic constantly criticize their transatlantic counterparts, the United States and EC have continued to actively pursue new trade negotiations, as evidenced by the trade negotiating round initiated in Doha in December 2001 and the granting of trade promotion authority to the Bush administration in July 2002. The legalization of international trade relations has not resulted in divergence; on the contrary, there is now greater *convergence* of U.S. and EC trade strategies toward challenging foreign trade barriers. The binding nature of the WTO dispute settlement system has somewhat constrained unilateralism in U.S. trade policy, even while U.S. unilateralism has intensified in most other policy areas, from global warming to Iraq.[27]

26. Great power management of the system is predicted by hegemonic stability theory. See Gilpin (2001, pp. 93–100): "The theory of hegemonic stability maintains that there can be no liberal international economy unless there is a leader that uses its resources and influence to establish and manage an international economy based on free trade, monetary stability and freedom of capital movement" (pp. 99–100). Richard Steinberg applies a variant of this theory based on U.S.-EC collaboration, which he terms the "great power management approach." See Steinberg (1998, p. 207): using "realist international relations theory to elaborate the assumptions and logic of a great power management approach to advancing liberal multilateralism."

27. See, for example, Bill Emmott, "Our Law, Your Law," *Economist*, June 29, 2002, p. 20 (survey), analyzing the increase in unilateralism in U.S. foreign policy under the Bush administration—exemplified by its withdrawal from the 1997 Kyoto Protocol on climate change; its rejection of the Comprehensive Test Ban Treaty, of the verification protocol for

Simultaneously, the EC—by adopting the Trade Barrier Regulation and other informal analogues to U.S.-style public-private trade litigation networks—has adjusted to a legalized WTO system initially promoted by the United States.

Enhanced public-private trade networks are not the primary cause of tension over the conduct of U.S. and EC trade policy. These tensions are rather a symptom of systemic political and cyclical economic developments: two primary ones being European discomfort with U.S. hegemonic power in the post–cold war era and new protectionist legislation and administrative measures in the wake of U.S. and European economic retrenchment. Trade tensions will always exist, but so far they have not triggered a "trade war" that itself could seriously undermine the global economy, although this concern is increasingly voiced.[28] The United States and EC have tools to manage transatlantic economic tensions, such as high-level summits and more regular lower-level meetings, as under the New Transatlantic Agenda and Transatlantic Economic Partnership.[29] That the United States and EC have the ability to manage politically sensitive cases is evident in the handling of the Helms-Burton case[30] and the foreign sales corporation tax subsidy introduced by the United States.[31]

---

the Biological Weapons Convention, and of the Rome treaty establishing a new International Criminal Court; and its "disregard for the Geneva conventions on prisoners of war."

28. See, for example, Gary Yerkey, "Blue-Ribbon Panel Calls for G-8 Standstill on New Trade Barriers through WTO Talks," *International Trade Reporter (BNA)*, June 27, 2002, p. 1123: "The risk of major trade conflict, particularly between the United States and the European Union, represents a real threat to the world economy." See also William Drozdiak, "EU May Hit U.S. with $4 Billion in Penalties; Commission Calls Tax Credits Illegal," *Washington Post,* August 21, 2001, p. E1: "U.S. Special Trade Representative Robert B. Zoellick has likened any EU sanctions of that magnitude to 'dropping a nuclear bomb' on the global trading system." And Daniel T. Griswold, *Wall Street Journal*, December 13, 2000, p. 10: "This growing threat of trade retaliation as an instrument of enforcement is an ominous development for trade."

29. See Pollack and Shaffer (2001c). Also Peterson (2001, p. 65): "The US and EU, after the bananas case, seemed gradually to be learning how to limit the political damage of what they decided—for whatever reason—to inflict upon each other juridically.") And Gary Yerkey, "U.S., EU Agree on New Guidelines to Improve Cooperation on Regulatory Policy," *International Trade Reporter (BNA)*, April 18, 2002, p. 696.

30. See Peterson (2001, p. 58).

31. See, for example, Gary G. Yerkey, "Trade Tensions between U.S. and EU Ease after Latest Zoellick-Lamy Meeting," *International Trade Reporter (BNA)*, June 27, 2002, p. 1127, noting an agreement between U.S. and EU trade officials "that—despite their differences—continued cooperation between the United States and the EU remains essential to ensuring progress in global trade negotiations . . . and that it was critical to keep bilateral disputes in perspective." See also Gary G. Yerkey, "EU Will Not Act against U.S. in Tax

Even the controversial U.S.-EC banana dispute was eventually settled.[32] Although tit-for-tat trade retaliation over noncompliance with WTO rulings could inflict severe economic harm, and justifiably stokes fears of trade restrictive policies spiraling out of control, the risk of a trade war lies less in strengthened public-private partnerships to challenge foreign trade restrictions than in old-fashioned private legislative and administrative lobbying for trade protectionism, on the one hand, and U.S.-European tensions over broader foreign policy issues, on the other. The greater risk for U.S.-EC trade relations lies in U.S. unilateralism in other policy areas that could spill over into the trade arena.[33]

Congress's increasing concern about WTO litigation is largely about challenges to U.S. trade remedy laws, which have been used, in particular, to protect the steel industry. As of February 2003, the last thirteen WTO panel decisions in which the United States was a defendant involved U.S. trade remedy laws and their deployment. WTO members initiated twelve new complaints against U.S. trade remedy laws between January 2002 and February 2003. Of the nine cases brought by the EC against the United States from January 2000 to January 2003, eight involved trade remedy laws.[34]

The three principal trade remedy laws provide for relief from foreign "dumping," relief from foreign subsidies, and "safeguard" relief from import surges causing serious injury. These U.S. trade remedy procedures, which are slanted to favor the U.S. private interests that initiate them, themselves are privatized. Under U.S. trade remedy laws, U.S. firms and trade associations can initiate legal claims before U.S. domestic agencies and courts, the results of which can shut out foreign competition from

---

Dispute if Congress Appears to Be Making Progress," *International Trade Reporter (BNA)*, July 11, 2002, p. 1219, citing an EU decision to "hold off on retaliation" despite a WTO ruling enabling such an action, "to give Congress time to work its way through the issue."

32. Anthony Depalma, "U.S. and Europeans Agree on Deal to End Banana Trade War," *New York Times*, April 12, 2001, p. C1, emphasizing the role of negotiation and compromise in the agreement bringing the nine-year trade dispute to an end.

33. See Elizabeth Becker, "U.S. Unilateralism Worries Trade Officials," *New York Times*, March 17, 2003, p. A8: "Top officials at the World Trade Organization say that they are worried that the Bush administration's go-it-alone policy is threatening international trade."

34. See appendix tables 3 and 4. Similarly, in its summary of WTO dispute settlement activity in 2001, the USTR reported that the United States was a defendant in twenty-two cases, seventeen of which involved challenges to U.S. import laws. See USTR (2002, pp. 28–36).

the U.S. market. Because of enhanced congressional concern over WTO constraints on the use of these import relief procedures, when USTR Robert Zoellick agreed to negotiations over the applicable WTO rules at Doha in November 2001, sixty-three senators immediately signed a letter "opposing any negotiations that could result in weaker U.S. trade laws."[35] As long as private pressure for protection remains, WTO cases will be brought and the affected enterprises, their lawyers, and their congressional representatives will vigorously, and self-righteously, protest.

Policymakers nonetheless need be aware of the dangers of granting private interests too great a role in WTO litigation, despite the resources that private firms and trade associations offer. These resources are not "free." Where a private party finances a WTO complaint, and the defendant WTO member does not comply with a WTO decision for domestic political reasons, whether involving its tax system or its food safety regulations, the private entity behind the lawsuit can exercise significant leverage to impede a harmonious settlement. Under the early GATT notion of reciprocity, the conflict could be settled through a "rebalancing" of trade concessions. "The legal procedures," Robert Hudec observed, "were not there to enforce obligations for the sake of enforcement. They were there to correct imbalances that might arise in the benefits governments were actually receiving from the agreement."[36] However, when a private interest has financed a WTO lawsuit, it is not interested in a "rebalancing" of trade concessions between governments. It is interested in the defense of legal "rights." The private interest presses the legislature to press the trade representative to inflict punitive measures on the offending country. Thus following the bananas litigation, the United States threatened "carrousel retaliation," pursuant to which tariff sanctions would be applied to different EC sectors, rotating periodically like cartridges through a weapon, injuring one export industry after another. Such an instrument is ingenious from the perspective of ratcheting up pressure on the offending country. But it is unlikely to facilitate transatlantic goodwill, much less harmonious trade relations.

35. Jenna Greene, "Grudge Match: Why the United States Is on a Losing Streak at the WTO," *Legal Times*, November 5, 2001, p. 1. When Congress finally agreed to grant the president trade promotion authority in July 2002, it wrote into U.S. negotiating goals the defense and preservation of U.S. import relief laws. See Rosella Brevetti, Fawn H. Johnson, and Chris Rugaber, "Senate Set to Clear Trade Package after House Approves Bill by 3 Votes," *International Trade Reporter (BNA)*, August 1, 2002, p. 1334.

36. Hudec (1993, p. 7).

## Implications for the System's Equity

A central attribute of WTO law, as compared with national or EC law, is that it can only be modified through consensus, with the result that the WTO political/legislative system remains extremely weak.[37] Governments modify WTO rules only through infrequent negotiating rounds (held about once every decade), involving complex trade-offs between more than 140 countries with widely varying interests, values, levels of development, and priorities. Because the bargaining process is complex, negotiators often draft rules in a vague manner as part of a political compromise. WTO members thereby delegate significant power to the WTO dispute settlement system to interpret and effectively make WTO law. Individual WTO cases function not only to resolve particular disputes but also to interpret and shape WTO law in the absence of an international legislative or executive check. Those governments that participate most actively in the dispute settlement system are best positioned to effectively shape the law's interpretation and application over time.

Since the United States and EC participate in most WTO cases, they exercise much greater influence in this shaping of WTO law than do other WTO members. As of January 2003, the United States had participated as a party or third party in 97 percent of WTO cases resulting in an adopted panel or Appellate Body decision, and the EC had participated in 81 percent of such WTO decisions (see tables 7-1 and 6-1). As repeat players, the United States and EC attempt to defend their systemic interests in shaping the interpretation of WTO rules over time. Legalization of international trade relations does not benefit all WTO members equally.

Moreover, not all private parties, including those within the United States and Europe, benefit equally from a more legalized international trading system. As in most litigation situations, given the financial demands and legal and factual complexity of bringing a successful

37. From a technical perspective, most WTO provisions can be amended by a two-thirds vote of the members. See WTO Agreement, Article X:1; and Bhala and Kennedy (1998, §4(f)(3)). In practice, WTO political decisions are made by consensus and thus are rare. See, for example, Posner and Rief (2000, pp. 504–05): "At least one thing is clear about WTO interpretations and amendments: they are not designed to be taken regularly or readily. In fact, there has not been a single interpretation or amendment adopted since the WTO came into effect in 1995, and there were only six amendments (the last in 1965) in the previous forty-eight years of GATT. Moreover, the interpretation or amendment process—particularly, achieving a consensus—is only likely to become more difficult as the number of WTO members grows."

Table 7-1. *Participation of All WTO Members in Cases Resulting in Adopted Panel or Appellate Body Reports, as of January 17, 2003*[a]

| | *Defendant* | | *Complainant* | | *Third party* | | *Aggregate total*[b] | |
|---|---|---|---|---|---|---|---|---|
| *Country* | *Count* | *Percent (of 69)* | *Count* | *Percent (of 69)* | *Count* | *Percent (of 69)* | *Count* | *Percent (of 69)* |
| United States | 26 | 37.7 | 19 | 27.5 | 24 | 34.8 | 67 | 97.1 |
| EC | 8 | 11.6 | 23 | 33.3 | 26 | 37.7 | 56 | 81.2 |
| Japan | 3 | 4.3 | 5 | 7.2 | 25 | 36.2 | 33 | 47.8 |
| Canada | 7 | 10.1 | 9 | 13.0 | 16 | 23.2 | 31 | 44.9 |
| India | 4 | 5.8 | 6 | 8.7 | 18 | 26.1 | 27 | 39.1 |
| Brazil | 2 | 2.9 | 5 | 7.2 | 9 | 13.0 | 16 | 23.2 |
| Australia | 2 | 2.9 | 3 | 4.3 | 11 | 15.9 | 14 | 20.3 |
| Korea | 4 | 5.8 | 4 | 5.8 | 6 | 8.7 | 14 | 20.3 |
| Mexico | 1 | 1.4 | 4 | 5.8 | 9 | 13.0 | 13 | 18.8 |
| Chile | 2 | 2.9 | 1 | 1.4 | 5 | 7.2 | 8 | 11.6 |
| Ecuador | | | 1 | 1.4 | 6 | 8.7 | 7 | 10.1 |
| Thailand | 1 | 1.4 | 2 | 2.9 | 4 | 5.8 | 7 | 10.1 |
| Argentina | 4 | 5.8 | 1 | 1.4 | 1 | 1.4 | 6 | 8.7 |
| Colombia | | | | | 5 | 7.2 | 5 | 7.2 |
| Costa Rica | | | 1 | 1.4 | 4 | 5.8 | 5 | 7.2 |
| Guatemala | 2 | 2.9 | 1 | 1.4 | 2 | 2.9 | 5 | 7.2 |
| El Salvador | | | | | 4 | 5.8 | 4 | 5.8 |
| Honduras | | | 1 | 1.4 | 3 | 4.3 | 4 | 5.8 |
| Hong Kong | | | | | 4 | 5.8 | 4 | 5.8 |
| Indonesia | 1 | 1.4 | 1 | 1.4 | 2 | 2.9 | 4 | 5.8 |
| New Zealand | | | 2 | 2.9 | 3 | 4.3 | 4 | 5.8 |
| Norway | | | | | 4 | 5.8 | 4 | 5.8 |
| Turkey | 1 | 1.4 | 1 | 1.4 | 2 | 2.9 | 4 | 5.8 |
| Venezuela | | | 1 | 1.4 | 3 | 4.3 | 4 | 5.8 |
| Israel | | | | | 3 | 4.3 | 3 | 4.3 |
| Jamaica | | | | | 3 | 4.3 | 3 | 4.3 |
| Pakistan | | | 2 | 2.9 | 1 | 1.4 | 3 | 4.3 |
| Philippines | | | 1 | 1.4 | 2 | 2.9 | 3 | 4.3 |
| Cuba | | | | | 2 | 2.9 | 2 | 2.9 |
| Dominica | | | | | 2 | 2.9 | 2 | 2.9 |
| Egypt | 1 | 1.4 | | | 1 | 1.4 | 2 | 2.9 |
| Malaysia | | | 1 | 1.4 | 1 | 1.4 | 2 | 2.9 |
| Nicaragua | | | | | 2 | 2.9 | 2 | 2.9 |
| Paraguay | | | | | 2 | 2.9 | 2 | 2.9 |

*(continued)*

Table 7-1 *(continued)*

| | *Defendant* | | *Complainant* | | *Third party* | | *Aggregate total*[b] | |
|---|---|---|---|---|---|---|---|---|
| *Country* | *Count* | *Percent (of 69)* | *Count* | *Percent (of 69)* | *Count* | *Percent (of 69)* | *Count* | *Percent (of 69)* |
| Peru | | | 1 | 1.4 | 1 | 1.4 | 2 | 2.9 |
| Poland | | | 1 | 1.4 | 1 | 1.4 | 2 | 2.9 |
| Singapore | | | | | 2 | 2.9 | 2 | 2.9 |
| Sri Lanka | | | | | 2 | 2.9 | 2 | 2.9 |
| St. Lucia | | | | | 2 | 2.9 | 2 | 2.9 |
| Switzerland | | | | | 2 | 2.9 | 2 | 2.9 |
| Barbados | | | | | 1 | 1.4 | 1 | 1.4 |
| Dominican Republic | | | | | 1 | 1.4 | 1 | 1.4 |
| Hungary | | | | | 1 | 1.4 | 1 | 1.4 |
| Iceland | | | | | 1 | 1.4 | 1 | 1.4 |
| Mauritius | | | | | 1 | 1.4 | 1 | 1.4 |
| Nigeria | | | | | 1 | 1.4 | 1 | 1.4 |
| Senegal | | | | | 1 | 1.4 | 1 | 1.4 |
| Uruguay | | | | | 1 | 1.4 | 1 | 1.4 |
| Total[c] | 69 | — | 97 | — | 233 | — | 390 | — |

Source: WTO Secretariat, *Update of WTO Dispute Settlement Cases,* WT/DS/OV/10 (January 22, 2003).

a. Caveat: this chart needs to be read with caution. Because of the way disputes are recorded by the WTO, various methods of counting can be used to generate statistics. For example, the EC filed two separate complaints against Chile for its taxes on alcoholic beverages (WT/DS87 and WT/DS110). A panel was established for the first complaint, but after the filing of the second one, the two complaints were brought before a single panel pursuant to Article 9.1 of the DSU. Accordingly, this chart treats them as one case, so Chile is counted as a defendant only once. In addition, countries such as the Unied States, which joined as a third party to the first panel in that case, and joined a second time as a third party before the merged panel, are counted as a third party only once. In other instances where panels concerning the same matter were not joined, such as the Canadian and U.S. complaints against the EC for its measures affecting livestock and meat (hormones) (WT/DS48 and WT/DS26, respectively), the two are treated separately. Percentages are based on the number of cases resulting in adopted Panel and/or Appellate Body reports listed on the WTO website as of January 17, 2003 (69). This figure includes the Appellate Body report for United States—Continued Dumping and Subsidy Offset Act of 2000 (WT/DS217, 234), which was circulated prior to January 17, 2003, and adopted on January 27, 2003.

b. In cases where a WTO member first reserved its rights as a third party but went on to become a complainant, its having joined as a third party is not reflected in the aggregate total column.

c. As of January 17, 2003, ninety-six WTO members had never participated as a party or a third party in a case resulting in adopted Appellate Body or Panel reports.

complaint, large and well-organized interests are best positioned to avail themselves of new legal rights by hiring lawyers, economists, and other consultants. Shifting litigation to the international level exacerbates the imbalance. The legal forum is distant. Legal expertise is less widespread and thus more expensive. The political process is more complex. While many WTO critics crudely characterize the WTO as a system designed to benefit footloose multinational firms, it remains true that large firms and well-organized industries are typically best informed and most likely to make use of international trading rights. As the world's largest traders, they are the most directly affected by the details and interpretive nuances of agreed rules.[38] They have *high per capita stakes* in the outcome of disputes. They thus have the incentive to inform themselves, organize, and generally play an active role. They also hold the resources to engage in complex, prolonged litigation in a remote forum, which they are willing to dedicate to these issues because of their stakes.

Small and medium-sized enterprises, on average, have lower per capita stakes and thus reduced incentives to engage the process. The costs of informing themselves of the issues and organizing to have their views represented often outweigh the potential, but uncertain, benefits of pursuing their interests through international trade litigation. Moreover, public officials have limited resources to help them overcome collective action barriers. Public officials can create databases and file a few publicized cases. But overall, large and well-organized interests remain best situated to use the process. Because of the weakness of the WTO political structure, private parties too can shape WTO law by working with U.S. and EC officials in the litigation process. To give just one example, the U.S. and European spirits industry, by working with U.S. and EC trade lawyers in disputes against Japan, Korea, and Chile, helped shape the interpretation of GATT Article III and induced countries around the world to reduce their taxes on U.S. and European hard alcohol.

With the creation of the WTO, an area of international law may have become more like law as commonly perceived. Yet it is not the neutral technocratic process some of its proponents idealize it to be. Even the richest WTO members have come to depend on the assistance of private

38. In the early 1980s, for example, approximately 40 percent of global trade was intrafirm trade conducted by 350 of the world's largest multinational corporations. See World Bank (1992). The same held true in the 1990s. See Graham (1996, p. 14), stating that intrafirm trade of multinational corporations with their affiliates accounted for about one-third of world trade and about 50 percent of U.S. imports and exports.

parties. If the United States and EC depend on assistance from private firms and trade associations, what does this bode for developing country participation in the system? Those who support the creation of international trading rights need be cognizant of how they will be used—that is, of the *law-in-action.*

And yet, forsaking such law will not rid the world of systemic biases either. As always, the choice is among imperfect alternatives.[39] The central issue is to identify which alternative is relatively less imperfect. Given the systemic biases of the WTO judicial system toward the wealthy and politically connected, one obvious alternative would be to curtail cross-border trading rights, which would result in more closed economies throughout the world. Such curtailment, however, would arguably reduce aggregate national welfare in developed and developing countries alike. Furthermore, it would not eliminate coercive political and economic pressures but could exacerbate them, since there would be no international legal check on great power coercion.

If one opposes or is skeptical about trade liberalization endeavors, or if one fears that excess private influence can trigger the bringing of inopportune, politically charged cases that could undermine the trading system, one will be wary of large and well-organized commercial interests working the system. Partnerships between the world's dominant economic powers (the United States and EC) and the world's largest private commercial enterprises (located in them) justifiably add fuel to these concerns. Just as in domestic litigation, the haves more likely come out ahead at the international level.[40] Even if one supports trade liberalization, one should be concerned about the appropriate public steering of these networks so that they are held accountable and pursue public, and not just private, ends.

On the other hand, public-private networks can also ensure more effective enforcement of WTO rules. Ultimately, WTO rule violations affect individual firms and industries. Those firms and industries most likely know the factual details of violations and can best judge their commercial

39. The phrase "imperfect alternatives" is used by Neil Komesar (1994) in the title of his book calling for an assessment of policy in terms of its likely handling by alternative institutions—be they courts, legislatures, or markets—in which different parties will be better, or less well, represented.

40. See Galanter (1974), assessing why the haves come out ahead in U.S. domestic litigation; and Conant (2002), concerning the role of organized interests in EC litigation. See also Braithwaite and Drahos (2000), Dezalay and Garth (1996, 2002), and Merry (2003) concerning global impacts, national regulatory policies, and the transformation of states.

significance. If one believes in the appropriateness of legal trading rights to open commerce across borders, public-private networks should possibly be expanded, not curtailed. Although firms pursue their self-interests in international trade litigation, their engagement can also give rise to public benefits (or, in the language of economics, positive externalities). Open trade policies can strengthen competition, increase consumer choice, and lower prices, all of which should result in higher standards of living. From this perspective, public-private networks in the United States and EC are competing models for successful implementation of WTO law.

Nonetheless, whatever one's perspective on trade liberalization and its enforcement, developing countries and developing country constituents clearly are at a disadvantage before the WTO's current dispute settlement system. Their participation in the system in terms of complaints against developed countries has declined since the establishment of the WTO compared with their participation under the less legalized GATT. Developing countries are shown to be "one-third less likely to file complaints against developed states under the WTO than they were under the post-1989 GATT regime." In contrast, "the fraction of cases targeting [developing countries] has risen dramatically, from 19 to 33 percent," which suggests that a developing country "is up to five times more likely to be subject to a complaint under the WTO."[41] Under the WTO, "the developing country share in terms of being a defendant rose to 37 percent" compared with "only 8 percent of all cases brought during the GATT years."[42] Developing countries' use of the WTO dispute settlement against developed countries is considerably less than their share of developed country trade:

> By mid 2000, 46 percent of the developed countries' complaints had been lodged against developing-country WTO members, while the latter accounted for only about 25 percent of developed-country trade. Just over 50 per cent of the developing countries' complaints, on the other hand, were lodged against developed countries, which was considerably less than the latter's share of trade with developing countries.[43]

41. See Busch and Reinhardt (2002, pp. 466–67), citing a table as well as other work by Reinhardt. They also note: "Developing countries constituted some 31 percent of GATT complainants, yet only 29 percent of WTO complainants, despite their ballooning proportion of the overall membership." These latter figures include the growing number of developing country cases against each other.

42. See Hoekman and Kostecki (2001, pp. 394–95).

43. See Michalopoulos (2001, p. 167), who also explains why the differential does not appear to reflect simply a greater compliance by developed countries with WTO obligations.

Moreover, developing countries' effective participation is overstated by reference to numerical charts, since the developing country, when it does participate, can be simply piggybacking on a U.S. or EC complaint.

Policymakers and scholars need to focus on mechanisms that can be developed to offset disadvantages under the WTO's legalized system. WTO remedies and procedures could be modified to offset structural biases favoring the WTO's most powerful members and their most powerful constituents, as is currently being discussed in Geneva.[44] Monetary damages and attorney fees could be awarded to developing country complainants when they successfully challenge a developed country trade barrier. Less costly arbitration procedures could be adopted in certain situations involving developing country complainants. Mechanisms for the mediation of politically sensitive claims could be incorporated.[45] Greater legal assistance could be provided so developing countries may defend WTO claims more cost-effectively, as through the new Advisory Center on WTO Law in Geneva.[46] Regional trade centers could also be developed through which developing countries pool their limited resources.

This book has documented the role of resource interdependencies and reciprocal public-private interests in explaining the rise of U.S. and European public-private trade litigation networks in the actual deployment of WTO law—its *law-in-action*. There is a reciprocal relationship between the judicialization of the WTO dispute settlement system and the rise of public-private partnerships pressing for the enforcement of trading commitments. The WTO has become more than an intergovernmental system based on a balancing of trade concessions. The organization has moved toward a system of defending interests in the pursuit of legal rights. The defining of these interests, whether the national interest or

44. See, for example, the numerous developing country proposals during WTO members' review of the WTO Dispute Settlement Understanding from the fall of 2002 through the winter of 2003. Also Shaffer (2003).

45. See, for example, Barfield (2001, pp. 112–25), proposing mediation by the WTO director-general or a panel of "eminent persons" for certain types of cases. The United States has proposed a mediation system to the European Union for transatlantic disputes. See Gary G. Yerkey, "U.S. Proposes New Mechanism for Settling Trade Disputes with EU Involving Early Talks," *International Trade Reporter (BNA)*, June 7, 2001, p. 889, referring to a "U.S. proposal for an enhanced 'dispute management procedure.'"

46. See "Welcome to the Advisory Center on WTO Law" at www.acwl.ch (August 9, 2002). The Advisory Center is to provide legal services to developing countries in WTO litigation at reduced rates. The center is funded through an endowment and user fees, the fees being imposed on a sliding scale in relation to the country's pro rata share of global trade and its per capita gross national product.

primarily private ones, involves behind-the-scenes negotiations between members of the public-private partnership. Although the system has not become purely privatized, private participation has increased. Public officials need to be aware of the challenges posed for public management of the enhanced resources offered through these litigation networks. In managing these networks, two central institutional challenges will remain. First, how can governments effectively maintain an open trade regime while safeguarding domestic social and regulatory choices? Second, when trade conflicts inevitably arise, how can governments best resolve them in a fair, objective, and peaceful manner with the assistance of a multilateral dispute settlement system?

Appendix Table 1. *Requests for Consultations by the United States: Panel and Appellate Body Reports, as of January 17, 2003*

| *WTO case* | *Section 301*[a] | *WTO procedure, request date* | *Summary* | *Status* |
|---|---|---|---|---|
| *WT/DS175* India: measures relating to trade and investment in the automotive sector. | No, a systemic case initiated by USTR, although with industry support. | 1 May 99 EC reserved 3d-party rights— 27 July 00 (EC also a complainant; see WT/DS149) | Panel found India's "indigenization" and "trade balancing conditions" relating to trade and investment in automotive sector for its policy 1997–2002 were inconsistent with Art. III:4 and XI of GATT. See WT/DS279 (EC follow-up request for consultations). | Panel report circulated: 21 Dec 01. U.S. prevailed. India withdrew appeal on 14 Mar 02. India removed conditions on 19 Aug 02 and 4 Sep 01, respectively. |
| *WT/DS170* Canada: patent protection term | No, though PhRMA behind case pursuant to Special 301 filing. | 6 May 99 | AB upheld the panel's determination that Canada's patent law does not provide for a 20-year protection term as required by TRIPS Art. 33. | AB report adopted: 12 Oct 00. U.S. prevailed. Canada initiated legislation that would extend patent term protection from 17 to 20 years. |
| *WT/DS163* Korea: measures affecting government procurement | No, initiated within U.S. Department of Commerce. | 16 Feb 99 EC reserved 3d-party rights— 16 June 99 | Panel found entities coordinating procurement for airport construction were not covered by Korea's obligations under Government Procurement Agreement. | Panel report adopted: 19 June 00. Korea prevailed. |

Appendix Table 1 (*continued*)

| *WTO case* | *Section 301*[a] | *WTO procedure, request date* | *Summary* | *Status* |
| --- | --- | --- | --- | --- |
| *WT/DS161* Korea: measures affecting imports of fresh, chilled, or frozen beef | No, but U.S. beef industry trade associations behind case. | 1 Feb 99 | AB upheld panel's determination that requirements for imported beef violated Art. III and XI:1 of GATT and Art. 4.2 of Agreement on Agriculture, but reversed panel's determination regarding excessive domestic support. | AB report adopted: 10 Jan 00. U.S. prevailed in part. Korea notified DSB that it had implemented panel recommendations: 25 Sept 01. |
| *WT/DS132* Mexico: antidumping investigation of high-fructose corn syrup from U.S. | USTR began investigation following petition from Corn Refiners Association on 17 Feb 98 (301-118). | 8 May 98 EC reserved 3d-party rights— 23 Oct 00, in Art. 21.5 proceeding | Panel found imposition of definitive antidumping measure on high-fructose corn syrup from the U.S. based on threat of injury determinations violated several articles of AD Agreement. Dispute was subject to political negotiation in early 2003. Mexico had challenged U.S. sugar tariff-rate quota under NAFTA. | Panel report adopted: 24 Feb 00. U.S. prevailed. Article 21.5 panel found Mexico failed to implement panel determinations: 22 June 01. |
| *WT/DS126* Australia: subsidies provided to producers and exporters of automotive leather | USTR initiated investigations for the second time in Nov 97 following complaint by Coalition against Leather Subsidies (301-107). | 4 May 98 EC reserved 3d-party rights— 14 Oct 99 | Panel found payments under grant contract from Australian government to Howe/ALH are subsidies that violate Arts. 1 and 3.1 of SCM Agreement. | Panel report adopted: 16 June 99. U.S. prevailed. Compliance panel determined Australia failed to implement recommendations. Parties notified DSB of mutual solution to compliance dispute: 24 July 00. |

| | | | | |
|---|---|---|---|---|
| *WT/DS103* Canada: measures affecting importation of milk and exportation of dairy products | National Milk Producers Federation, the U.S. Dairy Export Council, and International Dairy Foods Association filed petition: 5 Sept 97 (301-113). | 8 Oct 97 EC reserved 3d-party rights— 18 Dec 01, in Art. 21.5 compliance proceeding | AB upheld panel's determination that Canada's "special milk classes" constitute export subsidies that violate Arts. 3 and 8 of Agreement on Agriculture. | AB report adopted: 27 Oct 99. U.S. prevailed. AB compliance report circulated 20 Dec 02. Parties informed DSB of request to extend Art. 22.6 DSU arbitration. Canada announced provincial governments will discontinue existing programs. |
| *WT/DS90* India: quantitative restrictions on imports of agricultural, textile, and industrial products | No, a systemic issue initiated by USTR, although private parties interested. | 15 July 97 | AB upheld panel's determination that India's quantitative restrictions were inconsistent with Arts. XI and XVIII:11 of GATT and Art. 4.2 of Agreement on Agriculture. | AB report adopted: 26 May 99. U.S. prevailed. India announced it would remove quantitative restrictions by 1 Apr 01. |
| *WT/DS84* Korea: taxes on alcoholic beverages | No, but DISCUS behind case, following the initiative of the EC and Scotch Whisky Association. | 23 May 97 (EC also a complainant; see WT/DS75) | AB upheld panel's determination that soju is directly competitive with other distilled alcohol; therefore Korea taxed the imported products in dissimilar manner in violation of Art. III.2 of GATT. | AB report adopted: 17 Feb 99. U.S. prevailed. On 14 Jan 00, Korea informed DSB it had amended liquor tax law to impose flat nondiscriminatory liquor tax of 72 percent on all distilled alcoholic beverages. |
| *WT/DS76* Japan: measures affecting agricultural products | USTR self-initiated an investigation 7 Oct 97 and proceeded with WTO complaint (301-112). | 7 Apr 97 EC reserved 3d-party rights— 18 Nov 97 | AB upheld panel's determination that Japan's varietal testing of apples, cherries, and walnuts is inconsistent with Arts. 2.2, 5.6, and 7 of SPS Agreement. | AB report adopted: 19 Mar 99. U.S. prevailed. Parties informed DSB of solution: 23 Aug 01, regarding fruits and nuts st issue. |

Appendix Table 1 (*continued*)

| *WTO case* | *Section 301*[a] | *WTO procedure, request date* | *Summary* | *Status* |
|---|---|---|---|---|
| *WT/DS62, 67, 68* EC, Ireland, U.K.: customs classification of certain computer equipment | No, but USTR pressed by Cabletron and its supporters in Congress. | 11 Feb 97 | AB reversed panel's determination that EC tariff treatment was inconsistent with Art II:1 of GATT. | AB report adopted: 22 June 98. EC prevailed. However, tariffs were eliminated as of 1 Jan 00, when 29 countries signed Information Technology Agreement at Dec 96 WTO Ministerial Meeting. |
| *WT/DS59* Indonesia: certain measures affecting automobile industry | USTR self-initiated investigation: 4 Oct 96 (301-109). | 4 Oct 96 (EC also a complainant; see WT/DS54) | Panel found Indonesia's exemption from customs duties and luxury taxes on imports pursuant to its "national car" program violated Arts. I, II:2 of GATT, Art. 2 of TRIMS, and Art. 5 of SCM Agreement. | AB report adopted: 23 July 98. U.S. prevailed. Indonesia informed DSB it had adopted a new automotive policy implementing panel's recommendations on 24 June 99. Indonesia abandoned program in context of agreement with IMF during Asian financial crisis. |
| *WT/DS56* Argentina: certain measures affecting imports of footwear, textiles, apparel, and other items | USTR self-initiated investigation: 4 Oct 96 (301-108). Nike and Reebok pressed Congress and USTR. | 2 July 96 EC reserved 3d-party rights—25 Feb 97 | AB upheld panel's determination that Argentina's minimum specific duties violated Art. II of GATT and that its 3 percent ad valorem statistical tax on imports was inconsistent with Art. VIII of GATT. Compare subsequent EC challenge of Argentine safeguard on footwear imports, WT/DS121. | AB report adopted: 22 Apr 98. U.S. prevailed. Argentina entered agreement with U.S. that reduced statistical tax to .5 percent and capped specific duties on textiles and apparel at 35 percent, effective as of 30 May 99. |

| | | | | |
|---|---|---|---|---|
| *WT/DS50* India: patent protection for pharmaceutical and agricultural chemical products | USTR self-initiated an investigation: 2 July 96 (301-106). Requested by PhRMA. | 2 July 96 (EC also a complainant; see WT/DS79) | AB upheld panel's determination that India's failure to establish a mechanism that preserves novelty and priority with respect to patent applications for agricultural, chemical and pharmaceutical products violated Arts. 70.8 and 70.9 of TRIPS. | AB report adopted: 16 Jan 98. U.S. prevailed. On 28 Apr 99, India informed DSB it had enacted legislation to comply. U.S. dissatisfied with "exclusive marketing rights" provisions, but does not challenge them. |
| *WT/DS44* Japan: measures affecting computer photographic film and paper | USTR initiated investigation following petition by Eastman Kodak: 18 May 95 (301-99). | 13 June 96 EC reserved 3d-party rights— 16 Oct 96 | Panel found Japanese measures did not impair benefits to U.S. under Art. XXIII:1(b) of GATT nor accord less favorable treatment to imported film and photographic paper under Art. III:4 of GATT. | Panel report adopted: 22 Apr 98. Japan prevailed. |
| *WT/DS31* Canada: certain measures affecting periodicals | USTR self-initiated an investigation: 11 Mar 96 (301-102). Requested by Time Warner on account of *Sports Illustrated*. | 11 Mar 96 | AB upheld panel's determination that the tax treatment of "split-run" periodicals and favorable postal rates for Canadian periodicals were inconsistent with Art. III:2 of GATT. | AB report adopted: 30 July 97. U.S. prevailed. Parties agreed on a 15-month implementation period that expired 30 Oct 98. Canada and U.S. negotiated a compromise in June 99 so as to increase U.S. access. |
| *WT/DS27* EC: regime for importation, sale and distribution of bananas | USTR initiated investigation following petition from Chiquita Brands International, Inc. and Hawaii Banana Industry Association: 2 Sept 94 (301-94). | 28 Sept 95 | AB upheld Panel's finding that EC banana regime and licensing procedures were inconsistent with GATT Arts. I, III, XIII, provisions of Agreement on Import Licensing Procedures, and Arts. II and XVII of GATS. | AB report adopted: 25 Sept 97. U.S. prevailed. When AB found EC's amended banana regime failed to comply, DSB authorized U.S. to withdraw concessions worth US$191.4 million a year, which the U.S. applied. EC notified DSB of U.S.-EC settlement of dispute on 22 June 01. EC to adopt tariff-only system by 2006. |

Appendix Table 1 (*continued*)

| *WTO case* | *Section 301*[a] | *WTO procedure, request date* | *Summary* | *Status* |
|---|---|---|---|---|
| *WT/DS26* EC: measures affecting meat and meat products (hormones) complaint by U.S. | No. However, a Section 301 petition (301-60 & 62) in 1987 triggered U.S. sanctions and negotiation of an agreement for importation of U.S. non-hormone-treated beef. | 26 Jan 96 | AB upheld panel's finding that EC import prohibition on meat treated with hormones was inconsistent with Arts. 3.1 and 5.5 of SPS agreement. | AB report adopted: 13 Feb 98. U.S. prevailed. Arbitrator allowed suspension of tariff concessions up to $116.8 million a year, which U.S. applied. EC has conducted new risk assessments and might initiate a compliance procedure to have U.S. sanctions removed. |
| *WT/DS11* Japan: taxes on alcoholic beverages | No, but DISCUS behind case, following initiative of the EC and Scotch Whisky Association. | 7 July 95 (EC also a complainant; see WT/DS8) | AB upheld panel's determination that Japan's tax system that favors *shochu* over other distilled liquors was discriminatory in violation of Art. III:2 of GATT. | AB report adopted: 1 Nov 96. U.S. prevailed. Arbitrator determined an implementation period of 15 months to expire on 1 Feb 98. Japan presented modalities for implementation that were accepted by the complainants. |

a. As of August 9, 2002.

Appendix Table 2. *Requests for Consultations by the United States: Not Involving an Adopted Report, as of January 17, 2003*

| *WTO case* | *Section 301*[a] | *WTO procedure, request date* | *Summary of outcome of complaint* | *Status* |
|---|---|---|---|---|
| *WT/DS276* Canada: measures relating to exports of wheat and treatment of imported grain | North Dakota Wheat Commission filed a petition 9 Sept 00 (301-120). | 17 Dec 02 (EC requested to join consultations: 20 Dec 02) | U.S. alleges Canada's Wheat Board and government treat imported grain inconsistently with obligations under GATT Arts. III and XVII and Art. 2 of TRIMS. | Panel established: 31 Mar 03, but not composed |
| *WT/DS275* Venezuela: import licensing measures on certain agricultural products | No, a systemic case, although there was private party support. | 7 Nov 02 (EC requested to join consultations: 20 Nov 02) | U.S. alleges import licensing requirements for various agricultural products lack transparency and predictability in violation of Arts. III, X, XI and XIII of GATT, Art. 4.2 of the Agreement of Agriculture, Art. 2.1 of TRIMS, and various articles of the Agreement on Import Licensing Procedures. | Consultations held 26 Nov 02. |
| *WT/DS260* EC: provisional safeguard measures on imports of certain steel products | No, a tit-for-tat case after EC challenged U.S. steel safeguard. | 30 May 02 | U.S. alleges provisional safeguards on certain steel products under Commission regulation are inconsistent with various articles of Safeguards Agreement and Art. XIX:1(a) of GATT. Case linked to EC challenge of U.S. safeguard. See WT/DS248. | Panel established: 16 Sept 02, but not composed. U.S. has not challenged final EC safeguard measure. |

Appendix Table 2 (*continued*)

| *WTO case* | *Section 301*[a] | *WTO procedure, request date* | *Summary of outcome of complaint* | *Status* |
|---|---|---|---|---|
| *WT/DS245* Japan: measures affecting importation of apples | No, although Washington State Apple Commission and others behind the complaint. | 1 Mar 02 (EC reserved third-party rights 3 June 02) | U.S. alleges quarantine restrictions on apples from certain orchards to protect against "fire blight" are inconsistent with Art. XI of GATT, Art. 14 of Agreement on Agriculture, and several articles of SPS Agreement. Compare WT/DS76. | Panel composed: 17 July 02. Report circulated on 15 July 03. U.S. prevailed in panel report. |
| *WT/DS223* EC: tariff-rate quota on corn gluten feed from U.S. | No (related to U.S.-wheat gluten case). | 25 Jan 01 | U.S. alleges tariff-rate quota on corn gluten does not satisfy requirements of Arts. 8.1, 8.2 and 8.3 of Safeguards Agreement and Arts. I, II and XIX of GATT. | EC withdrew measure on corn gluten in connection with U.S. removal of wheat gluten TRQ. See WT/DS166 (EC complaint). |
| *WT/DS210* Belgium: administration of measures establishing customs duties for rice | No, although Uncle Ben's (rice) behind the complaint. | 12 Oct 00 | U.S. alleges Belgium's customs duties relating to rice imports were in violation of GATT Art. II, Customs Valuation Agreement, TBT Agreement, and Agreement on Agriculture when Belgium disregarded transaction values of imports. | U.S. requested suspension of panel's work on 19 Nov 01, and parties notified DSB of solution on 18 Dec 01. Belgium issued refund to affected U.S. companies. |
| *WT/DS204* Mexico: measures affecting telecommunications services | No, although U.S. telecommunications firms, such as AT&T and MCI, behind complaint. | 17 Aug 00 | U.S. alleges Mexico has maintained or adopted anticompetitive and discriminatory regulatory measures in violation of several articles of GATS. Mexico, however, did reduce interconnection rates. | Panel composed: 26 Aug 2002. |

| | | | | |
|---|---|---|---|---|
| *WT/DS203* Mexico: Measures affecting trade in live swine | No, although National Pork Producers Council behind the complaint. | 10 July 00 | U.S. alleges Mexico's AD measure on live swine was inconsistent with Arts. III:4 and XI:1 of GATT, Art. 4.2 of the Agreement on Agriculture, and that Mexico violated Arts. 2 and 5 of TBT Agreement, and several articles of SPS Agreement. | Consultations held on 7 Sept 00. Mexico issued a protocol allowing resumption of swine imports over 110 kg. Mexico self-initiated a review of threat of injury determinations. U.S. is monitoring and considering action on the AD matter. |
| *WT/DS199* Brazil: Measures affecting patent protection | No, although PhRMA behind the complaint under Special 301. | 30 May 00 | U.S. alleges that local working requirements under Brazilian patent law are inconsistent with Arts. 27 and 28 of TRIPS and Art. III of GATT. | On 1 Feb 01, U.S. dropped case after mounting pressure from activists. Brazil, however, agreed to notify the U.S. and hold consultations before issuing a compulsory license on a patent held by a U.S. company. |
| *WT/DS198* Romania: measures on minimum import prices | No, a systemic complaint, although supported by industry. | 30 May 00 | US alleges Romania established arbitrary minimum and maximum import prices for certain products in violation of Customs Valuation Agreement, and Arts. II, X and XI of GATT. | Parties notified DSB of solution: 26 Sept 01. Romania agreed to not use minimum reference prices for customs valuation purposes. |
| *WT/DS197* Brazil: measures on minimum import prices | No, a systemic complaint. USTR focused on long-standing customs valuation issues. | 30 May 00 | U.S. alleges minimum import prices for customs valuation purposes violate Arts. I and XI of GATT, Arts. 1 and 3 of Agreement on Import Licensing Procedures, Arts. 2 and 7 of Agreement on Textiles and Clothing, Art. 4.2 of Agreement on Agriculture, and several articles of Customs Valuation Agreement. | U.S. and Brazil held consultations on 18 July 00, and U.S. continues to monitor Brazil's customs valuation practices. See also EC case WT/DS183. |

Appendix Table 2 (*continued*)

| *WTO case* | *Section 301*[a] | *WTO procedure, request date* | *Summary of outcome of complaint* | *Status* |
|---|---|---|---|---|
| *WT/DS196* Argentina: certain measures on protection of patents and test data | No, although PhRMA behind the complaint under Special 301. | 30 May 00 | U.S. alleges Argentine patent law fails to, among other things, protect against unfair commercial use of undisclosed test data, improperly excludes certain subject matter from patentability, and fails to provide measures to prevent infringement in violation of several articles of TRIPS. | Parties notified DSB of solution to this dispute as well as related WT/DS171: 31 May 02. Argentina introduced legislation to be passed within one year to bring its patent law into conformity with TRIPS. Argentina refused to revise its laws on protection of test data unless required by a DSB interpretation of TRIPS. |
| *WT/DS195* Philippines: measures affecting trade and investment in automobile sector | No, a systemic complaint. | 23 May 00 | U.S. alleges Philippines' Motor Vehicle Development Program imposes local content requirements in violation of Arts. III and XI:1 of GATT, Arts. 2.1, 2.2 of TRIMS, and Art. 3.1(b) of SCM Agreement. Compare WT/DS175 decision against India under TRIMS. | Panel established: 17 Nov 00. An agreement to settle the dispute concluded on 18 Dec 01. Philippines is to phase out local content requirements by 1 July 03. |
| *WT/DS174* EC: protection of trademarks and geographical indications for agricultural | No, although Anheuser Busch and others behind complaint. | 1 June 99 | U.S. alleges EC regulations do not provide national treatment regarding geographical indications and do not provide sufficient protection to pre-existing trademarks that are similar | Consultations listed as pending. The geographical indications complaint continued in the context of Doha round negotiations regarding geographical indications. Concern |

| | | | | |
|---|---|---|---|---|
| products and food-stuffs | | | or identical to a geographic indication, in violation of TRIPS Arts. 3, 16, 24, 63, and 65. On 14 Apr 03, the U.S. filed a new complaint under GATT Arts. I and III. | involving Budweiser beer and Czech Republic. |
| *WT/DS173* France: measures relating to development of a flight management system | No, although Honeywell initially behind the complaint. | 21 May 99 | U.S. alleges preferential and non-commercial loans provided to a French company to develop a new flight management system are in violation of Arts. 1, 3, 5, and 6 of SCM Agreement. | Case dropped upon request of Honeywell for commercial reasons, possibly in relation to proposed merger with GE. USTR lists as "inactive." |
| *WT/DS172* EC: measures relating to development of a flight management system | No, although Honeywell initially behind the complaint. | 21 May 99 | See WT/DS173. | See WT/DS173. |
| *WT/DS/171* Argentina: certain measures on the protection of patents and test data | No, although PhRMA behind the complaint via Special 301 filing. | 6 May 99 | See WT/DS196. | Settled. See WT/DS196. |
| *WT/DS164* Argentina: measures affecting imports of footwear | USTR self-initiated investigations 4 Oct 96 (301-108). Nike behind complaint. | 1 Mar 99 | U.S. alleges safeguard duties including tariff rate quotas on footwear from non-MERCOSUR countries are inconsistent with Arts. 5.7, 7.4, and 12 of Safeguards Agreement. | Panel established: 26 July 99. See WT/DS121, EC complaint resulting in AB decision, in which U.S. is third party. |

Appendix Table 2 (*continued*)

| *WTO case* | *Section 301*[a] | *WTO procedure, request date* | *Summary of outcome of complaint* | *Status* |
|---|---|---|---|---|
| *WT/DS158* EC: regime for importation, sale, and distribution of bananas II, complaint by U.S. | No, although Chiquita behind former 301-94 petition. | 20 Jan 99 | U.S. alleges EC modified banana regime remains inconsistent with the EC's WTO obligations under DSB's rulings in case WT/DS27. | U.S. and EC settled the bananas dispute. See WT/DS27. |
| *WT/DS130* Ireland: certain income tax measures constituting subsidies | No (related to FSC case), though pressed by FSC beneficiaries. | 5 May 98 | U.S. alleges special tax rates applied to "special trading houses" constitute an export subsidy prohibited by Art. 3 of SCM Agreement. | Consultations listed as pending. Ireland approved changes in tax practices; however, change was not implemented before U.S. requested consultations. See also WT/DS131. |
| *WT/DS131* France: certain income tax measures constituting subsidies | No (related to FSC case), though pressed by FSC beneficiaries. | 5 May 98 | U.S. alleges French legislation contains measures equivalent to import substitution and export subsidies prohibited by Art. 3 of SCM Agreement. | Consultations listed as pending; were requested in response to FSC case. U.S. did not pursue cases when retaliation did not deter EC from continuing with FSC case. See WT/DS108 (FSC). |
| *WT/DS129* Greece: certain income tax measures constituting subsidies | No (related to FSC case), though pressed by FSC beneficiaries. | 5 May 98 | U.S. alleges Greek exporters entitled to special tax deductions constituting export subsidies prohibited by Art. 3 of SCM Agreement. | Consultations listed as pending. See also WT/DS131. |

| | | | | |
|---|---|---|---|---|
| *WT/DS128* Netherlands: certain income tax measures constituting subsidies | No (related to FSC case), though pressed by FSC beneficiaries. | 5 May 98 | U.S. alleges special "export reserve" for income derived from export sales constitutes an export subsidy prohibited by Art. 3 of SCM Agreement. | Consultations listed as pending. See also WT/DS131. |
| *WT/DS127* Belgium: certain income tax measures constituting subsidies | No (related to FSC case), though pressed by FSC beneficiaries. | 5 May 98 | U.S. alleges corporate taxpayers in Belgium receive a special tax exemption constituting an export subsidy prohibited by Art. 3 of SCM Agreement. | Consultations listed as pending. See also WT/DS131. |
| *WT/DS125, WT/DS124* Greece/EC: enforcement of intellectual property rights for motion pictures and television programs | No, although Motion Picture Association supports complaint under Special 301. | 30 Apr 98 | U.S. alleges TV stations in Greece regularly broadcast copyrighted motion pictures and television programs without authorization of copyright owners in violation of TRIPS Agreement. | Parties notified DSB of solution: 20 Mar 01. Greece passed legislation providing for additional enforcement remedies in copyright infringement cases. |
| *WT/DS115* EC: measures affecting the grant of copyright and neighboring rights | No, although IIPA supported complaint under Special 301. | 6 Jan 98 | U.S. alleges Ireland fails to grant copyright and neighboring rights under its law in violation of TRIPS Agreement. | Parties notified DSB of solution: 6 Nov 00. Ireland implemented legislation that brought Ireland into conformity with TRIPS. See WT/DS82. |

Appendix Table 2 (*continued*)

| *WTO case* | *Section 301*[a] | *WTO procedure, request date* | *Summary of outcome of complaint* | *Status* |
|---|---|---|---|---|
| *WT/DS109* Chile: Taxes on alcoholic beverages | No, although DISCUS supports complaint, following initiative of EC and Scotch Whisky Association. | 11 Dec 97 | In related EC case, AB upheld panel determination that Chile's system for taxation of distilled alcoholic beverages was inconsistent with Art. III.2 of GATT. | AB report adopted: 12 Jan 00. New legislation maintains 27 percent tax rate for *pisco* while progressively reducing all other taxes on spirits to 27 percent by 21 Mar 03. See WT/DS87, 110 (brought by EC). |
| *WT/DS106* Australia: subsidies provided to producers and exporters of automotive leather | USTR initiated investigations for second time in Nov 97 following complaint by Coalition against Australian Leather Subsidies (301-107). | 10 Nov 97 | U.S. alleges payments under grant and loans from Australian government to Howe/ALH are subsidies that violate Arts. 1 and 3.1 of SCM Agreement. | Parties notified DSB of solution: 11 June 98. However, dispute reemerged and was settled following a panel decision. See WT/DS126. |
| *WT/DS104* EC: measures affecting exportation of processed cheese | No, internally generated. | 8 Oct 97 | U.S. alleges EC classification of subsidies given on processed cheese violates Agreement on Agriculture and SCM Agreement. | Inactive. U.S. backed off. |
| *WT/DS102* Philippines: measures affecting pork and poultry. | No, although National Pork Producers Council behind the complaint. | 7 Oct 97 | U.S. alleges order to modify tariff-rate quota for pork and poultry and licensing system relating to WT/DS74 remains inconsistent with Arts. III, X, and XI of GATT, Art. 4 of Agreement on Agriculture, Art. 1 and 3 of the Import Licensing Agreement, and Art. 5 of TRIMS. | Parties notified DSB of solution: 12 Mar 98. Philippines modified the features of its tariff-rate quota for pork and poultry to U.S. satisfaction. U.S. had threatened to withdraw GSP benefits. |

| | | | | |
|---|---|---|---|---|
| *WT/DS101* Mexico: antidumping investigation of high-fructose corn syrup | USTR began investigation following petition of Corn Refiners Association on 17 Feb 98 (301-118). | 4 Sept 97 | U.S. alleges Mexico's preliminary dumping and injury determinations were inconsistent with several articles of AD Agreement. | U.S. requested consultations in respect to same dumping investigation after definitive antidumping measures were imposed on HFCS. See WT/DS132 (adopted panel decision). |
| *WT/DS86* Sweden: measures affecting enforcement of intellectual property rights | No, although Business Software Alliance behind complaint. | 28 May 97 | U.S. alleges Sweden's failure to provide provisional measures in civil proceedings (e.g., "unannounced searches") involving intellectual property rights violates Arts. 50, 63, and 65 of TRIPS. | Parties notified DSB of solution: 2 Dec 98. Sweden amended its laws to provide for provisional relief in civil proceedings. |
| *WT/DS83* Denmark: measures affecting enforcement of intellectual property rights | No, although Business Software Alliance behind complaint. | 14 May 97 | U.S. alleges Denmark's failure to provide provisional measures in civil proceedings (e.g., "unannounced searches") involving intellectual property rights violates Arts. 50, 63, and 65 of TRIPS. | Parties notified DSB of solution: 7 June 01. Danish parliament implemented legislation that included an "ex parte" search provision: 28 Mar 01. |
| *WT/DS82* Ireland: measures affecting the grant of copyright and neighboring rights | No, although IIPA supported complaint under Special 301. | 14 May 97 | U.S. alleges Ireland fails to grant copyright and neighboring rights under its law in violation of TRIPS Agreement. | Parties notified DSB of solution: 6 Nov. 00. Ireland implemented legislation that brought it into conformity with TRIPS. See WT/DS115. |

Appendix Table 2 (*continued*)

| *WTO case* | *Section 301*[a] | *WTO procedure, request date* | *Summary of outcome of complaint* | *Status* |
|---|---|---|---|---|
| *WT/DS80* Belgium: measures affecting commercial telephone directory services | No, although ITT behind the complaint. | 2 May 97 | U.S. alleges imposition of conditions for obtaining a license to publish commercial directories and regulations relating to telephone directory services violate Arts. II, VI, VIII, and XVII of GATS. | Inactive. ITT believed that filing the case helped in commercial discussions with Belgian authorities. |
| *WT/DS74* Philippines: measures affecting pork and poultry | No, although National Pork Producers Council behind the complaint. | 1 Apr 97 | U.S. alleges tariff-rate quota for pork and poultry and licensing system used to administer in-quota quantities is inconsistent with Arts. III, X, and XI of GATT, Art. 4 of the Agreement on Agriculture, Arts. 1 and 3 of the Agreement on Import Licensing Procedures, and Art. 5 of TRIMS. | Parties notified DSB of solution: 12 Mar 98. Philippines modified the features of its tariff-rate quota for pork and poultry to U.S. satisfaction. See WT/DS102. |
| *WT/DS65* Brazil: certain measures affecting trade and investment in the automotive sector. | USTR self-initiated an investigation: 11 Oct 96 (301-110). | 10 Jan 97 | U.S. alleges certain automotive investment measures taken by Brazilian government violate Arts. I:1 and III:4 of GATT, Arts. 3 and 27.4 of Subsidies Agreement, and Art. 2 of TRIMS. | U.S. and Brazil reached an agreement whereby Brazil committed to not extend its automotive trade-related measures beyond 31 Dec 99. |

| | | | | |
|---|---|---|---|---|
| *WT/DS57* Australia: textiles, clothing, and footwear import credit scheme | USTR initiated investigation following petition by the Coalition against Australian Leather Subsidies: 19 Aug 96 (301-107). | 7 Oct 96 | U.S. alleges subsidies granted on leather products under credit scheme violates Arts. 3 and 30 of SCM agreement. | USTR announced settlement of case in a 1996 press release. However, a new subsidies package resulted in a new request for consultations, leading to WT/DS126 concerning automotive leather. |
| *WT/DS52* Brazil: certain measures affecting trade and investment in automotive sector | USTR self-initiated an investigation: 11 Oct 96 (301-110). | 9 Aug 96 | See WT/DS65 re GATT, subsidies, and TRIMS claims. | Settled. See WT/DS65. |
| *WT/DS45* Japan: measures affecting distribution services | No, although related to Kodak 301 petition in photographic film case. | 13 June 96 | U.S. alleges measures regulating floor space, business hours, and holidays of supermarket and department stores ("large stores law") violate Arts. III and XVI of GATS. | Consultations listed as pending. This complaint initially was part of photographic film claim, but was not pursued. See WT/DS44. |
| *WT/DS43* Turkey: taxation of foreign film revenues | USTR self-initiated an investigation: 12 June 96 (301-105). Motion Pictures Association supports. | 12 June 96 | U.S. alleges Turkey's discriminatory taxation of revenues generated from showing of foreign films violates Art. III of GATT. | Parties notified DSB of solution: 14 July 97. Turkey equalized taxes imposed on box office receipts from showing of domestic and foreign films. |

Appendix Table 2 (*continued*)

| *WTO case* | *Section 301*[a] | *WTO procedure, request date* | *Summary of outcome of complaint* | *Status* |
|---|---|---|---|---|
| *WT/DS41* Korea: measures concerning inspection of agricultural products | No, although U.S. agricultural trade associations behind the complaint. | 24 May 96 | U.S. alleges measures including testing and inspection required for importation of agricultural products into Korea are inconsistent with Arts. III and XI of GATT, Art. 4 of Agreement on Agriculture, Arts. 2, 5, and 8 of SPS Agreement, and Arts. 2, 5, and 6 of TBT Agreement. | Inactive. Korea allegedly reduced inspection times following U.S. filing. |
| *WT/DS37* Portugal: patent protection under Industrial Property Act | USTR self-initiated an investigation: 30 Apr 96 (301-103). PhRMA behind complaint. | 30 Apr 96 | U.S. alleges Portugal's patent term is inconsistent with Arts. 33, 65, and 70 of TRIPS. | Parties notified DSB of solution: 3 Oct 96. Portugal implemented legislation that provides 15 years of protection from patent grant and 20 years from filing date, whichever is longer. |
| *WT/DS36* Pakistan: patent protection for pharmaceutical and agricultural chemical products | USTR self-initiated an investigation: 30 Apr 96 (301-104). PhRMA supports. | 30 Apr 96 | U.S. alleges Pakistan's failure to implement patent protection and exclusive marketing rights for pharmaceutical and agricultural chemicals violates Arts. 27, 65, and 70 of TRIPS. Similar to U.S. complaint against India, WT/DS50. | Parties notified DSB of solution: 25 Feb 97. Pakistan implemented legislation establishing a framework for a patent filing system. |

| | | | | |
|---|---|---|---|---|
| *WT/DS35* Hungary: export subsidies in respect of agricultural products | No. | 27 Mar 96 | U.S. alleges Hungary provided export subsidies on agricultural products in excess of its commitment levels, following a change in Hungarian government. | Parties notified DSB of solution: 30 July 97. Hungary received waiver of WTO commitment to phase out over time. |
| *WT/DS28* Japan: measures concerning sound recordings | No, although Recording Industry Association behind complaint. | 9 Feb 96 | U.S. alleges copyright regime for protection of sound recordings is inconsistent with Art. 14 of TRIPS. See also EC complaint, WT/DS42. | Parties notified DSB of solution: 9 Feb 96. Japan amended law to grant 50-year term of copyright protection for sound recordings. |
| *WT/DS21* Australia: measures affecting the importation of salmonids | No, although states of Alaska and Washington (and industry) support the complaint. | 17 Nov 95 (EC reserved third-party rights 16 June 99; U.S. was a third party in case brought by Canada) | U.S. alleges prohibition of salmon imports based on quarantine regulation is inconsistent with Arts. XI and XIII of GATT. | Parties notified DSB of solution: 27 Oct 00. Australia amended its quarantine policies on fresh salmon. It implemented DSB recommendations from dispute brought by Canada. See WT/DS18. |
| *WT/DS16* EC: regime for importation, sale, and distribution of bananas | See WT/DS27. | 28 Sept 95 | U.S. alleges EC banana regime is inconsistent with GATT, GATS, and Import Licensing Agreement. | Complaint renewed and settled after Appellate Body decision and U.S. retaliation. See WT/DS27. |

Appendix Table 2 (*continued*)

| *WTO case* | *Section 301*[a] | *WTO procedure, request date* | *Summary of outcome of complaint* | *Status* |
|---|---|---|---|---|
| *WT/DS13* EC: duties on imports of cereals | No, although USA Rice Federation and others support complaint. | 25 July 95 | U.S. alleges tariff-rate quotas on grain are in violation of GATT Agreement. | U.S. withdrew request for panel because EC implemented an agreement resolving the matter in context of EC enlargement: 30 Apr 97. |
| *WT/DS5* Korea: measures concerning shelf life of products | No, although linked to 301-95 petition leading to WT/DS3. | 3 May 95 | U.S. alleges requirements on imports resulted in import restrictions in violation of Arts. III and XI of GATT, Arts. 2 and 5 of SPS Agreement, Art. 4 of Agreement on Agriculture, and Art. 2 of TBT Agreement. | Parties notified DSB of solution: 31 July 95. Korea modified headings of products that remain subject to the shelf life requirement (though no agreement on sterilized milk). |
| *WT/DS3* Korea: measures concerning testing and inspection of agricultural products | USTR initiated investigation after petition by the National Pork Producers Counsel, American Meat Institute, and National Cattlemen's Beef Association: 18 Nov 94 (301-95). | 6 Apr 95 | U.S. alleges inspection and testing requirements on imports of agricultural products violate Arts. III and XI of GATT, Arts. 2 and 5 of SPS Agreement, Arts. 5 and 6 of TBT Agreement, and Art. 4 of Agreement on Agriculture. | U.S. and Korea reached an agreement modifying aspects of Korea's testing requirements, and USTR terminated its 301 investigation. But see WT/DS41. |

a. As of August 9, 2002.

Appendix Table 3. *Requests for Consultations by the EC: Panel and Appellate Body Reports, as of January 17, 2003*

| *WTO case* | *TBR* | *WTO procedure, request date* | *Summary of outcome of complaint* | *Status* |
|---|---|---|---|---|
| *WT/DS217* United States: continued dumping and subsidy offset act of 2000. | No, a systemic case. | 21 Dec 00 | AB upheld panel's determination that Byrd Amendment is a nonpermissible specific action against dumping or a subsidy contrary to the AD and SCM Agreements. | AB report circulated: 16 Jan 03. EC prevailed. |
| *WT/DS213* United States: countervailing duties on certain corrosion-resistant carbon steel flat products from Germany. | No, although four German companies supported, including ThyssenKrupp. | 10 Nov 00 | AB upheld panel's finding that U.S. sunset reviews were consistent with Arts. 21 and 10 of SCM Agreement and reversed panel's finding that U.S. law was inconsistent with Art. 21.3 of SCM Agreement regarding de minimis subsidization. Panel also found that DOC review lacked sufficient factual basis. | AB report adopted: 19 Dec 02. By and large, U.S. prevailed. |
| *WT/DS212* United States: countervailing measures concerning certain products from EC. Involved steel products. | No, although Corus and other steel companies provided support. | 10 Nov 00 | AB upheld panel's findings that U.S. CVD on EC products were inconsistent with SCM Agreement because U.S. failed to determine whether "benefit" from subsidy still exists. AB reversed panel finding that U.S. CVD statute is inconsistent with SCM Agreement but found arm's-length sale of government-owned firm creates rebuttable presumption that prior subsidies extinguished. | AB report adopted: 8 Jan 03. EC prevailed in part. See also WT/DS138. U.S. DOC published new methodology on privatization on 23 June 03. |

Appendix Table 3 (*continued*)

| *WTO case* | *TBR* | *WTO procedure, request date* | *Summary of outcome of complaint* | *Status* |
|---|---|---|---|---|
| *WT/DS189* Argentina: definitive antidumping measures on imports of ceramic floor tiles from Italy | No, although supported by Italian exporters. | 26 Jan 00 (U.S. reserved third-party rights: 17 Nov 00) | Panel found Argentina acted inconsistently with AD agreement by rejecting information from exporter for determination of normal value and export price, by not determining an individual dumping margin for each exporter, by failing to make due allowance for physical characteristics, and by not informing exporters of grounds for determination. | Panel report adopted: 5 Nov 01. EC prevailed. Argentina announced it revoked AD measures at issue on 24 Apr 02. |
| *WT/DS176* United States: Section 211 Omnibus Appropriations Act | No, although Pernod Ricard and France pushed for the case. | 8 July 99 | AB found the U.S. act violated MFN and national treatment obligations under TRIPS with respect to trademarks and reversed panel's determination that trade names are not covered by TRIPS. Bacardi behind U.S. act barring registration of trademarks confiscated under Cuban law, and Pernod Ricard behind EC complaint. | AB report adopted: 1 Feb 02. EC prevailed in part. Parties agreed to extend implementation period. |
| *WT/DS166* United States: definitive safeguard measure on imports of wheat gluten from EC | No, although wheat gluten trade association, AAC, pushed for the case. | 17 Mar 99 | AB upheld panel's finding that U.S. acted inconsistently under Safeguards Agreement regarding U.S. notification obligations, U.S. preferable treatment of NAFTA members, and causation analysis (in part). | AB report adopted: 19 Jan 01. EC prevailed. Parties agreed to implementation period. U.S. withdrew safeguard as of 2 June 01, three years after safeguard imposed. |

| | | | | |
|---|---|---|---|---|
| *WT/DS165* United States: import measures on certain products from EC | No, a systemic case. | 4 Mar 99 | AB found retaliatory measure sought to redress a WTO violation in EC-banana dispute was withdrawn. AB reversed panel's findings that the US acted inconsistently with Art. 23.2(a) of the DSU. | AB report adopted: 10 Jan 01. EC prevailed in part because U.S. did not appeal panel finding of inconsistency of increased U.S. bonding requirements under other GATT and DSU provisions. |
| *WT/DS160* United States: Section 110(5) of U.S. Copyright Act | Investigation initiated 11 June 97 following complaint by Irish Music Rights Organization. | 26 Jan 99 | Panel found that exemption, under U.S. Copyright Act, for payment of music royalties by bars and restaurants is inconsistent with Arts. 9.1 and 13 of TRIPS Agreement. | Panel report adopted: 27 July 00. EC prevailed. U.S. has yet to comply. DSB authorized EC to impose $1.08 million in annual trade sanctions on U.S. imports should the U.S. fail to implement the ruling. It agreed to pay financial compensation. Congress authorized funds in Apr 03. |
| *WT/DS155* Argentina: measures on export of bovine hides and import of finished leather | Investigation initiated 26 Feb 97 following complaint by COTANCE. | 24 Dec 98 | Panel found Argentina's de facto export prohibition on raw and semi-tanned bovine hides inconsistent with Art. III:2 of GATT and unjustified under Art. XX of GATT. | Panel report adopted: 16 Feb 01. Because of Argentina's economic hardship and its actions toward compliance, EC agreed to pursue discussions regarding compliance beyond DSB's expiration date of 28 Feb 02. |

Appendix Table 3 (*continued*)

| *WTO case* | *TBR* | *WTO procedure, request date* | *Summary of outcome of complaint* | *Status* |
|---|---|---|---|---|
| *WT/DS152* United States: Sections 301–310 of Trade Act of 1974 | No, a systemic case. | 25 Nov 98 | Panel found disputed sections of U.S. Trade Act were not inconsistent with any of the GATT or DSU provisions cited by EC base, subject to U.S. compliance with undertakings in U.S. Statement of Administrative Action approved by Congress and confirmed to the panel. | Panel report adopted: 27 Jan 00. U.S. prevailed, although put on notice that it must apply Section 301 in accordance with DSU requirements or panel finding will change. No appeal. |
| *WT/DS146* India: measures affecting automotive sector | No, but automobile trade association (ACEA) supported the case. | 6 Oct 98 (U.S. also a complainant; see WT/DS175) | Panel found India's local content and "trade balancing conditions" relating to trade and investment in automotive sector were inconsistent with Arts. III:4 and XI of GATT. Compare new EC request for consultations regarding India's policy 2002–07. See WT/DS279. | Panel report circulated: 21 Dec 01. EC prevailed. India withdrew appeal on 14 Mar 02. India removed conditions on 19 Aug 02. |
| *WT/DS142* Canada: certain measures affecting automotive industry | No, but automobile industry supported the case. | 17 Aug 98 (U.S. reserved third-party rights: 1 Feb 99) | Panel found conditions under which Canada granted its import duty exemption were inconsistent with Art. I and not justified by Art. XXIV of GATT. | AB report adopted: 19 June 00. Arbitrator determined that reasonable period of time for implementation would expire on 19 Feb 01. On 12 Mar 01, Canada informed DSB that it had complied. |

| | | | | |
|---|---|---|---|---|
| *WT/DS138* United States: imposition of countervailing duties on certain hot-rolled lead and bismuth carbon steel products originating in U.K. | No, although Corus and its U.S. lawyers pressed for the case and Legal Service engaged U.S. legal counsel to assist it. | 30 June 98 | AB upheld panel's findings that U.S. countervailing duties constituted a violation of Art. 10 of Subsidies Agreement because of U.S. presumption of continued benefit flowing from earlier subsidies following change in ownership in context of privatization of British Steel Corporation. | AB report adopted: 7 June 00. EC prevailed in part. U.S. announced it had implemented DSB recommendations on 5 July 00. EC filed a new complaint regarding US's "change in ownership" methodology in CV determinations and prevailed. See WT/DS212. |
| *WT/DS136* United States: Antidumping Act of 1916 | Investigation initiated 25 Feb 97 following complaint by EUROFER. | 9 June 98 | Panel found U.S. sanctions providing for treble damages, fines, or imprisonment were in violation of GATT and the AD Agreement. | AB report adopted: 26 Sept 00. EC prevailed. U.S. has yet to comply. |
| *WT/DS121* Argentina: Safeguard measures on imports of footwear | No. Primarily a systemic case, although Nike (U.S.) and European shoe companies supported it. | 3 Apr 98 (U.S. reserved third-party rights: 23 July 98) | AB upheld panel's finding that Argentina's safeguard measures are inconsistent with Arts. 2 and 4 of Safeguards Agreement. Compare WT/DS56 (U.S. complaint against Argentine duties and tax on footwear and other products). | AB report adopted: 12 Jan 00. EC prevailed. Argentina informed DSB measure would remain in force until 25 Feb 00, the date three years after imposition of safeguard. |
| *WT/DS114* Canada: patent protection of pharmaceutical products | No, although pharmaceutical industry supported the case. | 19 Dec 97 (U.S. reserved third-party rights: 1 Feb 99) | Panel found stockpiling exception of Canada's patent law was inconsistent with Art. 28.1 of TRIPS and was not covered by any Art. 30 exceptions. Panel found Canada's "regulatory review exception" covered by Art. 30. | Panel report adopted: 7 Apr 00. EC prevailed in part. Arbitrator determined that reasonable compliance period would end 7 Oct 00. Canada informed DSB that recommendations were implemented 7 Oct 00. |

Appendix Table 3 (*continued*)

| *WTO case* | *TBR* | *WTO procedure, request date* | *Summary of outcome of complaint* | *Status* |
|---|---|---|---|---|
| *WT/DS/110, WT/DS87* Chile: taxes on alcoholic beverages | No, although Scotch Whisky Association behind the case. | 15 Dec 97 & 12 Aug 97 (U.S. reserved third-party rights: 29 Nov 97) | AB upheld panel's determination that Chile's system for taxation of distilled alcoholic beverages was inconsistent with Art. III.2 of GATT. | AB report adopted: 12 Jan 00. Chile passed legislation that will progressively reduce taxes on spirits to 27 percent by 21 Mar 03, the tax rate for *pisco*. |
| *WT/DS108* United States: tax treatment for foreign sales corporations | No, a systemic case. | 17 Nov 97 | AB upheld panel findings that FSC was a prohibited subsidy. AB reversed panel's finding that FSC measure was inconsistent with Art. 3.3 of Agreement on Agriculture. U.S. revised FSC law, but AB finds amended law fails to comply. | AB report adopted: 20 Mar 00. EC prevailed. On 30 Aug 02, arbitrator determined value of trade concessions affected was US$4.043 billion a year. EC has yet to retaliate. |
| *WT/DS98* Korea: definitive measures on imports of certain dairy products | No, although Dutch milk association and Dutch government support case. | 12 Aug 97 (U.S. reserved third-party rights: 23 July 98) | AB upheld panel determination that Korea's import quota on certain dairy products from EC violated Art. 12.2 of Safeguards Agreement. | AB report adopted: 12 Jan 00. EC prevailed. Korea informed DSB that safeguard had been lifted on 20 May 00. |
| *WT/DS79* India: patent protection for pharmaceutical and agricultural chemical products | No, although pharmaceutical industry supported the case. | 28 Apr 97 (U.S. reserved third-party rights: 16 Oct 97; U.S. also a complainant) | Panel found India's failure to establish a mechanism that preserves novelty and priority with respect to patent applications for agricultural chemical and pharmaceutical products violated Arts. 70.8 and 70.9 of TRIPS. | Panel report adopted: 2 Sept 98. EC prevailed. On 28 Apr 99, India informed DSB that it had enacted legislation to implement DSB's rulings and recommendations. |

| | | | | |
|---|---|---|---|---|
| *WT/DS75* Korea: taxes on alcoholic beverages | No, although Scotch Whisky Association behind the case. | 4 Apr 97 (U.S. also a complainant; see WT/DS84) | AB upheld panel's determination that *soju* is directly competitive with other distilled alcohol; therefore Korea taxed the imported products in dissimilar manner in violation of Art. III.2 of GATT. | AB report adopted: 17 Feb 99. EC prevailed. On 14 Jan 00, Korea informed DSB it had amended liquor tax law to impose flat liquor tax rates of 72 percent on all distilled alcoholic beverages. |
| *WT/DS54* Indonesia: certain measures affecting automotive industry | No, although automobile industry supported the case. | 4 Oct 96 (U.S. also a complainant; see WT/DS59) | Panel found Indonesia's exemption from customs duties and luxury taxes on imports pursuant to "national car" program violated Arts. I & II:2 of GATT, Art. 2 of TRIMS, and Art. 5 of SCM Agreement. | Panel report adopted: 23 July 98. EC prevailed. Indonesia informed DSB it had adopted a new automotive policy implementing panel's recommendations on 24 June 99. Indonesia abandoned program in context of agreement with IMF during Asian financial crisis. |
| *WT/DS8* Japan: taxes on alcoholic beverages | No, although Scotch Whisky Association behind the case. | 25 Sept 95 (U.S. also a complainant; see WT/DS11) | AB upheld panel's determination that Japan's tax system that favors *shochu* over other distilled liquors was discriminatory in violation of Art. III:2 of GATT. | AB report adopted: 1 Nov 96. EC prevailed. Arbitrator determined an implementation period of 15 months to expire on 1 Feb 98. Japan presented modalities for implementation that were accepted by the complainants. |

Appendix Table 4. *Requests for Consultations by the EC: Not Involving an Adopted Report, as of January 17, 2003*

| *WTO case* | *TBR* | *WTO procedure, request date* | *Summary of outcome of complaint* | *Status* |
|---|---|---|---|---|
| *WT/DS279* India: import restrictions maintained under export and import policy 2002–07 | No, a systemic case, although certain industries support it. | 23 Dec 02 (U.S. joined consultations: 6 Feb 03) | EC alleges import restrictions maintained under India's Export and Import Policy violate Arts. III, X, and XI of GATT. Compare WT/DS175 (by U.S.) and WT/DS149 (by EC). | Consultations listed as pending. |
| *WT/DS273* Korea: measures affecting trade in commercial vessels | Yes. Initiated 2 Dec 00 by shipbuilding association. | 21 Oct 02 | EC alleges subsidies granted to commercial shipbuilding industry in Korea violate Arts. 1, 2, 3.1 ,5(a), 5(c), 6.3, and 6.5 of SCM Agreement. | Consultations held on 22 Nov and 13 Dec 02. |
| WT/DS262 United States: sunset reviews of antidumping and countervailing duties on certain steel products from France and Germany | No, although worked with Eurofer and some steel companies. | 25 July 02 | EC alleges U.S. sunset reviews proceeding regarding certain steel products from France and Germany violate several articles of AD and SCM Agreements. | Consultations held 12 Sept 02. Compare WT/DS213, in which U.S. by and large prevailed. |
| WT/DS248 United States: definitive safeguard measures on imports of certain steel products | No, although steel industry in close contact with the Commission. | 7 Mar 02 | EC alleges safeguard measures imposed by U.S. on certain steel products including tariff-rate quotas and increased duties violate Agreement on Safeguards and Arts. I:1, XIII, and XIX:1 of GATT. | Panel composed: 25 July 02. Report circulated on 11 July 03. EC prevails; status pending. |

| | | | | |
|---|---|---|---|---|
| *WT/DS225* United States: antidumping duties on seamless pipe from Italy | No, largely systemic. | 5 Feb 01 | EC alleges final sunset review results violate Arts. 5.8, 11.1, and 11.3 of AD Agreement, and that initiation of sunset review is inconsistent with Arts. 11.1, 11.3, and 18.4 of AD Agreement. | Consultations held on 21 Mar 01. Inactive. Issues overlap with those in WT/DS262 and WT/DS213, in which U.S. by and large prevailed. U.S. ITC found no injury, so case resolved. |
| *WT/DS214* United States: definitive safeguard measures on imports of steel wire rod and circular welded carbon-quality line pipe | No, although Eurofer and Germany pushed for the case. | 30 Nov 00 | EC alleges tariff rate quotas and duty increases on certain steel products violate Arts. I:1 and XIX:1 of GATT and Arts. 2, 4, and 5 of Safeguards Agreement. | Panel established: 10 Sept 01. Panel suspended after U.S. issued proclamation on 21 Nov 02 modifying allocation of tariff-rate quota on wire rod that satisfied EC export interests. |
| *WT/DS200* United States: Section 306 of Trade Act of 1974 and amendments thereto | No, a systemic case. | 5 June 00 | EC alleges Section 306, as amended in 2000 (providing for "carrousel retaliation"), is in breach of the DSU because it authorizes unilateral action absent use of WTO procedural requirements and allows threats of concessions not authorized by DSB in violation of Arts. 3.2, 21.5, 22, and 23 of DSU and GATT Arts. I, II, and XI. | Inactive. Resolution of bananas dispute reduced pressure on U.S. application of the statute. However, statute may have pressed EC to settle. |

Appendix Table 4 (*continued*)

| *WTO case* | *TBR* | *WTO procedure, request date* | *Summary of outcome of complaint* | *Status* |
|---|---|---|---|---|
| *WT/DS193* Chile: measures affecting transit and importation of swordfish | Investigation initiated following complaint by ANAPA: 26 May 98 | 19 Apr 00 (U.S. reserved third-party rights: 12 Dec 00) | EC alleges Chilean legislation disallowing EC ships with swordfish to land in Chilean ports is inconsistent with Arts. V and XI of GATT. | Parties agreed to suspend procedure day before panel to be established. Chile agreed to grant EC fishing boats limited access to its ports while the parties assess fisheries situation. |
| *WT/DS186* United States: Section 337 of Tariff Act of 1930 and amendments thereto | No, although earlier NCPI complaint resulted in GATT decision against U.S. | 12 Jan 00 | EC alleges Section 337 and rules of practice and procedure of ITC contained in U.S. Code of Federal Regulations are inconsistent with Art. III of GATT and several articles of TRIPS Agreement. | Consultations held on 28 Feb 00. EC continues to monitor the situation. |
| *WT/DS183* Brazil: measures on import licensing and minimum import prices. | Investigation initiated in 1998 following complaint by Febeltex. | 14 Oct 99 (U.S. participates as interested third party) | EC alleges Brazil's nonautomatic license system and minimum pricing practice restrict EC exports in violation of Arts. II, VIII, X, and XI of GATT. | Consultations listed as pending. See also U.S. complaint, WT/DS197. |
| *WT/DS157* Argentina: antidumping measures on imports of drill bits from Italy | No, largely a systemic case. | 14 Jan 98 | EC alleges antidumping measures imposed on drill bits from Italy resulted from an investigation that exceeded 18 months, violating Art. 1 of AD Agreement. | Inactive. |

| | | | | |
|---|---|---|---|---|
| *WT/DS151* United States: measures affecting textiles and apparel products | Yes. See WT/DS85. | 19 Nov 98 | EC alleges U.S. did not implement settlement agreement regarding changes in rules of origin for textile and apparel products, and violates Agreement on Rules of Origin, TBT Agreement, and Agreement on Textiles and Clothing. See WT/DS85. | Parties notified DSB of solution: 21 July 00. U.S. rules of origin determinations modified to recognize certain textiles as being made in EC. |
| *WT/DS150* India: measures affecting customs duties | No. | 30 Oct 98 | EC alleges increases in customs duties exceed India's WTO bound rates in violation of Arts. II.1(b) and III:2 of GATT. | Inactive, but consultations listed as pending. |
| *WT/DS149* India: import restrictions | No, largely a systemic case. See new filing under WT/DS279. | 29 Oct 98 | EC alleges India maintained import restrictions for reasons other than Art. XVIII:B of GATT; therefore the restrictions violate Arts. III, X, XI, XIII, and XVII of GATT. See U.S. case WT/DS/175. | Consultations listed as pending. Some liberalization took place, but Commission still evaluating. |
| *WT/DS147* Japan: tariff quotas and subsidies affecting leather | Investigation initiated by COTANCE: 9 Apr 97. | 8 Oct 98 | EC alleges tariff-rate quotas and subsidies benefiting leather industry violate Arts. 1(6) and 3(5)(g)–(j) of Agreement on Import Licensing Procedures and Art. 6 of SCM Agreement. | Inactive, but consultations listed as pending. EC discussing systemic issues in context of Doha negotiations. |

Appendix Table 4 (*continued*)

| *WTO case* | *TBR* | *WTO procedure, request date* | *Summary of outcome of complaint* | *Status* |
|---|---|---|---|---|
| *WT/DS145* Argentina: countervailing duties on imports of wheat gluten from EC. | No, although coordinated with trade association in CVD proceeding. | 23 Sept 98 | EC alleges CV duties imposed on wheat gluten imports from EC resulted from an investigation exceeding 18 months in violation of Arts. 11.11 and 10 of SCM Agreement. | Inactive. |
| *WT/DS120* India: measures affecting export of certain commodities | No, although supported by leather industry. | 16 Mar 98 | EC alleges India has effectively established an export embargo on raw hides and skins in violation of Art. XI of GATT. | Consultations listed as pending. Establishment of panel deferred: 23 Oct 00. |
| *WT/DS118* United States: harbor maintenance tax | No. | 6 Feb 98 | EC alleges harbor maintenance tax (HMT) violates Arts. I, II, III, VIII, and X of GATT. | Inactive. U.S. eliminated HMT on exports following U.S. Court of Appeals decision that unconstitutional, but tax remains on imports. |
| *WT/DS117* Canada: measures affecting film distribution services | No, although Polygram behind the case. | 20 Jan 98 | EC alleges Canada's 1987 policy decision on film distribution and its applicability to EC companies violates Arts. II and III of GATT. | Inactive. Polygram was bought out by Seagram, a Canadian company. |
| *WT/DS116* Brazil: measures affecting payment terms for imports | No. | 9 Jan 98 | EC alleges payment terms for imports introduced by Brazil's Central Bank violate Arts. 3 and 5 of Agreement on Import Licensing Procedures. | Consultations listed as pending, but case appears inactive. |

| | | | | |
|---|---|---|---|---|
| *WT/DS107* Pakistan: export measures affecting hides and skins | No, although supported by leather industry. | 7 Nov 97 | EC alleges prohibition of hides and skins and wet blue leather made from cow and calf hides limits access of EC industries to competitive sourcing of raw and semifinished materials. | Inactive. |
| *WT/DS100* United States: measures affecting imports of poultry products | No. | 18Aug 97 | EC alleges import ban on poultry products is inconsistent with Arts. 2, 3, 4, 5, and 8 of SPS Agreement, Arts. 2 and 5 of TBT Agreement, and Arts. I, III, X, and XI of GATT. | U.S. retaliated against EC ban on U.S. poultry products by imposing its own ban on EC poultry products. Contested issues part of negotiations surrounding U.S.-EC Veterinary Equivalency Agreement. |
| *WT/DS96* India: quantitative restrictions on imports of agricultural, textile, and industrial products | No. | 18 July 97 (U.S. continued to litigate; see WT/DS90) | EC alleges quantitative restrictions on textiles violate various articles of GATT. | Parties notified DSB of solution: 7 Apr 98. India agreed to phase out quantitative restrictions by 31 Mar 03. |
| *WT/DS88* United States: measure affecting government procurement | No, a systemic case, although affected European companies supported it. | 20 June 97 | EC alleges Massachusetts act that prohibits public procurement of goods or services from any persons who do business in Burma violates Arts. VIII(B), X, and XIII of Government Procurement Agreement. | Panel proceeding suspended at the request of the complainants: 10 Feb 99. U.S. Supreme Court held that Massachusetts act was unconstitutional. |

Appendix Table 4 (*continued*)

| *WTO case* | *TBR* | *WTO procedure, request date* | *Summary of outcome of complaint* | *Status* |
|---|---|---|---|---|
| *WT/DS85* United States: measures affecting textiles and apparel products | Investigation initiated 22 Nov 96 following complaint by FEDERTESSILE. | 23 May 97 | EC alleges U.S. rules of origin for textiles do not recognize certain products as being of EC origin in violation of Art. 4.2 of Agreement on Rules of Origin, GATT Art. III, Art. 2 of TBT Agreement, and provisions of Agreement on Textiles and Clothing. | DSB notified of solution: 11 Feb 98. U.S. failure to implement solution resulted in WT/DS151. |
| *WT/DS81* Brazil: measures affecting trade and investment in automotive sector | No. | 7 May 97 | EC alleges certain measures in trade and investment sector violate Arts. I and III:4 of GATT, Art. 2 of TRIMS, and Arts. 3, 5, and 27.4 of Subsidies Agreement. | EC benefited from U.S.-Brazil agreement whereby Brazil agreed not to extend its measures beyond 31 Dec 99. See WT/DS65. |
| WT/DS77 Argentina: measures affecting textiles and clothing | No. | 17 Apr 97 (U.S. litigated the case; see WT/DS56) | EC alleges increase in duties exceed 35 percent binding made by Argentina in violation of Art. II of GATT and Art. 7 of Agreement on Textiles and Clothing. | EC requested suspension of panel: 29 July 98. Authority of panel lapsed: 29 July 99. |

| | | | | |
|---|---|---|---|---|
| *WT/DS73* Japan: procurement of a navigation satellite | No. | 26 Mar 97 | EC alleges European bidders were unable to participate in Japanese tender to purchase a satellite for Air Traffic Management because specifications referred explicitly to U.S. specifications in violation of Art. VI(3) and XII(2) of Government Procurement Agreement. | Parties notified DSB of solution: 31 July 97. Japan and EC came to an agreement regarding requirements for procurement in the future. |
| *WT/DS63* United States: antidumping measures on imports of solid urea from former German Democratic Republic | No, although pushed by German government. | 28 Nov 96 | EC alleges U.S. antidumping duties on solid urea violate Arts. 9 and 11 of AD Agreement. | Case was resolved without formal notification to DSB. U.S. antidumping measure was repealed. |
| *WT/DS53* Mexico: customs valuations of imports | No. | 27 Aug 96 | EC alleges Mexico applies CIF value for basis of customs valuation of imports originating in non-NAFTA countries rather than FOB value used for NAFTA countries in violation of Art. XXIII:1(b) of GATT. | Inactive. |
| *WT/DS42* Japan: measures concerning sound recordings | No, although European association supported case. | 24 May 96 | EC alleges Japan's copyright regime violates Arts. 14.6 and 70.2 of TRIPS. See also U.S. complaint, WT/DS28. | Parties notified DSB of solution: 7 Nov 97. Japan amended patent law to provide for a 50-year term of protection for sound recordings. |

Appendix Table 4 (*continued*)

| *WTO case* | *TBR* | *WTO procedure, request date* | *Summary of outcome of complaint* | *Status* |
|---|---|---|---|---|
| *WT/DS40* Korea: laws, regulations and practices in the telecommunications sector | No. | 9 May 96 | EC alleges procurement practices of Korea's telecommunications sector discriminate against foreign suppliers in violation of Arts. I, III, and XVII of GATT. | Inactive. |
| *WT/DS39* United States: tariff increases on products from the European Communities | No. | 17 Apr 96, 15 July 96 | EC alleges retaliation against the "hormones" directive resulting in tariff increases on certain products from EC violate Arts. I, II, and XXIII of GATT. | EC requested panel suspend its work: 21 Apr 97. Case resolved after DSB authorizes U.S. withdrawal of concessions. |
| *WT/DS38* United States: Cuban Liberty and Democratic Solidarity Act | No, a systemic case. | 3 May 96 | EC alleges U.S. trade restrictions on goods of Cuban origin and exclusion of non-U.S. nationals from U.S. soil is inconsistent with GATT Arts. I, III, V, XI, and XIII, and Arts. I, III, VI, XVI, and XVII of GATS. | EC requested panel suspend its work: 21 Apr 97. Panel's authority lapsed: 22 Apr 98. EC reserves rights if Helms-Burton used against EC persons. |
| *WT/DS15* Japan: measures affecting purchase of telecommunications equipment | No. | 18 Aug 95 | EC alleges agreement reached between U.S. and Japan regarding telecommunications equipment is inconsistent with Arts. I:1, III:4, and XVII:1 of GATT. | Apparently bilaterally settled, although there was no official notification of settlement. |

# *References*


Abbot, Kenneth. 1989. "Modern International Relations Theory: A Prospectus for International Lawyers." *Yale Journal of International Law* 14: 335–411.

———. 1996. "'Economic' Issues and Political Participation: The Evolving Boundaries of International Federalism." *Cardozo Law Review* 18: 971–1010.

Abbott, Kenneth, and Duncan Snidal. 2000. "Hard and Soft Law in International Governance." *International Organization* 54(3): 421–56.

Abels, Tracy. 1996. "The World Trade Organization's First Test: The United States–Japan Auto Dispute." *UCLA Law Review* 44: 467–526.

Alston, Philip. 1993. "Labor Rights Provisions in U.S. Trade Law: 'Aggressive Unilateralism?'" *Human Rights Quarterly* 15: 1–35.

Alter, Karen. 2001. *Establishing the Supremacy of European Law*. Oxford University Press.

Aspinwall, Mark, and Justin Greenwood. 1998. "Conceptualising Collective Action in the European Union." In *Collective Action in the European Union*, edited by Justin Greenwood and Mark Aspinwall. London: Routledge.

Austin, John. [1832] 1971. "The Province of Jurisprudence Determined." In *The Great Legal Philosophers: Selected Readings in Jurisprudence*, edited by Clarence Morris. University of Pennsylvania Press.

Axelrod, Robert, and Robert Keohane. 1985. "Achieving Cooperation under Anarchy: Strategies and Institutions." *World Politics* 38: 226–54.

Barfield, Claude. 2000. "The Role of Interest Groups in the Design and Implementation of U.S. Trade Policies." In *Social Dimensions of U.S. Trade Policies*, edited by Alan V. Deardorff and Robert M. Stern. University of Michigan Press.

———. 2001. *Free Trade, Sovereignty, Democracy: The Future of the World Trade Organization*. Washington: Institute for International Economics.

Bauer, Raymond, Ithiel de Sola Pool, and Lewis A. Dexter. 1963. *American Business and Public Policy: The Politics of Foreign Trade*. New York: Atherton Press.

Bayard, Thomas O., and Kimberly Ann Elliott. 1994. *Reciprocity and Retaliation in U.S. Trade Policy*. Washington: Institute for International Economics.

Bellis, Jean-Francois. 1989. "The EEC Antidumping System." In *Antidumping Law and Practice: Comparative Approach*, edited by John H. Jackson and Edwin A. Vermulst. University of Michigan Press.

Bello, Judith H. 1997. "Some Practical Observations about WTO Settlement of Intellectual Property Disputes." *Virginia Journal of International Law* 37: 357–67.

Bello, Judith H., and Alan F. Holmer. 1990a. "The Heart of the 1988 Trade Act: A Legislative History of the Amendments to Section 301." In *Aggressive Unilateralism*, edited by Jagdish Bhagwati and Hugh T. Patrick. University of Michigan Press.

———. 1990b. "'Special 301': Its Requirements, Implementation, and Significance." *Fordham International Law Journal* 13: 259–75.

Bhagwati, Jagdish. 1994. "Comment by Jagdish Bhagwati." In *The New GATT: Implications for the United States*, edited by Susan M. Collins and Barry P. Bosworth. Brookings.

Bhagwati, Jagdish, and Hugh T. Patrick, eds. 1990. *Aggressive Unilateralism: America's 301 Trading Policy and the World Trading System*. University of Michigan Press.

Bhala, Raj. 1999. "The Myth about Stare Decisis and International Trade Law." *American University International Law Review* 14: 845–955.

———. 2000. *International Trade Law: Theory and Practice*. 2d ed. Charlottesville, Va.: Lexis Law.

Bhala, Raj, and David Gantz. 2001. "WTO Case Review 2000." *Arizona Journal of International and Comparative Law* 18: 1–101.

———. 2002. "WTO Case Review 2001." *Arizona Journal of International and Comparative Law* 19: 457–642.

Bhala, Raj, and Kevin Kennedy. 1998. *World Trade Law: The GATT-WTO System, Regional Arrangements, and U.S. Law*. Charlottesville, Va.: Lexis Law.

Braithwaite, John, and Peter Drahos. 2000. *Global Business Regulation*. Cambridge University Press.

Brand, Ronald. 1992. "GATT and United States Trade Law: The Incomplete Implementation of Comparative Advantage Theory." *Journal of Legal Economics* 2: 95–109.

———. 1996. "Direct Effect of International Economic Law in the United States and the European Union." *Northwestern Journal of International Law and Business* 17: 556–608.

Bronckers, Marco C. E. J. 1984. "Private Response to Foreign Unfair Trade Practices—United States and EC Complaint Procedures." *Northwestern Journal of International Law and Business* 6: 651–759.

Bronckers, Marco C. E. J., and Natalie McNelis. 2001. "The EU Trade Barriers Regulation Comes of Age." *Journal of World Trade* 35 (4): 427–82.

Busch, Marc, and Eric Reinhardt. 2000. "Bargaining in the Shadow of the Law: Early Settlement in GATT/WTO Disputes." *Fordham International Law Journal* 24 (November–December): 158–72.

———. 2002. "Testing International Trade Law: Empirical Studies of GATT/WTO Dispute Settlement." In *The Political Economy of International Trade Law: Essays in Honor of Robert E. Hudec*, edited by Daniel L. M. Kennedy and James D. Southwick. Cambridge University Press.

———. 2003. "Developing Countries and GATT/WTO Dispute Settlement." Draft as of January 20, 2003.

Caine, Christopher G. 2000. "Powers of Persuasion: Behind the Scenes with the World's Top Lobbyists." *Corporate Legal Times* 10: 20–28.

Cerny, Philip. 1997. "Paradoxes of the Competition State: The Dynamics of Political Globalization." *Government and Opposition* 32: 251–74.

Chang, Seung Wha. 2000. "Taming Unilateralism under the Multilateral Trading System: Unfinished Job in the WTO Panel Ruling on U.S. Sections 301–310 of the Trade Act of 1974." *Law and Policy in International Business* 31 (Summer): 1151–1226.

Charnovitz, Steve. 2001. "Rethinking WTO Trade Sanctions." *American Journal of International Law* 95 (October): 792–832.

Cheek, Marney. 2001. "The Limits of Informal Regulatory Cooperation in International Affairs: A Review of the Global Intellectual Property Regime." *George Washington International Law Review* 33: 277–323.

Coen, David. 1997. "The Evolution of the Large Firm as a Political Actor in the European Union." *Journal of European Public Policy* 4: 91–108.

———. 1998. "The European Business Interest and the Nation State: Large-Firm Lobbying in the European Union and Member States." *Journal of Public Policy* 18: 75–100.

Coleman, William, and Eric Montpetit. 2000. "Multitiered Systems and the Organization of Business Interests." In *Organized Business and the New Global Order*, edited by Justin Greenwood and Henry Jacek. New York: St. Martin's Press.

Colombatto, Enrico, and Jonathan Macey. 1999. "The Decline of the Nation-State and Its Effect on Constitutional International Economic Law: A Public Choice Model of International Economic Cooperation and the Decline of the Nation-State." *Cardozo Law Review* 18: 925–56.

Conant, Lisa. 2002. *Justice Contained: Law and Politics in the European Union.* Cornell University Press.

Cortner, Richard C. 1975. *The Supreme Court and Civil Liberties Policy.* Palo Alto, Calif.: Mayfield.

Cowles, Maria Green. 1996. "The EU Committee of AmCham: The Powerful Voice of American Firms in Brussels." *Journal of European Public Policy* 3 (3): 339–58.

———. 2001a. "Private Firms and U.S.-EU Policy-Making: The Transatlantic Business Dialogue." In *Ever Closer Partnerships: Policy-Making in U.S.-EU Relations,* edited by Eric Philippart and Pascaline Winand. New York: P.I.E.-Peter Lang.

———. 2001b. "The Transatlantic Business Dialogue and Domestic Business-Government Relations." In *Transforming Europe: Europeanization and Domestic Change*, edited by Maria Green Cowles, James Caporaso, and Thomas Risse. Cornell University Press.

Cunningham, Richard. 1998. "Trade Law and Trade Policy: The Advocate's Perspective." In *Constituent Interests in U.S. Trade Policies*, edited by Alan V. Deardorff and Robert M. Stern. University of Michigan Press.

Cunningham, Richard, and Eric Emerson. 2001. "Section 301 and Dispute Settlement in the World Trade Organization: An Update." Unpublished manuscript, October 18 draft. On file with author.

Cutler, Claire. 1997. "Artifice, Ideology and Paradox: The Public/Private Distinction in International Law." *Review of International Political Economy* 4: 261–85.

Cutler, Claire, Virginia Haufler, and Tony Porter. 1999. "The Contours and Significance of Private Authority in International Affairs." In *Private Authority and International Affairs,* edited by Claire Cutler, Virginia Haufler, and Tony Porter. State University of New York Press.

Dahl, Robert. 1976. *Modern Political Analysis*. 3d ed. Englewood Cliffs, N.J.: Prentice-Hall.

Dahl, Robert, and Charles Lindblom. 1976. *Politics, Economics and Welfare.* 2d ed. University of Chicago Press.

Dam, Kenneth, 1970. *The GATT: Law and International Economic Organization.* University of Chicago Press.

———. 2001. *The Rules of the Global Game: A New Look at U.S. International Policymaking.* University of Chicago Press.

Davey, William. 2003. "The WTO Dispute Settlement Mechanism." Unpublished manuscript. On file with author.

Deardorff, Alan. 1990. "Should Patent Protection Be Extended to All Developing Countries?" *World Economy* 13: 497–507.

De Bièvre, Dirk. 2003. "International Institutions and Domestic Coalitions: The Impact of the World Trade Organization on the European Union." Manuscript on file.

Degregorio, Christine. 1998. "Assets and Access: Linking Lobbyists and Lawmakers in Congress." In *The Interest Group Connection: Electioneering, Lobbying, and Policymaking in Washington*, edited by Paul S. Herrnson, Ronald G. Shaiko, and Clyde Wilcox. Chatham, N.J.: Chatham House.

Destler, I. M. 1995. *American Trade Politics*. 3d ed. Washington: Institute for International Economics.

Devuyst, Youri. 1995. "The European Union and the Conclusion of the Uruguay Round." In *The State of the European Union*, vol. 3: *Building a Polity?* edited by Carolyn Rhodes and Sonia Mazey. Boulder, Colo.: Lynne Rienner.

———. 2000. "The European Union's Constitutional Order? Between Community Method and Ad Hoc Compromise." *Berkeley Journal of International Law* 18: 1–52.

———. 2001. "Transatlantic Competition Relations." In *Transatlantic Governance in the Global Economy*, edited by Mark Pollack and Gregory Shaffer. Lanham, Md.: Rowman & Littlefield.

De Witte, Bruno, Dominik Hanf, and Ellen Vos, eds. 2001. *The Many Faces of Differentiation in EU Law*. New York: Intersentia.

Dezalay, Yves, and Bryant Garth. 1996. *Dealing in Virtue: International Commercial Arbitration and the Construction of a Transnational Legal Order*. University of Chicago Press.

———. 2002. *The Internationalization of Palace Wars: Lawyers, Economists, and the Contest to Transform Latin American States*. University of Chicago Press.

Dinan, Donald. 2003. "An Analysis of the United States-Cuba 'Havana Club' Rum Case before the World Trade Organization." *Fordham International Law Journal* 26 (January): 163–208.

Drake, William, and Kalypso Nicolaidis. 1992. "Ideas, Interests and Institutionalization: 'Trade in Services' and the Uruguay Round." *International Organization* 46 (Winter): 37–100.

Eichmann, Erwin, and Gary Horlick. 1989. "Political Questions in International Trade: Judicial Review of Section 301?" *Michigan Journal of International Law* 10: 735–64.

Emiliou, Nicholas, and David O'Keeffe. 1996. *The European Union and World Trade Law: After the GATT Uruguay Round*. New York: Wiley.

Epstein, Jeffrey. 1998. "Americans Distrust Their Government." *Futurist* 32 (October): 12–13.

Epstein, Lee. 1991. "Courts and Interest Groups." In *The American Courts: A*

*Critical Assessment*, edited by John B. Gates and Charles A. Johnson. Washington: CQ Press.

Featherstone, Kevin, and Roy H. Ginsberg. 1993. *The United States and the European Community in the 1990's: Partners in Transition.* New York: St. Martin's Press.

Feketekuky, Geza. 1990. "U.S. Policy on 301 and Super 301." In *Aggressive Unilateralism*, edited by Jagdish Bhagwati and Hugh T. Patrick. University of Michigan Press.

Felsteiner, William, Richard Abel, and Austin Sarat. 1980–81. "The Emergence and Transformation of Disputes: Naming, Blaming and Claiming." *Law and Society Review* 15: 631–54.

Finnemore, Martha, and Stephen J. Toope. 2001. "Comment on 'Legalization and World Politics.'" *International Organization* 55 (Summer): 743–58.

Frost, Ellen L. 1997. *Transatlantic Trade: A Strategic Agenda.* Washington: Institute for International Economics.

Galanter, Marc. 1974. "Why the 'Haves' Come Out Ahead: Speculations on the Limits of Legal Change." *Law and Society Review* 9: 95–160.

Gardner, Anthony Laurence. 1997. *A New Era in U.S.-EU Relations? The Clinton Administration and the New Transatlantic Agenda.* Brookfield, Vt.: Ashgate.

Gero, John, and Kathleen Lannan. 1995. "Trade and Innovation: Unilateralism v. Multilateralism." *Canada-U.S. Law Journal* 21: 81–98.

Gilligan, Michael. 1997. *Empowering Exporters: Reciprocity, Delegation, and Collective Action in American Trade Policy.* University of Michigan Press.

Gilpin, Robert. 1975. *U.S. Power and the Multinational Corporation: The Political Economy of Foreign Direct Investment.* New York: Basic Books.

———. 1987. *The Political Economy of International Relations.* Princeton University Press.

———. 2001. *Global Political Economy: Understanding the International Economic Order.* Princeton University Press.

Goldstein, Judith. 1993. *Ideas, Interests, and American Trade Policy.* Cornell University Press.

Goldstein, Judith, Miles Kahler, Robert O. Keohane, and Anne-Marie Slaughter, eds. 2000. Special issue on "Legalization and World Politics." *International Organization* 54 (Summer): 385–703.

Gordon, Bernard K. 2003. "A Step in the Wrong Direction. *Foreign Affairs* (July–August).

Gormley, William. 1998. "Interest Group Interventions in the Administrative Process: Conspirators and Co-Conspirators." In *The Interest Group Connection: Electioneering, Lobbying, and Policymaking in Washington*, edited by Paul S. Herrnson, Ronald G. Shaiko, and Clyde Wilcox. Chatham, N.J.: Chatham House.

Gottlieb, Gidon. 1985. "The Nature of International Law: Toward a Second Concept of Law." In *International Law: A Contemporary Perspective*, edited by Richard Falk, Friedrich Kratochwil, and Saul H. Mendlovitz. Boulder, Colo.: Westview Press.

Graham, Edward M. 1996. *Global Corporations and National Governments.* Washington: Institute for International Economics.

Greenwood, Justin. 1997. *Representing Interests in the European Union.* New York: St. Martin's Press.

———. 2000. "Organized Business and the European Union." In *Organized Business and the New Global Order*, edited by Justin Greenwood and Henry Jacek. New York: St. Martin's Press.

Grieco, Joseph M. 1990. *Cooperation among Nations: Europe, America, and Non-Tariff Barriers to Trade.* Cornell University Press.

Grygiel, Heidi. 1997. "Now They GATT Worry: The Impact of the GATT on the American Generic Pharmaceutical Industry." *Baltimore Intellectual Property Law Journal* 6: 47–69.

Hart, H. L. A. 1994. *The Concept of Law.* 2d ed. Oxford: Clarendon Press.

Hasenclever, Andreas, Peter Mayer, and Volker Rittberger, eds. 1997. *Theories of International Regimes.* Cambridge University Press.

Hayes, J. P. 1993. *Making Trade Policy in the European Community.* New York: St. Martin's Press for the Trade Policy Research Center, University of Reading.

Hayes-Renshaw, Fiona, and Helen Wallace. 1997. *The Council of Ministers.* New York: St. Martin's Press.

Heclo, H. 1978. "Issue Networks and the Executive Establishment." In *The New American Political System*, edited by Anthony King. Washington: American Enterprise Institute for Public Policy Research.

Helfer, Laurence R. 2000. "World Music on a U.S. Stage: A Berne/TRIPs and Economic Analysis of the Fairness in Music Licensing Act." *Boston University Law Review* 80: 93–204.

Hix, Simon. 1999. *The Political System of the European Union.* New York: St. Martin's Press.

Hoekman, Bernard, and Michel M. Kostecki. 2001. *The Political Economy of the World Trading System: The WTO and Beyond.* 2d ed. Oxford University Press.

Hoeller, Peter, Nathalie Girouard, and Alessandra Colecchia. 1998. "The European Union's Trade Policies and Their Economic Effects." OECD Working Paper 194. Paris: Organization for Economic Cooperation and Development, Economics Department.

Hollingsworth, J. Rogers, Philippe C. Schmitter, and Wolfgang Streeck, eds. 1994. *Governing Capitalist Economies: Performance and Control of Economic Sectors.* Oxford University Press.

Horwitz, Morton J. 1982. "The History of the Public/Private Distinction." *University of Pennsylvania Law Review* 30: 1423–28.

Hudec, Robert E. 1990a. *The GATT Legal System and World Trade Diplomacy.* Salem, N.H.: Butterworth Legal.

———. 1990b. "Thinking about the New Section 301: Beyond Good and Evil." In *Aggressive Unilateralism*, edited by Jagdish N. Bhagwati and Hugh T. Patrick. University of Michigan Press.

———. 1993. *Enforcing International Trade Law: The Evolution of the Modern ATT Legal System.* London: Butterworth.

———. 1996. "International Economic Law: The Political Theater Dimension." *University of Pennsylvania Journal of International Economic Law* 17 (Spring): 9–15.

———. 1998. "GATT/WTO Constraints on National Regulation: Requiem for an 'Aim and Effects' Test." *International Lawyer* 32 (Fall): 619.

Irwin, Douglas A. 1996. *Against the Tide: An Intellectual History of Free Trade.* Princeton University Press.

International Trade Administration (ITA). 1999. "GDP and U.S. International Trade in Goods and Services, 1970–1998." In *U.S. Foreign Trade Highlights.* Washington.

Jackson, John. 1998. *The World Trade Organization: Constitution and Jurisprudence.* London: Royal Institute of International Affairs.

Johnson, Michael. 1998. *European Community Trade Policy and the Article 113 Committee.* London: Royal Institute of International Affairs, International Economics Programme

Kagan, Robert. 1995. "Adversarial Legalism and American Government." In *The New Politics of Public Policy*, edited by Marc K. Landy and Martin A. Levin. Johns Hopkins University Press.

———. 2000. "How Much Do National Styles of Regulation Matter?" In *Regulatory Encounters: Multinational Corporations and American Adversarial Legalism*, edited by Robert Kagan and Lee Axelrad. University of California Press.

Katzenstein, Peter. 1976. "International Relations and Domestic Structures: Foreign Economic Policies of Advanced Industrial States." *International Organization* 30: 1–45.

Kelsen, Hans. 1942. "The Nature of International Law." In *Law and Peace in International Relations: The Oliver Wendell Holmes Lectures: 1940–1941.* Harvard University Press.

Kennan, George Frost. 1951. *American Diplomacy, 1900–1950.* University of Chicago Press.

Kennedy, Kevin C. 1987. "Presidential Authority under Section 337, Section 301 and the Escape Clause: The Case for Less Discretion." *Cornell International Law Journal* 20: 127.

Keohane, Robert O. 1984. *After Hegemony: Cooperation and Discord in the World Political Economy.* Princeton University Press.

———, ed. 1986. *Neorealism and Its Critics*. Columbia University Press.

Kettl, Donald. 1993. *Sharing Power: Public Governance and Private Markets.* Brookings.

Koh, Harold Hongju. 1992. "The Fast Track and United States Trade Policy." *Brooklyn Journal of International Law* 18: 143–80.

Komesar, Neil. 1994. *Imperfect Alternatives: Choosing Institutions in Law, Economics and Public Policy.* University of Chicago Press.

Kooiman, Jan. 1993. "Findings, Speculations and Recommendations." In *Modern Governance: New Government-Society Interactions*, edited by Jan Kooiman. Newbury Park, Calif.: Sage Publications.

Kosterlitz, Julie. 1998. "Trade Crusade." *National Journal* 30 (1054).

Kouwenhovern, Vincent. 1993. "The Rise of the Public Private Partnership: A Model for the Management of Public-Private Cooperation." In *Modern Governance: New Government-Society Interactions,* edited by Jan Kooiman. Newbury Park, Calif.: Sage Publications.

Krueger, Anne O. 1995. *American Trade Policy: A Tragedy in the Making.* Washington: American Enterprise Institute.

Lawrence, Robert. 2003. *Crimes and Punishments.* Washington: Institute for International Economics (manuscript on file).

Lijphart, Arend. 1999. *Patterns of Democracy: Government Forms and Performance in Thirty-Six Countries.* Yale University Press.

Lindberg, Leon N., John L. Campbell, and J. Rogers Hollingsworth. 1991. "Economic Governance and the Analysis of Structural Change in the American Economy." In *Governance of the American Economy*, edited by John L. Campbell, J. Rogers Hollingsworth, and Leon N. Lindberg. Cambridge University Press.

Lindsey, Brink, and Daniel Ikenson. 2001. "Coming Home to Roost: Proliferating Antidumping Laws and the Growing Threats to U.S. Exports." *Trade Policy Analysis* no. 14 (July). Washington: Cato Institute, Center for Trade Policy Studies.

Llewellyn, Karl. 1931. "Some Realism about Realism—Responding to Dean Pound." *Harvard Law Review* 44: 1222–64.

Loomis, Burdett, and Allan Cigler. 1998. "Introduction: The Changing Nature of Interest Group Politics." In *Interest Group Politics,* edited by Burdett Loomis and Allan Cigler. 5th ed. Washington: CQ Press.

Low, Patrick. 1993. *Trading Free: The GATT and U.S. Trade Policy*. New York: Twentieth-Century Fund Press.

Lowi, Theodore J. 1979. *The End of Liberalism: The Second Republic of the United States.* 2d ed. New York: Norton.

Macaulay, Stewart. 1986. "Private Government." In *Law and the Social Sciences*, edited by Leon Lipson and Stanton Wheeler. New York: Russell Sage Foundation.

Maclean, Robert. 1999. "The European Community's Trade Barrier Regulation Takes Shape: Is It Living Up to Expectations?" *Journal of World Trade Law* 33 (6): 69–96.

Macleod, I., I. D. Hendry, and Stephen Hyett. 1996. *The External Relations of the European Communities: A Manual of Law and Practice*. New York: Clarendon Press.

Maresceau, Marc, ed. 1993. *The European Community's Commercial Policy after 1992: The Legal Dimension.* Dordrecht: Martin Nijhoff.

Maskus, Keith. 2000. "Intellectual Property Issues for the New Round." In *The WTO after Seattle*, edited by Jeffery Schott. Washington: Institute for International Economics.

Mavroidis, Petros C. 2000. "Remedies in the WTO Legal System: Between a Rock and a Hard Place." *European Journal of International Law* 11: 763–813.

Mavroidis, Petros C., and Werner Zdouc. 1998. "Legal Means to Protect Private Parties' Interests in the WTO." *Journal of International Economic Law* 1 (3): 407–32.

McDougal, Myres, and Howard D. Lasswell. 1996. "The Identification and Appraisal of Diverse Systems of Public Order." In *International Rules: Approaches from International Law and International Relations*, edited by Robert J. Beck, Anthony Clark Arend, and Robert D. Vander Lugt. Oxford University Press.

McGinnis, John, and Mark Movsiean. 2000. "The World Trade Constitution: Reinforcing Democracy through Trade." *Harvard Law Review* 114: 511–605.

Merry, Sally Engle. 2003. "From Law and Colonialism to Law and Globalization." *Law and Social Inquiry* 28(2): 569–90.

Meunier, Sophie. 2000. "What Single Voice? European Institutions and EU-U.S. Trade Negotiations." *International Organization* 54 (Winter): 103–35.

Meunier, Sophie, and Kalypso Nikolaidis. 1999. "Who Speaks for Europe? The Selection of Trade Authority in the EU." *Journal of Common Market Studies* 37 (September): 477–501.

———. 2000. "EU Trade Policy: The 'Exclusive' versus Shared Competence Debate." In *The State of the European Union,* vol. 5: *Risks, Reform Resistance, and Removal*, edited by Maria Green Cowles and Michael Smith. Oxford University Press.

Michalopoulos, Constantine. 2001. *Developing Countries in the WTO*. New York: Palgrave.

Milner, Helen. 1990. "The Political Economy of U.S. Trade Policy: A Study of the Super 301 Provision." In *Aggressive Unilateralism*, edited by Jagdish N. Bhagwati and Hugh T. Patrick. University of Michigan Press.

Molyneux, Candido Garcia. 1999. "The Trade Barriers Regulation: The European Union as a Player in the Globalisation Game." *European Law Journal* 5 (4): 375–418.

———. 2001. *Domestic Structures and International Trade: The Unfair Trade Instruments of the United States and European Union.* Oxford: Hart.

Morgenthau, Hans Joachim. 1963. *Politics among Nations: The Struggle for Power and Peace.* 3d ed. New York: A. A. Knopf.

North, Douglas. 1997. "Institutions [role in the performance of economies]." *Journal of Economic Perspectives* 5 (Winter): 97–112.

Novak, Viveca. 1993. "How Drug Companies Operate on the Body Politic." *Business and Society Review* (Winter): 58–64.

Nugent, Neill. 1994. *The Government and Politics of the European Union.* 3d ed. Duke University Press.

Olson, Mancur. 1965. *The Logic of Collective Action: Public Goods and the Theory of Groups.* Harvard University Press.

Ostry, Sylvia. 1990. *Governments and Corporations in a Shrinking World : Trade and Innovation Policies in the United States, Europe and Japan.* New York: Council on Foreign Relations Press.

Paemen, Hugo, and Alexandra Bensch. 1995. *From the GATT to the WTO: The European Community in the Uruguay Round.* Leuven University Press.

Pauwelyn, Joost. 2000. "Enforcement and Countermeasures in the WTO: Rules are Rules—Toward a More Collective Approach." *American Journal of International Law* 94 (April): 335–47.

Petersmann, Ernst-Ulrich. 1991. *Constitutional Functions and Constitutional Problems of International Economic Law: International and Domestic Foreign Trade Law and Foreign Trade Policy in the United States, the European Community and Switzerland.* Boulder, Colo.: Westview Press.

———. 2000. "Prevention and Settlement of Trade Disputed between the European Union and United States." *Tulane Journal of International and Comparative Law* 8 (Spring): 233–60.

Peterson, John. 2001. "Get Away from Me Closer, You're Near Me Too Far: Europe and America after the Uruguay Round." In *Transatlantic Governance in the Global Economy*, edited by Mark Pollack and Gregory Shaffer. Lanham, Md.: Rowman & Littlefield.

Pollack, Mark, and Gregory Shaffer. 2001a. "The Challenge of Reconciling Regulatory Differences: Food Safety and GMOs in the Transatlantic Relationship." In *Transatlantic Governance in the Global Economy*, edited by Mark Pollack and Gregory Shaffer. Lanham, Md.: Rowman & Littlefield.

———. 2001b. "Transatlantic Relations in Historical and Theoretical Perspective." In *Transatlantic Governance in the Global Economy*, edited by Mark Pollack and Gregory Shaffer. Lanham, Md.: Rowman & Littlefield.

———. 2001c. "Who Governs?" In *Transatlantic Governance in the Global Economy*, edited by Mark Pollack and Gregory Shaffer. Lanham, Md.: Rowman & Littlefield.

Porges, Amelia. 1995. *Guide to GATT Law and Practice.* Analytical Index. Geneva: WTO Secretariat.

Posner, Theodore, and Timothy Rief. 2000. "Homage to a Bull Moose: Applying Lessons of History to Meet the Challenges of Globalization." *Fordham International Law Journal* 24: 481–518.

Powell, Walter W. 1991. "Neither Market nor Hierarchy: Network Forms of Organization." In *Markets, Hierarchies and Networks: The Coordination of Social Life*, edited by Jennifer Frances, Rosalind Levacic, Jeremy Mitchell, and Grahame Thompson. Newbury Park, Calif.: Sage Publications.

Ragosta, John. 2000. "Unmasking the WTO—Access to the DSB System: Can the DSB Live Up to Its Moniker 'World Trade Court?'" *Law and Policy in International Business* 31: 739–84.

Raustiala, Kal. 2002. "The Architecture of International Law: Transgovernmental Networks and the Future of International Law." *Virginia Journal of International Law* 43: 1–92.

Reich, Robert B. 1991a. "Global Economics and the Ecumenical Corporation." *New Perspectives Quarterly* 10 (1): 47–50.

———. 1991b. *The Work of Nations: Preparing Ourselves for 21st-Century Capitalism.* New York: A. A. Knopf.

Rhodes, R.A.W. 1996. "The New Governance: Governing without Government." *Political Studies* 44: 652–67.

———. 1997. *Understanding Governance: Policy Networks, Governance, Reflexivity and Accountability.* Philadelphia: Open University Press.

———. 2000. "Introduction: The ESCR Whitehall Programme: A Guide to Institutional Change." In *Administering the Summit: Administration of the Core Executive in Developed Countries,* edited by B. Guy Peters, R. A. W. Rhodes, and Vincent Wright. New York: St. Martin's Press.

Rometsch, Dietrich, and Wolfgang Wessels. 1994. "The Commission and the Council of Ministers." In *The European Commission*, edited by Geoffrey Edwards and David Spence. Harlow, England: Longman Current Affairs.

Rosenau, James. 1992. "Governance, Order and Change in World Politics." In *Governance without Government: Order and Change in World Politics*, edited by James N. Rosenau and Ernst-Otto Czempiel. Cambridge University Press.

Ruggie, John. 1995. "At Home Abroad, Abroad at Home: International Liberalisation and Domestic Stability in the New World Economy." *Millennium: Journal of International Studies* 24: 507–26.

Schattschneider, E. E. 1935. *Politics, Pressures and the Tariff; A Study of Free Private Enterprise in Pressure Politics, as Shown in the 1929–1930 Revision of the Tariff.* New York: Prentice-Hall.

Schmertz, John R., and Mike Meier. 1997. "U.S. Imposes Trade Sanctions on Argentina for Failure to Protect U.S. Intellectual Property Rights." *International Law Update* 3: 34.

Schmidt, Vivien. 1996. *From State to Market? The Transformation of French Business and Government.* Cambridge University Press.

Schmitter, Philippe C. 1974. "Still the Century of Corporatism?" *Review of Politics* 36 (1): 85–131.

Schwok, Rene, 1991. *U.S.-EC Relations in the Post–Cold War Era: Conflict or Partnership?* Boulder, Colo.: Westview Press.

Sell, Susan. 1998. *Power and Ideas: North-South Politics of Intellectual Property and Antitrust.* State University of New York Press.

———. 1999. "Multinational Corporations as Agents of Change: The Globalization of Intellectual Property Rights." In *Private Authority and International Affairs*, edited by Claire Cutler, Virginia Haufler, and Tony Porter. State University of New York Press.

Shaffer, Gregory. 1994 "United States' Import Prohibition of Certain Shrimp and Shrimp Products." *American Journal of International Law* 93 (April): 507–14.

———. 2001. "The WTO's Blue-Green Blues: The Impact of U.S. Domestic Politics on Trade-Labor, Trade-Environment Linkages." *Fordham International Law Journal* 24: 608–51.

———. 2002. "Reconciling Trade and Regulatory Goals." *Columbia Journal of European Law* 9 (Fall): 29–77.

———. 2003. "How to Make the WTO Legal System Work for Developing Countries: Some Proactive Developing Country Strategies." In *Fostering the Development Interests of Developing and Least Developed Countries through the WTO Dispute Settlement System.* Issues Resource Paper 5. Geneva: International Centre for Trade and Sustainable Development.

Shaiko, Ronald. 1998. "Lobbying in Washington: A Contemporary Perspective." In *The Interest Group Connection: Electioneering, Lobbying, and Policymaking in Washington*, edited by Paul S. Herrnson, Ronald G. Shaiko, and Clyde Wilcox. Chatham, N.J.: Chatham House.

Shaw, Josephine. 2000. *Law of the European Union.* 3d ed. New York: Palgrave.

Slaughter, Anne-Marie. 1997. "The Real New World Order." *Foreign Affairs* 76 (5): 183.

———. 2000. "Governing the Global Economy through Government Networks." In *The Role of Law in International Politics: Essays in International Relations and International Law*, edited by Michael Byers. Oxford University Press.

Snidal, Duncan. 1985. "Coordination Versus Prisoners' Dilemma: Implications for International Cooperation and Regimes." *American Political Science Review* 79: 923.

Steinberg, Richard. 1998. "Great Power Management of the World Trading System: A Transatlantic Strategy for Liberal Multilateralism." *Law and Policy in International Business* 29 (Winter): 205–56.

———. 1999. "The Prospects for Partnership: Overcoming Obstacles to Transatlantic Trade Policy Cooperation in Europe." In *Partners or Competitors? The Prospects for U.S.-European Cooperation on Asian Trade*, edited by Richard Steinberg and Bruce Stokes. Lanham, Md.: Rowman & Littlefield.

———. 2002. "In the Shadow of Law or Power? Consensus-Based Bargaining and Outcomes in the GATT/WTO." *International Organization* 56 (Spring): 339–74.

Steinberg, Richard, and Bruce Stokes, eds. 1999. *Partners or Competitors? The Prospects for U.S.-European Cooperation on Asian Trade*. Lanham, Md.: Rowman & Littlefield.

Stephen, Paul B. 2000. "American Hegemony and International Law: Sheriff or Prisoner? The United States and the World Trade Organization." *Chicago Journal of International Law* 1 (Spring): 49–74.

Stern, Paula. 1990. "Commentary." In *Aggressive Unilateralism*, edited by Jagdish N. Bhagwati and Hugh T. Patrick. University of Michigan Press.

Stewart, Alistair. 1996. "Market Access: A European Community Instrument to Break Down Barriers to Trade." *International Trade Law and Regulation* 2: 123.

Stone Sweet, Alec. 2000. *Governing with Judges*. Oxford University Press.

Stopford, John, and Susan Strange. 1991. *Rival States, Rival Firms: Competition for World Market Shares*. Cambridge University Press.

Strange, Susan. 1985. "Protectionism and World Politics." *International Organization* 39 (Spring): 233–59.

Swan, Alan C. 1999. "'Fairness' and 'Reciprocity' in the International Trade Section 301 and the Rule of Law." *Arizona Journal of International and Comparative Law* 16: 37–75.

Sykes, Alan. 1992. "Constructive Unilateral Threats in International Commercial Relation: The Limited Case of Section 301." *Law and Policy in International Business* 23: 263–330.

Symposium. 1998. "Is the WTO Dispute Settlement Mechanism Responsive to the Needs of the Traders? Would a System of Direct Action by Private Parties Yield Better Results?" *Journal of World Trade Law* 32 (2): 147–65.

Trachtman, Joel. 2003. "Whose Right Is It Anyway? Private Parties in EC-U.S. Settlement at the WTO." In *Dispute Prevention and Dispute Settlement in the Transatlantic Partnership*, edited by Ernst-Ulrich Petersmann and Mark Pollack. Oxford University Press. Manuscript on file.

Turkel, Gerald. 1992. *Dividing Public and Private: Law, Politics, and Social Theory.* Westport, Conn.: Praeger.

United States Trade Representative (USTR). 1999. *National Trade Estimate Report on Foreign Trade Barriers*. Washington.

———. 2000. *2000 Trade Policy Agenda and 1999 Annual Report*. Washington.

———. 2001. *2001 Trade Policy Agenda and 2000 Annual Report*. Washington.

———. 2002. *2002 Trade Policy Agenda and 2001 Annual Report*. Washington.

Van den Bossche, Peter. 1997. "The European Community and the Uruguay Round Agreements." In *Implementing the Uruguay Round,* edited by John H. Jackson and Alan O. Sykes. Oxford University Press.

Vander Schueren, Paullette, and David Luff. 1996. "The Trade Barrier Regulation and the Community's Market Access Policy." *European Foreign Affairs Review* 2: 2.

Van Eeckhaute, Jean Charles. 1999. "Private Complaints against Foreign Unfair Trade Practices: The EC's Trade Barriers Regulation." *Journal of World Trade Law* 33 (6): 199–213.

Van Schendelen, M. P. C. M. 1993. "Introduction: The Relevance of National Public and Private EC Lobbying." In *National Public and Private EC Lobbying,* edited by M. P. C. M. Van Schendelen. Brookfield, Vt.: Dartmouth.

Wallach, Lori, and Michelle Sforza. 1999. *Whose Trade Organization? Corporate Globalization and the Erosion of Democracy.* Washington: Public Citizen.

Watal, Jayashree. 2000. "Pharmaceutical Patents, Prices and Welfare Losses: Policy Options for India Under the WTO TRIPS Agreement." *World Economy* 23 (5): 733–52.

Weber, Max. 1946. *From Max Weber: Essays in Sociology,* translated by H. H. Gerth and C. Wright Mills. Oxford University Press.

———. 1947. *The Theory of Social and Economic Organization*, translated by A. M. Henderson and Talcott Parsons. Oxford University Press.

Weingast, Barry. 1993. "Constitutions as Governance Structures." *Journal of Institutional and Theoretical Economics* 149 (March): 286–311.

Wilcox, Clyde. 1998. "The Dynamics of Lobbying the Hill." In *The Interest Group Connection: Electioneering, Lobbying, and Policymaking in Washington*, edited by Paul S. Herrnson, Ronald G. Shaiko, and Clyde Wilcox. Chatham, N.J.: Chatham House.

Williamson, Oliver E. 1975. *Markets and Hierarchies, Analysis and Antitrust Implications: A Study in the Economics of Internal Organization.* New York: Free Press.

———. 1985. *The Economic Institutions of Capitalism: Firms, Markets, Relational Contracting.* New York: Free Press.

———. 1996. *The Mechanisms of Governance.* Oxford University Press.

Wilson, Graham. 2003. *Business & Politics: A Comparative Introduction.* 3d ed. Chatham, N.J.: Chatham House.

Winham, Gilbert R. 1986. *International Trade and the Tokyo Round Negotiations.* Princeton University Press.

Wolff, Alan William. 1985. "International Competitiveness of American Industry: The Role of U.S. Trade Policy." In *U.S. Competitiveness in the World Economy*, edited by Bruce R. Scott and George C. Lodge. Harvard Business School Press.

———. 1998. "Reflections on WTO Dispute Settlements." *International Lawyer* 32: 951–58.

Woolcock, Stephen. 2000. "European Trade Policy: Global Pressures and Domestic Constraints." In *Policy-Making in the European Union*, edited by Helen Wallace and William Wallace. 4th ed. Oxford University Press.

Woolcock, Stephen, and Michael Hodges. 1996. "EU Policy in the Uruguay Round." In *Policy-Making in the European Union*, edited by Helen Wallace and William Wallace. 3d ed. Oxford University Press.

World Bank. 1992. *Global Economic Prospects and the Developing Countries 1992*. Washington.

World Trade Organization (WTO). 2000, 2001, 2002. *World Trade Annual Report*. Geneva.

Yarbrough, Beth, and Robert Yarbrough. 1990. "International Institutions and the New Economics of Organization." *International Organization* 44: 235–59.

Young, Alasdair. 1998. "European Consumer Groups: Multiple Levels of Governance and Multiple Logics of Collective Action." In *Collective Action in the European Union*, edited by Justin Greenwood and Mark Aspinwall. London: Routledge.

———. 2001. "Extending European Cooperation: The European Union and the 'New' International Trade Agenda." Working Paper 2001/12. European University Institute.

Young, Oran R. 1997. "Rights, Rules, and Resources in World Affairs." In *Global Governance: Drawing Insights from the Environmental Experience*, edited by Oran R. Young. Cambridge, Mass.: MIT Press.

Zoller, Elisabeth. 1985. "Remedies for Unfair Trade: European and United States Views." *Cornell International Law Journa*l 18: 227–45.

Zonnekeyn, Geert A. 1995. "The EC 'Trade Barriers Regulation': More Opportunities for Community Industries?" *International Trade Law and Regulation* 1: 143–48.

# *Index*

Gregory C. Shaffer is associate professor of law and senior fellow at the Center on World Affairs and the Global Economy at the University of Wisconsin. In addition to *Transatlantic Governance in the Global Economy* (with Mark Pollack, Rowman & Littlefield, 2001), he has published over thirty articles and book chapters on international trade and transatlantic relations. He recently was a research fellow at the American Bar Foundation and at Columbia University.